'The Moth connects us a: [...]
all have stories. And the g[...]
us as people is that when w[...]
might see faces, skin colour, gender, race
or attitudes, but we don't see, we can't see, the
stories. And once we hear each other's stories we
realise that the things we see as dividing
us are, all too often, illusions, falsehoods.'

Neil Gaiman

'Some stories are heartbreakingly sad;
some laugh-out-loud funny; some momentous
and tragic; almost all of them resonant or
surprising. They are stories that attest to
the startling varieties and travails of human
experience, and the shared threads of love,
loss, fear and kindness that connect us.'

Michiko Kakutani, *New York Times*

'The stories retain the vulnerability and
rawness inherent in the situation of one
person, alone at the mic, telling a room
full of strangers something personal.'

Hermione Hoby, *Observer*

Also from The Moth

The Moth: This is a True Story

The Moth: All These Wonders

This paperback edition published in 2020

First published in Great Britain in 2019 by
SERPENT'S TAIL
29 Cloth Fair
London EC1A 7JQ

www.serpentstail.com

Compilation copyright © The Moth 2019, 2020

Copyrights in the individual works are
retained by the contributors.

1 3 5 7 9 10 8 6 4 2

Typeset in Lino Letter to a design by Henry Iles

Printed and bound in Great Britain by
CPI Group (UK) Ltd, Croydon, CR0 4YY

The moral right of the authors has been asserted.

All rights reserved. Without limiting the rights under
copyright reserved above, no part of this publication
may be reproduced, stored or introduced into a retrieval
system, or transmitted, in any form or by any means
(electronic, mechanical, photocopying, recording or
otherwise), without the prior written permission of both
the copyright owner and the publisher of this book.

A CIP catalogue record for this book is available from the
British Library.

ISBN 978-1781256671
eISBN 978-1782830689

Occasional Magic

True Stories of Defying the Impossible

THE MOTH

EDITED BY

Catherine Burns

CONTENTS

On the Other Side of That Wall

It's Messy, But It Works

The Wattage of Our Inner Light

We'll Come with Lions

FOREWORD

Meg Wolitzer

When I was first asked to be a storyteller at The Moth, a nonprofit that sends people out in front of audiences to tell their true stories, I was a little leery. The word "storyteller" made me uneasy; I pictured myself sitting somberly with a group of people in a circle, wearing a special storyteller cloak. But of course telling a story at The Moth is nothing like that.

It wasn't that I was afraid of standing up before an audience. I'm a novelist, so reading aloud to a roomful of people (or even a handful of people and a loud bookstore cappuccino machine) is something I know how to do. But at The Moth you can't hold notes. While the artistic director had been working with me on my piece, helping me turn it from an anecdote into a fully realized story, I was still hung up on the remembering part.

The Moth, which has become something of an international phenomenon, puts on story nights and slams and has worked with countless people from a variety of backgrounds, helping them sift through their own histories and think about what has mattered to them. At a Moth evening, which is often a lively and raucous event, you might find a country music icon, a dentist, an Iraqi interpreter, an Arctic explorer. You never know who or what will be in the mix.

I chose a story from my adolescence, which to me remains a startlingly vivid time. I tried hard to memorize all the parts of it, but in the days leading up to the big night, whenever I banished my husband from the living room and stood there with a timer, practicing, I found that I was leaving out entire chunks of story. I started to panic.

Then I realized that, instead of focusing on memorizing, I should focus on memory. I simply remembered the experience of being at summer camp in the 1970s, feeling young and excited and open. And once I really felt it all over again, I found the words. They weren't the exact same words as during my last rehearsal, but they weren't supposed to be. A Moth story is like a living thing: it changes and moves.

Finally, onstage under a spotlight in front of an enormous audience, I was like a better-coiffed, much older version of that girl I'd been at camp. I would say to anyone who is thinking of getting up onstage and telling a story: what you need to do, most of all, is feel like yourself. Once you do that, the words will come.

And also, as it turns out, the applause. I left the stage gratified, hot-faced, exorcised, thrilled, thinking, *I would do this again.* Hell, I would even do it wearing a special storyteller cloak.

Here, in this new collection, you will find fifty storytellers from all over the world. Some of them, I'm sure, experienced the same mix of nerves and excitement that I did when I walked up to the microphone. How fortunate we are that they were willing to channel their memories into these strong and radiant stories, and how wonderful it is that we now have the chance to read them here.

INTRODUCTION

Catherine Burns

The title of this collection, *Occasional Magic,* comes from a story told by Vietnam veteran Larry Kerr. It's about his intense love for a young woman named Omie, whom he describes as "smart, meltingly lovely, and strong, with a fierce belief in the possibility of occasional magic."

Occasional magic refers to those moments of beauty, wonder, and clarity, often stumbled upon, where we suddenly see a piece of truth about our life. As Moth directors we spend our days helping people shape their stories. We help people identify the most important moments of their lives (as we sometimes put it, "the moments when you became *you*") so the audience will understand why they mattered *so much.*

All the stories on the following pages were first told in front of live audiences. They showcase the great range of humanity – from a fifteen-year-old kid saving a life in Chicago to a Russian facing down the KGB – and cover all seven continents.

To select them we read transcriptions of hundreds of stories before narrowing it down to these fifty, which were chosen for their ability to convey emotion, humor, and vulnerability in print. They were then edited with an emphasis on preserving the live voices as much as possible – so you'll find tense changes, sentence fragments, and even the occasional grammatical mistake.

The authenticity of those voices is what can make a show in a three-thousand-seat theater feel like being in someone's living room. The feeling that the person onstage isn't *presenting* a story, but *sharing* one, the same way we might with a friend over dinner. The warmth and investment of the audience is as much a part of the show as the stories themselves.

We will forever try to live up to the way British writer and Moth storyteller Lemn Sissay described the feel of Moth evenings: "Imagine The Moth to be an encampment in the desert. Take a seat. Someone will make space for you. It's dusk in the land of story. What's happening? Who knows? Someone's gonna stand up and speak? Something about their life – something that means something to them, something that may mean something to you. The sun dips and fires, rising stars spill across the sky like shoals of silver fish. You see there are as many small fires as there are stars. This is not an encampment. It is the world. The air is perfect body temperature. It is. The Moth is by the people, for the people. That's you."

For more than two decades, tens of thousands of people have shared stories on Moth stages around the world, and millions more have shown up with open hearts to listen.

If the warm response of Moth audiences assures us of anything, it's that empathy is alive and well in the world, and for that we have a reason to feel hopeful.

Catherine Burns is Artistic Director of The Moth

*To the stories that
give us perspective,
clarity, and hope.*

Put Your Curry Down, Sweetheart

Anaïs Bordier

So Much, and Enough

Growing up, I always felt that my birthday wasn't the day I was born, but rather the day I arrived in Paris. When I was three months old, my parents came to pick me up at Charles de Gaulle Airport, and this was the day we became a family.

I always knew I was adopted, and my mom told me that I was always in her heart, but that it was another woman who gave birth to me.

I grew up in the suburbs of Paris as an only child. I was a happy, balanced kid, but I could sometimes feel really lonely, and this loneliness couldn't be filled by friends. In darker moments I felt abandoned. I wondered if my birth parents didn't love me, and if that was the reason why they decided to put me up for adoption.

Whenever I had questions my parents would sit me down, take my adoption files out of the desk drawer, and start reading the story to me.

My birth parents were from Pusan. They met when they were really young, and they started dating, but my birth father had to leave Pusan for a job. My birth mother had gotten pregnant with me, and because of social stigma at the time in Korea – and that she wasn't married and she was still studying at university – she and her family decided to put me up for adoption.

I never felt the need to reach out to them or wanted to meet them because I had my mom and my dad who loved me. They were my real parents, so it didn't matter.

But one day, I had just turned twenty-five, and I was studying fashion at Central Saint Martins in London. My friend sent me a screenshot of a YouTube video featuring me, except I had never made such a video, and no one had filmed me. I clicked on the link and discovered a short, humorous video entitled *High School Virgin*.

It was made by a kid called KevJumba in Los Angeles, and it starred a girl who looked very much like me, except she had an American accent.

I was startled. I was trying to look for her name or a little bit of information about her, but there was nothing. And so I thought it was just a coincidence, and I dropped it.

Then, a few months later, my friend told me that he saw that "look-alike girl" again in a trailer for the film *21 & Over*. I found her credits in the cast list; she was listed as "Asian Girl." Her name was Samantha Futerman. She was an American actress who had been in films such as *Memoirs of a Geisha*. She was born in South Korea on the 19th of November, 1987.

I stopped right there. I thought I had read it wrong, because it said that she was born the same day as me.

So, we had the same birthdates, we looked really similar, except I knew my adoption records by heart, and I knew it had to be just a coincidence.

I really wanted to talk to my parents, so I immediately called them. As my mom got on the phone, she said, "Do you think she could be your twin sister?"

I was relieved because I thought I wasn't totally insane for thinking the same thing and now I felt I was allowed to think something that was supposed to be impossible.

Then I got my dad on the phone, and as I told him the same thingwards, he was Googling her, and found another website with a different birthdate. He told me that I must have got it wrong, but that it was indeed quite a funny coincidence. Except that, to me, it wasn't just a coincidence.

I couldn't really focus that day, I was just a zombie, wandering around. So I thought I would spend the rest of the day casually stalking her on social media.

I discovered that she was an American actress living in Los Angeles, that we were indeed born the same day, that she was also adopted from South Korea, and she recently had discovered that she wasn't born in Seoul, but in Busan. And I was also born in Busan.

So I decided I should try and reach out to her. But how do I do it? I didn't have her email address.

I could Tweet at her: "Hi. It seems we might be related, so private message me."

Didn't seem quite appropriate.

So I decided I would send her a friend request on Facebook, as well as a message, where I introduced myself quickly. I told her about the video, about the common birthdates and birthplace. I made a joke about *The Parent Trap* film and asked her not to freak out.

As I was waiting for her answer for three days, I started feeling really down and thought I was crazy. And then all of a sudden, I receive a notification on my phone saying that she had accepted my friend request.

My heart was beating. I was jumping all around, waiting for what she might say. She wasn't typing anything to me. She just sent me a picture of her adoption records. She also said that she didn't have much time to talk to me, but we would chat more in the coming days.

I had made first contact.

And as I was reading through her file, it confirmed that we were born the same day, the same year. We were both adopted from South Korea, both born in Pusan. But apart from this, none of our background stories matched. So I started thinking that maybe my dad was right, and maybe it was all just a coincidence.

For the next week I was looking at all her pictures, trying to discover what her life might be. And as we got to know each other a little more chatting on Facebook, we decided it was time to Skype.

And that was the weirdest experience. When both our faces appeared on the screen, I didn't know where to look. I was confused: which was her and which was me?

And I was like, "Uh, no, that's her."

We looked identical.

And where do you start? I wanted to say so many things that our Skype session lasted about three hours in the middle of the night. And when it was time to hang up, I didn't really want to.

As we were chatting more, she started feeling like a long-lost friend or a friend that you haven't seen in a while that you miss, except we had never met.

We decided it might be time to meet in person, but my dad, who was quite protective, said that we might want to take a DNA test before everyone got too emotionally involved.

We found a doctor that specialized in twins. She offered to help us with the DNA test results, but she warned us that there was a great chance we might be just doppelgängers. And it would take a few weeks to get the test results.

It was so intense that we decided, regardless of what the outcome might be, we really wanted to meet. So, we arranged to meet in London to get the test results together.

Samantha, her two older brothers and her parents flew from America, and my parents came from Paris.

I remember the day we were going to meet. I woke up, I got dressed, I was looking up at the sky, walking towards the Airbnb in Shoreditch, where we were supposed to meet. And I was thinking, *Oh my god, she might be in that plane right now. She's getting really close.*

So my parents and I get to the flat. And as I stood in front of the door, I could hear loud voices behind it, and I knew it was about to happen.

So I stepped into the room, and it felt like two parallel universes had suddenly merged together. She was sitting right in front of me. It looked like a mirror image of myself, except she wasn't moving as I was moving, so my brain had to readjust.

She started laughing hysterically. I did too.

We felt like two magnets that were attracted to each other, but also had this very special force that would repel us from each other.

My mom, who was standing behind me the whole time, said, "Oh my god, I have another daughter."

And my dad, who had been trying to warn us that we might be just doppelgängers, said, "Okay. I don't think you need a DNA test."

We then went for lunch, and we were just observing and staring at each other. Everyone was chatting, and we were amazed by our resemblance. We had the similar loud laughter, and our mannerisms were the same.

After all this emotion, I really needed to rest, and so did she, so when we got back to the Airbnb, we decided to take a nap together, in the same bed. That might seem quite strange, but at the time it felt really natural. We were just chatting, got tired, and fell asleep next to each other.

When I woke up, I felt this incredible sense of relief, because it felt as if we were being born again, but in the same world this time.

Later that evening, we sat down in front of our laptop, and we waited for Dr. Segal to call us on Skype.

She was quite serious. She looked at us and asked us to turn towards each other, and hug and kiss our identical twin sister.

She said, "DNA doesn't lie."

She had given us the final proof that this was all true.

We were really twins, separated at birth, adopted on two different continents, who had found each other through social media at twenty-five years old.

Today we still don't know what happened to our birth parents or why we were given up separately, or which of our stories is true. But I do know that I'm not that young girl who felt abandoned anymore.

I suddenly went from being an only child to having a twin sister, two older brothers, and even more parents living in America. Sam and I both have a big extended family, and this is so much, and enough, to be happy about.

The fact that we met is a miracle. But the most important thing is that, from now on, we have so much to live together. And we know that our lives are intertwined forever.

ANAÏS BORDIER is a thirty-year-old French designer. She was adopted from South Korea and grew up in Paris, where she graduated with a degree in textiles. She has further developed her creative skills studying fashion design at Central Saint Martins in London. She also obtained an MBA in luxury brand marketing and is now working with her family for the French luxury leather goods company Jean Rousseau. Anaïs and her sister Samantha are the authors of the book *Separated @ Birth: A True Love Story of Twin Sisters Reunited* (Putnam/Berkley, 2014), unveiling the story behind their documentary film *Twinsters* (2015).

Phyllis Marie Bowdwin

Quiet Fire

It was 1979, and it was summer in New York City. I was interviewing for a promotion from secretary to coordinator of daytime casting at ABC. I was thrilled. I put on a beautiful new blouse and matching skirt and two-inch heels.

I was ready.

But there were some who felt that I wasn't tough enough to manage a job like that. And somewhere deep inside there was a small part of me that suspected they might be right.

I actually had one friend, a colleague at the office, blurt out, "Phyllis, you're just too nice."

I said, "Thank you."

I was supposed to meet a friend across the street for lunch before my interview. When I got across the street, there was this horde of people filling up the sidewalk. They formed a human oval three people deep.

I didn't know what was going on, but I needed to get into the building. So I found a gap and I worked my way through, got into the opening, and was about to climb the stairs to go in when someone came up behind me and pinned my arms to my sides and prevented me from moving. I looked over both shoulders to try to figure out who it was, but I couldn't see anything, so I struggled, and the more I struggled, the tighter the grip became on my body.

When I looked out, I saw a sea of faces, and I was searching them for some clue about what was wrong, who was holding me, what was going on, but they were just eating their lunches, chewing, and watching me.

Suddenly the pressure eased, and a set of rough hands groped my entire body and then gave me a sharp push in my lower back. I stumbled forward, almost falling, but I regained my balance and whirled around and found a six-foot mime leering at me.

He was in full dress, with the beret, the striped shirt, the suspenders, the black pants, and the black sneakers, and he was dancing and bobbing and weaving around this human oval. He bent over, and he started to show me his behind, and he beckoned to me: *Come and hit me.* That's what he was indicating.

So I obliged.

I wrapped the strap of my bag around my hand, and I swung at him. The minute the bag was about to make contact, he sprang away and moved to another side of the oval.

Then he did it again: beckoned, pointed, beckoned.

I went after him this time in such earnest, and I swung my bag so hard that when he dodged (and he did dodge), I was pulled forward by the momentum and stumbled, and the crowd began to laugh.

I was so embarrassed. So when he invited me a third time, common sense prevailed. I was in a straight skirt with heels on, and he was bouncing around like a ball. I was outmatched.

I said, "You got it." I turned around and proceeded to go up the stairs when he rushed up, squeezed my behind, and then darted to safety in another part of the oval.

People laughed. I stood there so humiliated that waves of rage began to run through my body. But I finally got myself together, went up the stairs, went into the building, and went to the cafeteria, where they were serving my favorite dish, turkey Tetrazzini.

But I couldn't eat.

I sat down at that table feeling so dejected about what had just happened. I had been blindsided, bullied, and blatantly violated by a strange man in front of a group of strangers in the street.

I said to myself, *They must be giving him really big tips for him to do such a thing to me.* I couldn't defend myself. I couldn't protect myself in any way. So I just sat there feeling powerless.

Then I remembered something that I had dropped in my purse about four months ago. I had bought it in the 99-Cent Store as a joke. So I started digging down in the bag. And when my fingers made contact with that cold canister, I figured I had some options after all.

I pulled it out, wrapped a paper napkin around it, said, "Got to go," and I turned around and rushed outside to see if he was still there.

Of course he was. And by now the human oval had grown to *five* people deep. He had lots more audience.

As I looked at him, another woman cut in, a beautiful blond woman with a flared red dress on. She came through the crowd just as I had, and she was about to climb those stairs when this man got down on the ground and insinuated himself between her legs and stood up.

I was astounded. He basically had her mounted on his lower back like a rider on a horse. He grabbed her legs and proceeded to gallop around the oval. And the poor woman's arms were flailing as she was trying to hold on to her purse and keep from falling backwards. He let her down and promptly lifted her dress up over her head and held it there to the hoots and whistles from the crowd. When he finally let her go, the woman staggered into the building and disappeared.

I was saying to myself, *Is this New York City in 1979, or am I in the Twilight Zone? How could this happen here in the city, in broad daylight? Where are the police?*

And just as I thought that, an elderly gentleman – tall, handsome, salt-and-pepper gray, maybe about eighty-five – stepped out from the oval, and he approached the mime with an elderly woman in tow. She was holding on to his jacket, and she was peering out at the mime and cringing, peering out and cringing.

And I thought, *I wonder what he did to that old woman.* Sure enough, the man walked up to the mime, and he was shaking his finger in the mime's face and chastising him.

The mime feigned innocence. He threw his hands up in the air, and he put on that sad face, and he mimed crying.

Somebody from the crowd yelled, "Boo, BOO! Leave the mime alone!"

And the crowd picked up the chant: "BOO, BOO! Leave the mime alone!" The man looked up, startled, into the hostile eyes of the wolf pack consisting of executives, messengers, and clerks.

There was a UPS driver there, a postal worker, men of all ages, all races, out there enjoying the show. The man shook his head and gently took the woman by her hand and led her out of the crowd.

By then I was beginning to understand that this was a show, this was theater in the round, and any woman who made the mistake of stepping through that crowd became a player, whether she liked it or not. That woman, any woman, became the catch of the day on the mime's lunchtime menu for entertaining his patrons.

So when he started looking around for a new player, I stepped back into the arena, and I waited for him to see me. Sure enough, he saw me out of the corner of his eye, and he started coming toward me.

When he got a little closer, his eyes narrowed, and I couldn't tell whether it was because he remembered me from our past encounter or whether he was trying to figure out how he was going to launch a frontal attack, because every time he did something, he always attacked from behind.

I didn't wait. When he got two feet closer, I said, "Hi. Remember me?"

And I smiled.

And lifted my can of pepper spray.

And I sprayed him in his face.

His eyes got wide, and he reached for my throat, and I stepped backwards, and I sprayed him again and again.

I sprayed him like a roach.

He began coughing, and sneezing, and wheezing, and staggering about, because now he couldn't see, and he started heading towards the street.

His loyal supporters parted, and they let him go. He landed on the hood of a parked car, coughing, sneezing, wheezing. But while I was enjoying watching him, someone karate-chopped my right hand, and I dropped my canister.

And I turned around, and it was *another mime,* only this one was twice the size of the first one, and this hulking Goliath of a man was glowering at me and looked like he wanted to kill me.

We both heard the canister rolling slowly but noisily down the sidewalk, and he lumbered toward it. I turned around, and I started rushing toward it, and the two of us scrambled to get to that canister, but I got there first. And

I grabbed it, and I scooped it up, and I looked at him. He came at me, and I stepped back, and I took a wide stance, and I got all the way down on the ground, and I started rocking back and forth on my heels, and said:

"YOU WANT THIS, MOTHERFUCKER?!

"COME

"AND

"GET

"IT!"

And he stopped cold.

Now, we both knew he was four times my size. If he ever got his hands on me, he would have been able to break me in two. But at what cost? Because that was the day that I was prepared to die ... and when I left the planet, I was taking him with me.

He must have seen it in my eyes – *Kill. The. Mime.* – because he turned around and disappeared back into the crowd.

By now the spray was spreading, and some of the lovely supporters were starting to cough, and sneeze, and choke, and wheeze, and they quickly dispersed without leaving a dime in the mime's hat.

It was then that I realized that from all that rocking on the ground, I had bent the heel on my shoe and split my skirt all the way up to my butt, and I had an interview at two o'clock!

So I hobbled across the street, and I got upstairs to my office. I grabbed my Scotch tape and my stapler. I got myself into the ladies' room, locked the door, took off my skirt, pulled the seam back together, and stapled, stapled, stapled, stapled. I flattened it out, took some Scotch tape, taped down one edge, taped down the other edge, and placed one in the center for good measure.

I went back to my desk, where I had a pair of flats, thank the Lord. I put them on, and I waited for that call. When they called, I went upstairs.

I aced that interview and got the job.

That was the day that I got in touch with my other side. She doesn't make many appearances. She's available on an as-needed basis.

I call her my quiet fire, and we both thank you.

PHYLLIS MARIE BOWDWIN is a Bronx-born artist, jeweler, and griot. A former teacher trainer for the New York City Department of Education, crisis-intervention counselor, and coordinator of daytime casting at ABC, Phyllis was a panelist on the UN's 2013 Pre-Commission on the Elimination and Prevention of Violence Against Women and Girls. Phyllis's Middle Passage Maafa brooch was featured in the *New York Times* and is in the permanent collection of the Cooper Hewitt, Smithsonian Design Museum. Phyllis won a 2013 BRIO Award for literature. Her stories have been published in the *Bronx Memoir Project*, the UFT's *Reflections* magazine, and the *Independent*.

Liel Leibovitz

Real Men Don't Rob Banks

I grew up in Israel in the 1980s, and my father's mission in life was to make sure that his only son – me – grew up to be a real man.

As soon as I turned four, every Saturday he would take me shooting, which was funny because my arm was exactly the size of a Smith & Wesson .45. Two or three years later, when I was six or seven, my father would take advantage of Israel's surprisingly relaxed car-rental insurance policies and rent a car to take me on driving lessons (which were terrifying because even sitting in his lap I didn't reach the wheel).

Every two or three weeks, there was a special treat. We would stop the rental car by the side of the road and my father would make me go out and change tires, whether the car needed it or not, because in his mind knowing how to change a tire was the epitome of manhood.

I really hated changing tires.

And I really hated spending these Saturday afternoons with him. But he didn't care, because he was inducting me to the International Brotherhood of Macho Men.

Every chance he got, he would take me to the movies to see his heroes – men like Sylvester Stallone or Chuck

33

Norris or Burt Reynolds. I didn't mind these guys too much, but they were not *my* idols.

My idol was a real live person called the Motorcycle Bandit. He appeared on the scene shortly after my twelfth birthday, robbing bank after bank after bank all over Israel. He was in and out of the banks in under forty seconds, never leaving behind any clues to his real name or identity.

He got so popular that Israel's most famous comedy sketch show – sort of the local version of *Saturday Night Live* – devoted an entire episode to the bandit, speculating in one bit that he probably never robbed a bank in Jerusalem because he didn't particularly care for that city. So you can imagine what the reaction was the next day, when, in an apparent tribute to his favorite television show, the Motorcycle Bandit robbed his one and only Jerusalem bank.

People went *insane*. Women who worked at banks would write their names and phone numbers on little notes so that if the sexy heart-throb robber happened to hit their bank, maybe he would find their number and give them a call.

But the people who loved the bandit most were us teenage boys. For us he was a hero, and on Purim, which is more or less the Jewish equivalent of Halloween, we all dressed up like him – in a leather jacket and a motorcycle helmet and a big shiny gun.

So about a year and a half later, I'm thirteen. I'm walking home from the eighth grade, and no one's home, so I mosey over to the kitchen to make myself a snack. I hear a knock on the door, but it's not a *tap-tap-tap*. It's a *boom-boom-BOOM*.

I open the door, and there are three police officers standing there. They're not looking at me, and none of them are saying anything.

Finally, after about half a minute, one of them looks up and says, "Son, we arrested your father a while ago with a motorcycle helmet and a leather jacket and a big shiny gun."

And I remember my first thought was, *NO WAY!*

You think, you think MY DAD, with a beer belly and a receding hairline and the terrible jokes, you think THAT GUY is the Motorcycle Bandit?

But in the hours and the days and the weeks that passed, I learned that he *was*.

The real story, as I soon came to learn, began when my father, who was thirty-five at the time and the son of one of Israel's wealthiest families, was summoned by his father to have "the talk." Now, if you've watched a couple episodes of *Dallas* or *Dynasty* or *Knot's Landing,* you know "the talk." It's when the rich guy calls his wayward playboy son over and says, "Son, it's time for you to grow up and be a man, take responsibility for your life and get a job."

My father didn't like that at all. So he stormed out of my grandfather's office, and he hopped on his motorcycle (because, of course), and he drove to the beach. He'd later tell me that as he was sitting there watching the sun set over the Mediterranean, he was thinking about his life. My father grew up in the sixties, so he believed in things like "do what you love" and "follow your heart."

So he decided to follow his heart, and his heart led him to robbing banks.

Now, as it turns out, he was good at it; he was *great* at it; he was an inventor, an innovator.

He was the Elon Musk of the stickup job.

And later I learned how he did it, and it was incredible. To rob a bank in under forty seconds, he'd take the money at gunpoint, then run out of the bank, jump on his motorcycle, and drive around a corner, up a ramp he had custom-built, and into a van, where he would pause.

So here's a seminal existential question of bank rob-bing: *Where's the last place you would ever look for a bank robber?*

And the answer is: the last place you would ever look for a bank robber is *inside the bank he just robbed.*

So my father would take off his jacket and his helmet and tuck the gun back into his pants. He'd calmly walk out of the van and around the corner and go back into the bank, which at that point was a crime scene crawling with police officers.

One of these police officers would inevitably run up to my father and say, "You can't be here, sir, this is a crime scene!"

And my father would give him this dopey look and say, "Oh, can I please just make a quick deposit? My wife will kill me if I don't."

The police officer would say something like "Sure, but be quick about it," and my father would walk up to the bank teller and deposit the *same exact cash he had stolen three minutes earlier.* This being the 1980s and computers were still kind of new, he made the cash virtually untraceable.

It was a work of genius. He was so good at it and he became so popular that eventually he got cocky. He robbed one bank a day, and then two, and then two banks in two different cities.

One time he was riding in a cab on his way to the air-port when the urge struck.

He asked the cab driver, "Would you mind stopping? I promise I'll only be a minute."

It was literally true – he was only a minute. He robbed the bank, hopped back into the cab, drove to the airport, and flew off for an all-expenses-paid vacation in New York.

But you know how this story ends. Eventually he was caught. And after he was arrested, life got really weird,

in no small part because Israel, being a small state surrounded by enemies, has its own ideas about prison.
Prisoners get one weekend out of the month off to go
home on vacation, the logic being that the country only
has one airport, and it's extremely secure, and if you want
to go ahead and try to escape through Gaza or Syria, you
know, be our guest!

So, every fourth Friday, I would go to the prison to pick
my father up, and we would go out and have ourselves a
weekend on the town.

People would come up to him and high-five him and
pat him on the back and say things like "Bandit, we love
you, you're cool."

But to me he *wasn't* cool. And he wasn't even the bandit. He was my dad, who had just done something so
incredibly stupid that it had landed him a twenty-year
prison sentence.

But even weirder than that one weekend a month we
spent together were the three weekends a month apart.
Because here I would be, and it was Saturday, and there's
no shooting practice, there's no driving lesson, no changing tires, no Burt Reynolds, and I didn't know what to do.

So one afternoon I got dressed, which, by the way, was
also an ordeal, because when the police searched our
house, they took not only all of my father's belongings
but, because we were more or less the same size, also
all of mine. So I put on one of the few outfits I had – this
really ratty, disgusting purple sweatsuit with the Batman
logo on front, which I assume the police thought no self-
respecting bank robber would ever wear.

I walked out and started walking around town, looking
for a sign.

And then I saw it – a literal sign. It was a sign above a
theater advertising an all-male Japanese modern dance

show. I thought about it for maybe five seconds, and then I did something that I'm pretty sure my father would disown me for: I bought a ticket, and I went in.

And I *loved* it. Here onstage were these amazing, elegant, graceful men, and guess what? They weren't punching each other in the face, they were not riding Harley-Davidsons. They were *dancing*. And yet they were so secure in their bodies and their masculinities.

I thought to myself, *If that's another way of being a man, what* other *ways are there?*

And thus began a two-decade-long process of trial and error – of trying to figure out what kind of man I wanted to be. And look, some of the things I learned didn't surprise me at all. I love bourbon, and I'm the kind of guy who would watch as much sports as you would let him in a given day.

But other things were really surprising, like some French poets moved me to tears. And even though bourbon was great, you know what else tastes really good? Rosé wine. And even though I'm really, really good at changing tires, if I get a flat now, I'm calling AAA.

I didn't share any of these insights with my father, because for one thing he's not really the kind of guy who's into insights. But, for another, by the time he got out of prison, I was already a man in full – it was too late for him to shape who I became in any meaningful way.

From time to time, he still comes to visit New York, where I live with my family. And on one of these recent visits, he and I are sitting in my living room, not talking, as men do. And my son comes prancing into the room – my three-year-old boy.

Now, that boy looks exactly like me. Just as I look exactly like my father.

And if there's one thing in the world that boy loves, it's his older sister.

And if there's one thing in the world that his older sister loves, it's Disney princesses.

And in prances the child dressed like Princess Anna from *Frozen*.

I look at my son, and I look at my father looking at my son (who, by the way, looked amazing in this light green taffeta with a black velvet bodice and some lovely lacing).

And I know that my father is judging me.

But you know what? I don't care. Because at that moment I realize, strangely, that by going to jail when he did, he didn't just free *me* from the burden of this macho nonsense, he also freed up *my son* to grow up as a happy boy who can pretend to be whoever he wants to be, even – or especially – a pretty, pretty princess.

And I can't tell you how grateful I am that, instead of going through life mindlessly as two tough guys, my son and I are free to become whatever kind of real men we want to be.

LIEL LEIBOVITZ writes for *Tablet* magazine, the world's finest Jewish publication, and co-hosts its podcast, *Unorthodox*. He has written some books, most of which are about the beautiful and desperate things people do when searching for redemption. He also has a Ph.D. in video games, which would have made his seven-year-old self very happy. He's married, a father of two, and a religious fundamentalist when it comes to good coffee.

Martha Ruiz-Perilla

Opposing Forces

I was about to graduate from dental school when I told my mother I had been assigned to do my residency at a hospital in a small town in Colombia called Neiva.

She was very upset. It was 1992. I was twenty-one years old. This was the Colombia of Pablo Escobar, of daily assassinations and bombings, of government corruption and kidnappings, paramilitary groups and massacres.

It was also the Colombia of the FARC, one of the oldest guerrilla movements in modern history.

It was a Colombia where we had gotten used to the war between all these opposing forces. We heard a loud noise, like when a car backfired, and went down on the ground; we waited, we got up, we dusted off, and we moved on. Neiva, where I was going, was small, hot, and violent. Add to that the possibility of guerrillas and narcotraffic, and the prospects were pretty scary, especially for a young woman like me who had never left home.

So my mother called my dad, who at the time lived in Granada, another very violent town in Colombia.

He asked me if I was scared.

I said yes.

He said, "*M'ija,* you know how I live here in Granada, and you know how violent and dangerous it is. You know why I stay? Because if the good people don't stay to serve, the bad people take over. So you go where you're being called to serve, and you help those who need you the most. Just be smart, be careful, and call your mother."

And with that I went to Neiva. I arrived one April afternoon. My first impression was that this was an overcrowded and underfunded hospital. But there were plenty of people helping it stay afloat.

My workday at the hospital began early in the morning, doing the rounds with the resident physicians. After that I took care of my outpatients until 5:00 p.m., focusing strictly on general dentistry. I took one patient every fifteen minutes, with two short breaks during the day.

At night and on the weekends, I would be on call at the ER for any emergencies that dealt with superficial injuries above the neck. That's how I learned to put noses, eyelids, and ears back onto people.

The room where I lived at the hospital during my residency faced a roof terrace, which I quickly came to find out was inhabited by hundreds of bats. At night I had to sleep with the window open, because temperatures rose up to 105 degrees, and there was no A/C at the hospital.

To combat the heat and avoid the bats, I wrapped myself in a soaking-wet beach towel. This I decided after I woke up one night to the horror of a baby bat comfortably sleeping on my pillow next to me and another one bathing in the glass of water I'd left on my night table.

Then, one hot night, I went to sleep and the next thing I remember is standing in the dark next to a man holding a rifle. I didn't know what time it was. Early in the morning, I guessed – it was dark outside.

In the shadows I could see another person, also armed, guarding my bedroom door. The man pointing the rifle at me ordered me to get dressed. It was then that I realized

I was in my underwear standing in front of them; I had been pulled out of my beach towel.

I rushed to look for my uniform in the dark. As I looked, I began thinking of my parents, and the stories I had heard of doctors and nurses being taken by the guerrillas and never returned.

Once I was dressed, I turned to him and I asked if I could leave my parents a note.

He said, "No."

He grabbed my arm and rushed me out of the room. We went down the emergency stairwell, which was lined with men dressed like him, wearing rags that covered their heads and faces and only left their eyes visible.

I didn't want to look at them. I didn't want them to think that I could recognize them or remember any of them. All of these men addressed the man holding me as "Commander." I knew immediately this wasn't the army. I had seen men like this when we visited my father in Granada.

These were rebels.

When we got to the first floor, I realized they had seized the hospital. I was ordered not to speak and to go to my office.

I headed down this long corridor, and the farther away we got, the more hopeless I felt. We got to the office, and they had broken the doorknob. Inside, in the dark, two men awaited.

The man holding me told me that I had three hours to help him or I would have to come with them. I was terrified.

So I just asked, "Who is the patient?"

And from within the shadows, one of these men turned on a flashlight and revealed a boy about fifteen years old, wearing this ripped T-shirt and dirty pants and soiled boots.

His face was completely deformed by an exacerbated abscess that made the left side look like a water balloon about to burst.

The man holding me let me go. But when I approached the child and tried to touch his face, I felt a rifle firmly pressed against my spine.

He said to me, "Can you help us or not?"

I said, "Yes, I can."

I told him to sit the child on the chair and that I would have to turn on all the lights and instruments. He agreed but continued to point the rifle at me.

Once inside, I realized that I was going to need assistance holding the child down. I couldn't make him drowsy, because I knew they needed to leave the hospital on foot. I couldn't apply any anesthesia, because given the degree of the infection no anesthesia would catch.

So I knew I was going to have to do this procedure without numbing him, and it was going to hurt – *a lot.*

I explained this to the Commander, and he pointed to one of his men, who immediately put his rifle on the floor and jumped on the child, straddled him at the thighs, grabbed his arms, and held them by the side of the kid's body.

So I had my assistant ready.

I was shaking. I had an idea what needed to be done. I'd seen it in books and in enormous slide projections in our oral pathology classes. But I had never done anything like this myself; it would be the first time.

What I did know was if I made a mistake in my incision and touched the nerve that runs by that area of the face, I could cause the paralysis of half of this kid's face for life.

I also knew that if I let the infection progress, this kid could go into sepsis and die.

In the back of my mind, I also knew that, if the army had been informed that the rebels were in the hospital, they could burst in at any time. There could be a crossfire, and I could become collateral damage by the end of the morning.

So I grabbed a towel, wet it with cold water, and rubbed the kid's forehead. He was burning with fever.

I didn't want to ask his name, so I called him *pelao,* which means "kid" in the area of Colombia where I come from.

I explained to him what I was going to do. I told him that it was going to hurt a lot and that he could cry or scream. But he could also tell me when he couldn't take it anymore, and I would stop and let him rest.

He looked up at me, and his little eyes filled with tears. He nodded.

My heart shrunk. This boy was in so much pain. And he was terrified.

But so was I. I had a rifle on my back. So I put on my protective gear, and I wrapped my arm around him to prevent him from hitting me. I prepared the scalpel and a handful of gauze.

I took a deep breath. I calculated the position of the nerve in that inflated balloon of skin. And I made my first incision on that cheek, slowly and carefully.

I began to drain. The kid was screaming and twitching in the chair. I felt the rifle shake on my back. Greenish yellow pus came bursting out of his cheek. The man holding him closed his eyes and turned away – the smell was nauseating.

I made a wider cut. But suddenly the child began to cry uncontrollably, so I stopped.

I reached down for his hand and grabbed it. It was this small, cold, rough hand.

I told him that he was a brave boy. He closed his eyes and nodded. We were both sweating profusely.

I went back to squeezing and draining.

When the kid couldn't take it anymore, he suddenly yelled out, *"¡Ay, no más, Papá!"* and it was then that I felt strongest the pressure of that rifle on my back.

The man, the Commander, who had been pointing the rifle at me this whole time, broke his silence, and he said, "Almost there, *m'ijo.*"

And I was petrified. Because it was then that I realized whose child I was cradling in my arm.

This was the Commander's son.

I couldn't screw this up. I had to do this right.

I knew that if this kid got worse, or if he died, this guy would come back for me – I was sure about that.

I went back to working as fast as I could.

When the inflammation went down enough for me to look into his mouth, I found the culprit – a rotten molar. I had to pull it out. It was part of the procedure.

I explained this to the Commander and his son, and they agreed.

With every piece of tooth that I pulled, a scream came along. And with every scream, the barrel of that rifle shook on my back. This man was feeling his son's pain. As I worked, however, I began to see relief on the kid's face.

It was close to dawn. We were running out of time. So I finished preparing the wound. I got up and grabbed some free samples of antibiotics and some medical supplies.

I gave them to the Commander, and I explained how to clean the wound. I told him the boy should be okay in two weeks.

And that's when he said, "I hope so, *Doctora*, because I don't want to come back, and you don't want to come where we're going."

He ordered the kid off the chair, and he obeyed immediately. They circled around me and walked out the door.

I felt the rifle pressure ease off my back. I closed my eyes, and I prayed to God that he wouldn't shoot me right there. That's when I heard them saying from the door that if I didn't speak or move for at least a half an hour, I would be okay.

I nodded. And then I heard the door close.

When I opened my eyes, the kid's blood was still drying on my latex gloves. My hands were drenched in sweat inside them. I kept reviewing the procedure: *Had I done everything right? Had I forgotten something? Had I left anything out?*

For the next two weeks, I was cold. I couldn't eat anything. Everything made me nauseous.

I didn't want to answer questions about the incident. I didn't even tell my parents.

At night I couldn't sleep. I would lie on my bed and stare at that door, hoping that nobody would break into the room again. I continued to take care of my outpatients, but every time one walked in, I feared it would be the child.

I was excused from the ER. They said that I didn't have to volunteer if I didn't want to.

And then one day I was at the office and the phone rang. It was from the front desk. They said I had a package there. I froze, but I went. The girl handed me this crumpled envelope and said that a man had stopped by and left me a note and *that* (she was pointing at a sack of oranges with a live chicken tied to it).

I opened the envelope and pulled out a note. In almost illegible writing it said, *"The pelao is okay, Doctora, no need to come back – gracias."*

I felt this relief. I put the note quickly in my uniform, and I went back to work. Later that night when I went to my room, I climbed out of the window onto the roof terrace. I could hear the bats flapping their wings above my head. I didn't care.

I brought the note and matches with me. I pulled it out, and I burned it.

And I burned it because it reminded me of how scared I had been that night, of how frightened I had been for the last two weeks. I also burned it because I thought it connected me to the bad people.

But then I thought, *What bad people?* This was a sick child. I had to help him.

And besides, in Colombia in the nineties, who knew who the bad guys and the good guys were? Nobody knew.

We were just people trying to get by in this battle of warlords that nobody knew how to stop, that, as you know, to this day we're still trying to stop. These people that had come in search of my help were just people with mothers and fathers and sons and toothaches, capable of love and hate and gratitude, amidst this violence. Capable, too, of killing, and kidnapping, and hurting.

And yet that man had risked his life that day for his son. Like my own father would. And he had respected my life.

Then I thought about my father's words, about serving the people who need it the most.

Since then I've come to think that in times of war it's very hard to tell the good people from the bad people. And if you're gifted with the opportunity to help another

47

human being, you do it. Because that's how you serve –
not a faction, not a party, not a cause, but the people.

So the following night, I volunteered at the ER.

I went down again to serve the people of Neiva.

MARTHA RUIZ-PERILLA is a New York-based artist. Born and raised in Colombia, Martha graduated dental school in 1992. Her love for storytelling, a family tradition, is evident in her artwork, which includes painting, sculpture, and installation. Martha's work is part of private and public collections around the world. She was a graduate fellow and salutatorian at Christie's Education, earning a master's degree in modern and contemporary art in 2002. Martha has captivated audiences with her stories since the age of five. She lives with her husband, Marc; her children, Fermín Adrián and Zeta Simöne; and their dog, Quesito.

Peter Aguero

Me and Mama vs. Christmas

I just finished my first semester of college, and I have a big bag of laundry. I come through the door of the house, and things aren't looking too good for me and my mom.

The first thing I notice is that the piano is gone, and she had that ever since she was a little girl and took piano lessons. We always put the nativity on top of it around Christmastime. I took piano lessons, too (for two weeks, but still, I took piano lessons on that piano), and now it's gone.

I go through the living room, and the only thing that's left is one couch with broken springs sticking out of it.

There are two televisions, one on top of the other – one has a picture that works, and one has sound that works. One of the TVs is hooked up to cable, and the other one gets the antenna so the sound doesn't quite jibe up, you know?

Over in the corner are the impressions from my dad's La-Z-Boy that has been gone for four years now.

I walk into the dining room and I see that it's empty. There used to be this big, beautiful dining-room set with carved chairs and a glass breakfront and a buffet table, and that's gone.

In the kitchen there's a small table and two chairs. There used to be four, but I broke one of them, and the other chair I also broke, and so there's only two left.

I go upstairs to the bedrooms, and in my mom's room there's nothing left but her mattress on the floor. And there's nothing quite as damning as a bedroom without furniture, because you see all the dings and the scratches in the wallpaper, all the mistakes that can usually be covered up.

My sister's room is exactly the way it looked when she moved out two years ago to go live with my dad: Pepto-Bismol-pink walls, and a canopy bed, and this big toy box in the shape of a rubber strawberry, as if she was gonna move back in and be the little girl that she was before she moved out.

My room looks exactly the way it was when I left for college. There's posters all over the walls, and it's ridiculous, like me.

I start to do my laundry. My mom comes home from work, and she immediately takes over, doesn't let me do it myself. I end up helping her with it, and she's happy to see me – she's happy that I'm home.

When we're done with that, we have dinner. My mom makes tomato casserole. It was one of my favorite things. It was canned tomatoes with cubes of Wonder bread and American cheese baked in the oven. If you put enough shaky cheese on it, it's delicious, you know?

So we're sitting there in the two kitchen chairs, and I'm telling her all about my first semester of college and how I finished up. She's so proud of me.

And she's telling me about work. My mom's a nurse, and she's been taking all the shifts that she can. But she had warned me that she was starting to have to sell stuff in the house to be able to catch up on the bills, because the house is too big for the two of us, and now that I am away at school, it is just her.

So she was doing everything she could, and she warned me, but it was still shocking, you know? She had just taken a second job, a part-time seasonal job at the mall, behind the perfume counter. My mom didn't like people telling her what to do, so I knew that wasn't gonna last very long.

While we're sitting there at dinner, she says, "Pete, we're not going to have a lot of money this year for Christmas, so I don't think we're going to be able to give each other presents."

I said, "That's okay, Mom" – and I'm being completely honest. I'm just happy to be home with her. I don't need anything, and that's the truth.

We sit there eating quietly for a minute, and then she says, "You know what'd be funny? What if we cut out pictures of things from magazines that we would give to each other if we could?"

And we laughed about it.

And then we cried about it, because it's sad – it's a really sad thing.

But then we laughed again, because no matter how hard things are, you just have to laugh, you know?

The next day I decided I wanted to make the house look as Christmassy as possible. I went up to the attic, and I got down the boxes with the lights, and I hung the lights on the bushes out front and around the gutters. I wanted to go get a Christmas tree.

I grew up in a little town in New Jersey called Delanco. It was a small town, twenty-five hundred people. It was mostly farms. At that time there wasn't Walmart or big stores or anything, so I went over to the local Christmas-tree farm to get a tree.

I figured they'd give me a deal because I used to date their daughter. But it turns out they didn't give me a deal, because I used to date their daughter. And the Christmas tree was like forty bucks – man, I couldn't afford that. So I went back home, and I got an old saw out of the garage, and I cut out a tree from the side yard, and I brought it in.

It wasn't even a pine tree, it was like a stunted maple tree. I put it in the tree holder. It had like five branches. I put twenty ornaments on each branch and just kinda put the lights on it and called it a day. My mom came home from work, and she just laughed about it.

When I visited my friends who were also home from college, I would steal their mom's fancy catalogs and bring them home and cut out pictures of stuff. My mom always wanted a green Jaguar convertible. I found a picture of one of those. I cut out pictures of gold and diamonds and jewelry and an island, all these things that I would love to be able to give my mom for Christmas.

I kept collecting them and folding them up and tying them up with ribbons and hiding them in my room, and I was waiting to put them under the tree. And, like I said, I knew it was a sad thing, but it was also something that would bring us together. I knew it was something that we would be able to hold on to together.

There is one night toward the end of December, close to Christmas, when we're sitting there in the living room watching the TVs and the Charlie Brown Christmas special is on. And we're sitting there right next to each other on the couch, but we're worlds apart.

My mom's exhausted. I've been trying to get her to sell the house for years, because I knew it was just too big for her to be in by herself. If I'm being honest, it was too big when all four of us were living there. I don't know why they got it in the first place.

Four years before that, my parents – who had been separated on and off the whole time that they were married – were giving it one last try. The plan was that they were going to sell the house and take the money, and we were gonna move to Georgia from Jersey and have a fresh start. That was the big plan.

It went along okay for a couple of weeks, and then they started to fight and things went back to normal. So that fresh start never really happened, and it culminated with the four of us in the third pew at St. Casimir's church in Riverside, New Jersey, for Christmas Eve midnight Mass.

Right before the priest started the Mass in the packed church, my dad stood up, and he walked out of the church. The only sound you could hear in the silent church was the hydraulic door just go *shooo*.

The three of us stood up, and we went past the priest and everyone we knew, and we walked the two blocks to where the car was parked. My dad was nowhere to be found, but he left the keys to the car sitting on the hood.

And that year my parents were done. That was it.

I got what I wanted for Christmas that year: my parents never got back together.

But here we are now, today, the two of us sitting on this couch and trying to watch this thing and be happy, something. And she's a million miles away.

It's all killing her, trying to pay the bills, trying to keep it together. She did everything she could to try to keep the house so there would be some semblance of normalcy. I knew that she took a big hit on her pride. She's a very prideful woman, and I knew that when everyone she knew in her life saw our family disintegrate at that midnight Mass, it ripped her apart.

My mom was my best friend. It was the two of us, man. She was my partner. She was like my road dog, you know?

It was like me and her against the world, and being there with her and having her be a million miles away was killing *me,* just like I knew this house was killing her.

Well, it got to be Christmas Eve, and my buddy Brian came over and picked me up, and we went to a different church for midnight Mass. When you're under twenty-one, you can't go to a bar, so you go see your friends at Mass. We split a jug of wine in the parking lot, and we went in. Mass was awesome, and afterwards I came home.

The next morning I wake up, and it's Christmas morning. So I go and gather up all the little pictures of the gifts that I want to give to my mother, all wrapped up and tied in ribbon, and I put them under the tree.

I hear my mom stirring upstairs, and she comes down. Her hair's in corkscrews, and she's got this big flannel housecoat on and her big, red plastic Sally Jessy Raphael morning glasses with the broken ear thing on the side taped up.

I say, "Merry Christmas, Mom."

She goes, "Oh, honey, oh – hold on."

And she goes upstairs, and she's upstairs for a minute. Then she comes back down, and she has a few pictures of gifts.

I give her hers first. There's the Jaguar and the jewelry and the island and a picture of a baby grand piano. A picture of a new dining-room set and of a new mahogany bedroom set, and all these things I wish I could replace for her. And she's smiling and laughing the whole time.

When it's all done, she gives me mine, and there's three of them: there's a picture of a bag of Reese's Peanut Butter Cups, there's a picture of a pair of Homer Simpson slippers, and there's a picture of a karaoke machine.

And they were all from the same Rite Aid catalog that was up in her bathroom, because she was working so hard *she had completely forgotten about this thing that I thought was going to bring us together.*

So we're stuck in the middle of this O. Henry story that he never would have written, and I thank her so much for the gifts.

We go to the kitchen, and my mom makes the best pancakes in the world. (You might think your mom does, but I'm so sorry, you're wrong.) But this morning she burns them a little bit. So I'm sitting in the kitchen eating these pancakes, cutting around the burnt pieces. And I'm looking out through our backyard at everybody else's house, and all the light in their houses looks orange and colorful and friendly, with all these people inside. And our house just feels empty and stark and white under the fluorescent light, as we eat these pancakes in silence together, just the two of us.

A couple of months later, she finally did send me my present. I was back in college, and man, I had taken out all the tuition in loans, because we couldn't afford it otherwise, but it was important to her that I go.

I had just finished a day of classes, and I was heading to the dining hall. I stopped over to check my mail. Remember mail? I opened up the mailbox, and there was an envelope with my mother's postmark on it.

I take it up to the dining hall, and I fill up my tray with too much food (because that's what you do). I go over to a table, and I sit down. And before I start eating, I open up that envelope.

Inside there's no note, there's just one photograph. It's of her standing in front of the house with a For Sale sign.

The house sold pretty quickly. She offloaded it, and she took a little bit of a hit financially, and she took an even bigger hit on her pride. She moved into a much smaller place that she could afford. And it hurt her, I know it hurt her.

But the most important thing to me was right then, when looking at that picture ... I got my girl back.

PETER AGUERO was born and raised in the wilds of South Jersey. He's been working with The Moth since 2007 as a storyteller, instructor, and host. His solo show *Daddy Issues* has played the far reaches and middle grounds of North America, mostly to acclaim (except for one guy in Fresno, California. That guy hated it). He spends most of his time listening to The Allman Brothers while making weaponized, profane pottery in Queens. Some of those pieces can be acquired at www.etsy.com/shop/PotterAguero.

Lynn Ferguson

Before Fergus

I'm Scottish.

A friend of mine is Bosnian, and he married a Serbian, and together they had a child. They had to flee their country, because their child – being of mixed race – was in danger by just *being*. They called their son Trim, which means "courage."

My friend said he called his son "Courage" because he felt that as soon as the child was born, he'd lost all of his own courage, and that anything that he'd fought for in his previous life had gone, and now he'd fight for nothing but the life of that child.

You know, I've thought about that a lot since I've had my son, about the things that I've lost. I thought that maybe I should have called him "Dress Sense" or "Whole Night's Sleep" or "The Ability to Watch a Grown-Up Movie the Whole Way Through."

Then I settled for "Peace of Mind."

I was thirty-seven when I first fell pregnant.

Well, I didn't *fall* pregnant. There wasn't some incident with a sidewalk and a flip-flop.

I did stuff. I got pregnant. I was thirty-seven.

The point is, I'd lived a bit, but suddenly, after twenty years of self-imposed hedonism, I found myself unable to smoke or drink alcohol and taking a little sabbatical from pâté, caffeine, and soft cheese.

The discovery wasn't the kind of romantic one you get in black-and-white movies. I had been touring France on the back of a motorcycle with my husband when I started to feel a bit unwell.

Now, a word of advice: if you're feeling sick, don't do it at eighty miles an hour, leather pants on one end, crash helmet on the other, in a country where they eat snails because they can.

We arrive back home, and my husband decides he wants some take-out food. I have this bizarre thing where I want to do a pregnancy test. It's positive.

So my husband arrives back with his little brown paper bag to be greeted with the immortal phrase, "Put your curry down, sweetheart, there's something really big I have to tell you!"

I've heard it said that you feel most like a woman when you're pregnant. It's complete rubbish. It's not so. I felt most like a beached whale. It's a completely bizarre thing, because you suddenly find yourself entirely responsible for this other person. And this other person has only got you, and so even though the two of you are together twenty-four hours a day, it's not like you can just go to a bar and have a discussion about it.

Before I got pregnant, my greatest fear about getting run down by a car was that I wouldn't be wearing matching underwear. After I got pregnant, the whole idea of getting run over by a car took on a whole different meaning. Never mind the eating for two, it's the *thinking* for two that wears you out, you know?

There was a lot of difficulty around my pregnancy, because thirty-seven is considered quite an old age to be having your first child, so anybody here who's thirty-six and thinking about becoming a parent, get your skates on.

In fact, in the medical profession they define it as "clinical geriatric," and I am not even joking.

So almost as soon as everybody agreed that I was in the family way, they decided that I should have an amniocentesis. An amniocentesis is an invasive test where they put a needle through the mother's belly and into the amniotic fluid, and it can tell you whether the baby has Down syndrome or not. But there's also a one percent risk that it will cause damage to the fetus or the fetus will miscarry.

Now, I'm totally not against risk; I think it's a matter of choice, and I like risk, and I am completely and utterly pro-choice.

But there was no way that I figured they were going to do it. It wasn't the baby's fault I was thirty-seven. That was entirely on me. That was my decision.

So I was like, *No*. But every appointment it would come up about the amniocentesis, and initially I would deal with it that way you do when you don't want to have coffee with someone.

When you go, "Oh, damn, the amniocentesis – we will, we'll do it. I can't do it this week, though. Maybe next week? Oh, no, my mother's coming. No, I can't do that."

But, as they became more insistent about it, I kind of felt like I had to, too.

So I was like, "You know, can this test tell me whether this child will be a jerk? Can your test tell me whether this kid is going to be one of those really screamy ones that annoys the hell out of everybody on airplanes? Can your test tell me whether this small, tiny, growing human being will mature into a fully grown adult who has some horrific affinity with Peruvian pan-flute music? Because I'm worried about Down's syndrome, hands up, but I'm pregnant, and I'm worried about *a lot* of things. So thanks very much and everything, but no."

Then came the twenty-week scan.

We were told we were having a boy. Woo-hoo! Then the lady scanning the baby said that my son had statistically a very large head.

I looked across at my husband for the first time, I swear, noticing *his* statistically large head. I silently cursed love for being blind.

She told me I was thirty-seven. I knew that.

Then, scanning the baby's head, she said there were choroid plexus cysts all down one side of the baby's brain.

Okay. That wasn't something I was expecting.

We were told that everything was going to be "fine," in that way where you just know it's not, and we had to wait for a specialist.

The specialist we went to see told us we were having a boy. We knew that.

She told me I was thirty-seven. *I know.* She said the baby had a statistically large head.

Then she said that the choroid plexus cysts were a problem.

We'd kind of guessed that.

And then, scanning the baby again, she said that there was a vessel missing on the umbilical cord.

She said we needed to do the test. But because I had waited so long, they didn't want to do an amnio, they wanted to do something called a cordio, which is pretty much the same brand as an amnio. They insert a big needle into the womb, and they take a little bit of the umbilical cord, and that can tell them what's going on with the baby. Now, this is an umbilical cord that they have just told me isn't fully functioning.

We didn't even need a discussion for the decision.

I was like, "Okay, the Down syndrome thing, it's not exactly what we'd planned, and I know it's going to be difficult, probably – for us and for him and in ways that I don't even know yet. But actually, personally, I think there are worse things than having Down syndrome, you know?

"I mean, having Down's syndrome doesn't mean you're a bad person, does it?"

So I said no.

But that's when they told me that Down's syndrome was off the table and what we were talking about now was Edwards, a syndrome that means the baby will likely die, either in the womb or within the first year of life.

We'd had so many scans, and I'd seen my son. I'd seen his heart, seen the inside of his eyes. I'd seen his hands and his feet, and in fact, during one of the scans, he'd held his hand out to the front of my body as if to say, *Will you go away? I'm busy. Do not disturb.*

I'd felt my son move inside my body. What did it matter whether he had a disorder or not?

And if he was going to die, well, we're all going to die, right?

So we should meet first.

He was my son, and he needed me. He was depending on me to make the right decision.

So I said no.

We had no choice but to change hospitals after they offered me a termination at twenty-five weeks. It became really clear that they wanted to win a battle, and I just wanted to see my boy.

At precisely thirty-five weeks and five days, my son decided it was time to be born. My husband drove us to the hospital in our car, neither of us talking about what lay ahead.

The conversation was made up of the same four phrases:

"Are you okay?"

"Yeah."

"You do know I love you?"

"Yeah."

The birth process was the true definition of laborious. My husband waited and gave me water and held my hand, and the midwives were brilliant. They were really patient and reassuring. It would be okay, they said, everything was really early, but it would be okay.

I have no idea how long labor lasted, but eventually, after one final push, my son appeared – shot out, in fact, doing a kind of handbrake turn on the table as he did so. He was purple in color, and my husband cut the cord. But, whereas before there had been noise and bustle and shouting, suddenly there was silence.

It was like the whole world had gone underwater.

The door burst open, and people in white coats came in. They bundled my son over onto a metal table, where they hurriedly tried to resuscitate him.

I had failed my son. He was depending on me, and I had failed him, and the whole world was underwater.

Then suddenly he choked, gagged, coughed up something, and started to breathe. The people in the white coats wandered off, and with my husband standing next to me, they handed me my son.

He. Was. Perfect.

"Fine," they said. "He's absolutely fine."

My son looked up at me. He was curious. He was amazing.

I was so, so very tired.

He looked up at me as if to say, *Ooh, that was all a bit of a trial.* So very sleepy.

"I am so glad you're here," I said.

My son is ten years old now, and he's still perfect (some

of the time).

And, like his father, he still has a statistically large head.

I haven't seen my Bosnian friend for such a long time, but I often wonder how he's getting on in his self-imposed exile.

I called my son Fergus. In Irish it means "the right choice," but it has a different meaning in Scottish. It means "courage," too.

LYNN FERGUSON is a writer/performer and general show-off, hailing from the Scottish cosmopolitan metropolis of Cumbernauld. Since leaving the metropolis, she's worked on two Oscar-winning movies, grabbed a Stage Award for Acting, and appeared periodically on TV. She's written for CBS, Pixar, three series of her own sitcom for BBC radio 4, along with some afternoon dramas, and a cluster of plays for Edinburgh and beyond. She lives in Los Angeles with husband, Mark and sons Fergus and Lachlan. She co-founded www.YouTellYours.com in 2015 to coach people in all things narrative, and to teach them how to be show-offs, too.

David Montgomery

Spicy

There is a very special place in heaven for those who grow up gay in a small, backwoods town. Myself, I grew up extremely gay outside of Pittsburgh, Pennsylvania. If you've never been, it's pretty much the Manhattan of West Virginia, so things weren't super-duper easy for me growing up.

I remember I was about twelve years old, and my huge, poor family – my six brothers and sisters, my mom, and me – were all sitting down to dinner, and my sister said something about a Melissa Etheridge song, because it was the nineties and that's what people talked about at dinner back then.

My mother turned to her, and she just snapped. She got so ugly.

She said, "I wouldn't listen to her music. She's a dyke. She's better off dead, so do not bring her music into this house."

And my emotional growth is stunted by five seconds of dialogue from the one person in the world who is supposed to love me unconditionally, no matter what. I'm a child, and by the transitive property my own mother had just said that I was better off dead. It made me hate myself, which made it really easy for other people to hate me.

I would sit alone in my room at night and cry to myself, thinking, *Is this what my whole life is going to be like, just sitting here, never connecting with anyone, while the world outside rages on and laughs and has fun without me?*

I was worth less than nothing.

But when I was fourteen years old, I had a deeply meaningful experience, something so real, so raw, almost divine, that I knew it was going to shape who I was to become for the rest of my life.

I saw the Spice Girls on MTV.

When I first saw their debut video, "Wannabe," my jaw hit the floor in disgust. These five British women, not terribly older than me, were screaming and running around this super-fancy hotel. Were they not at all concerned about people's opinions of them? I kept watching, and my disgust turned into awe around the time Sporty Spice did that backflip off the buffet.

I realized this is what I want to do – metaphorically.

I wanted to have a voice.

I wanted to be loud and brash and in-your-face and not care what people thought about me.

I wanted to be Spicy.

Now, I promise that outside of the Spice Girls I have impeccable taste in music; I'm always about two drinks away from a Joni Mitchell tattoo at any given moment. But I have this theory, as a music person, that if something gets you in your adolescence, no matter how poppy it is, it always holds this little special place in your heart. And if something traumatic happens to you during your fragile adolescence, then that tiny, poppy thing can turn into a huge obsession later on in life, an obsession sometimes so big that every now and then you might have to take a step out of the real world and step into Spice World for a while instead.

Flash forward to 2007. I'm a big boy now. I'm a grown-ass man, if you will. I got my degree in elementary education. I moved to Philadelphia, and I was working within my field.

I was doing something called curriculum development, which is just as much fun as it sounds. You basically take all those fun, wonderful, inspiring parts of teaching *out* of the job, and then you replace them with paperwork and emails and meetings-that-definitely-should-have-been-emails, but you keep the low pay.

I was feeling so squashed by the heavy weight of adult life. My boss *hated* me (and I'm a delight). I was making so little money I couldn't pay my bills, and I was having a hard time meeting friends in this new, big city.

Suddenly I'm that teenager all over again, alone in my room, not connecting, while the world rages on without me.

But one glorious day, I am sitting at my workstation and a colleague comes over to inform me that it was just announced via CNN that the Spice Girls are embarking on a worldwide reunion tour with only eight shows across the globe. Now, the question on everybody's lips was which of the three American shows was I obviously going to be going to?

Full disclosure, I've always jokingly referred to my savings account as my Spice Girls Reunion Tour Fund, and it became a reality that day when, like a crazy person, I purchased tickets to *all three* of the American shows.

So I go to talk to my boss, and I ask for a week off (obviously unpaid), and she gave me a soft no.

I returned to my desk, and on my computer screen I still have the Spice Girls tour map up. It's suddenly covered in blue dots and, a split second later, even more blue dots, and it becomes clear that this tour is quickly selling out and then rapidly expanding to meet the demand.

It looked like one of those time-lapse Ebola-outbreak maps. Like [*in a deep, serious, announcer voice*], "If we do nothing, in five months' time the Spice Girls will have infected the entire United States. We will all become victims of girl power."

I knew that my boss had told me no. But like some out-of-body experience, my hand, independent of my body, kept clicking *Purchase ticket, Purchase ticket, Purchase ticket,* over and over and over again.

I was like a zombie. But instead of mindlessly, instinctively feasting on human flesh like a zombie would, I was mindlessly, instinctively buying tickets to no less than *twenty-two* Spice Girls concerts.

Twenty-two Spice Girls concerts.

Let that sink in.

This was *every* American show they were doing.

I'm obviously not big on sports references – my nickname in high school was "faggot." But in a matter of minutes, I just became the equivalent of a Spice Girls season ticket holder.

Now I have to talk to my boss again. This is going to go great.

So I walked in and said, "Hey . . . uh, remember that week that I needed off? It . . . uh, it needs to be a little bit more like four to six months off instead."

Her no was not as soft this time around. I went back to my seat feeling so defeated and so deflated.

I thought to myself, *David Montgomery, you're not being very Spicy right now. What would Ginger Spice do?*

Now, for the uninitiated, she left the group at the height of their fame. And, in this momentary rush of inspiration, I walked out of my job that day, becoming the first grown man in world history to leave his big-boy job to follow the Spice Girls around.

I mean, at this point in my life, I really want to be a teacher. But I really, *really* wanna zig-a-zig-ah.

I was now broke as a joke, but goddamn it was I being Spicy.

The tour began, and I was everywhere – New York, Vegas, LA, Chicago, *everywhere*. Just for the bragging rights, I had this little YouTube show documenting my experience in Spice World, and it was kind of a hit, making me *pretty notorious* in the Spice community (which is an actual thing).

I had people at every show and every airport coming up to me and asking for pictures with me. I had people quoting me.

I had this tagline at the end of every episode where I'd say, "Remember, it's a Spice World. We're just living in it."

Strangers are walking up to me saying my stupid words.

And I mean it's always nice to meet a fan, but I had this bittersweet encounter with one on the road in New Jersey after a show. This teenage boy, obviously gay, comes up to me, and he tells me a very familiar story. He tells me how he came to the show by himself because he doesn't have any friends. And he told me how he had to take the bus into the city by himself. His mother wouldn't give him a ride, because she was worried that driving her son to a Spice Girls concert would make him gay.

(In her defense, that *is* usually how it happens.)

But he said to me, "I wish that I could be like you. I wish that I could do something that made me so happy and not care what anybody thought about me."

And I did not know what to say back to him. I wanted to comfort him in some way, but I didn't want to lie to him.

I could say, "It gets better."

But honestly . . . does it? At the end of the tour, this money's not coming back to me, and this feeling of me being liked by everybody is going to prove to be fleeting. Like, at the end of this tour, I might possibly be homeless, but I'm definitely going to go back to being plain old unspecial, next-to-nothing me.

But the tour marches on. I'm still recognized everywhere. Even the Spice Girls recognize me at this point. I mean, granted I'm one of very few adult men with a bleached-blond Posh Spice haircut in the front row every night, but I'll take it.

Then came a moment that will possibly define my life. Victoria Beckham, Posh Spice, the laziest Spice Girl, *my favorite* Spice Girl, was doing a signing the morning of their show in Chicago. She was promoting her designer women's clothing fashion line, and you were only guaranteed to meet her if you had a receipt for like five hundred dollars' worth of merch from this line. This was obviously not in my tour budget. I was mostly living off coffee and airline peanuts at this point.

But I pressed my luck. I went to the event anyway, and I was very discouraged to find that hundreds, even thousands, of people would eventually get to cut in front of me if they had the receipt for these clothes. Before I know it, the event's nearly over and, despite being the first one there that morning, I am pretty much dead last in line.

This guy comes up to me out of nowhere and says, "Excuse me, did you already go through the line once, and you're trying to meet her again?"

I said, "No, I've been here since four o'clock this morning, but I don't have money for these clothes, so I'm not going to get to meet her."

And he goes, "You're kidding me. Follow me."

I followed him down some service hallways and pop-up corridors. And, as we walk and talk, he tells me he's their tour photographer, and he has recognized me from seeing me every single night. He wants the photo op of Posh Spice with her number-one fan.

Before I know it, I am thrust into brightness, now three feet away from my lazy idol, and she squeals, "Oh, my God, it's you!"

Like, not only was she not afraid of me, she seemed genuinely excited to see me.

Now, at these events she sits at a little table, and she does not stand up for anyone or anything. If you want to get a picture, you have to lean across the table, and they take a Polaroid from the side, real personal-like.

She asked how many shows I was actually seeing and did not believe me until I pulled out the evidence of the twenty-two ticket stubs. She got up out of her seat, grabbed me by the hands, pulled me to the red carpet, and said, "*You* are fabulous. We've got to get some pictures."

Mind: blown.

My presence has just moved the laziest Spice Girl to get up out of her seat and do something? What power do these hands hold in Spice World?

We return to her little seating area, and I ask her to sign a CD very specifically.

She agrees, so I dictate the following to her: "Dear David, you're really thin. You should eat something. Love, Victoria Beckham."

And this smug pop star, who has made a career out of not laughing or smiling, cackled and then covered her mouth so the press wouldn't get a picture of her looking happy.

And at that moment, it started to click.

You know what, David? You're not better off dead.

You might even be special outside of Spice World, too.

But all good things must come to an end. And in February 2008 the Spice Girls called it quits yet again, cutting their tour just a tiny bit short and thus ending my walkabout.

Now what?

The tour was over, but the reviews kept rolling in.

I was doing all right. I waited a really long time, thinking that that feeling of me being someone special was going to go away, and I'm so happy to report that it never did. Because during my little walkabout I learned so much about the world. I gained so much perspective. I realized that when I was a kid, my mother was a young single mother with seven kids. *Of course* she was angry and stressed out.

She's since realized that I'm a human being with feelings and worth, no matter who I fall in love with.

I learned that the world wasn't necessarily hating me while I couldn't connect. The world was waiting for me to find my voice. (And good luck getting me to shut up now!)

And there's one more thing that I learned about the world that I think I probably knew all along.

It's a Spice World.

We're just living in it.

DAVID MONTGOMERY learned comedy from his terrible childhood and the Upright Citizens Brigade. He's been featured on *Risk!* and *True Story*. His solo show *How The Queen Found His Crown* enjoyed sellouts in Los Angeles and Pittsburgh, where it won the Fringe Festival Audience Choice Award. David's blog, www.RideshareStorytime.com, recounts terrible tales from his days rideshare driving, and his podcast, *Two-Story Building*, is available on iTunes. His live album *The Queen of Small-Town Gossip* is available on iTunes. David coaches storytelling; details at www.buymeahotdog.com, where his memoir, *Here's the Story from A to Z*, is available.

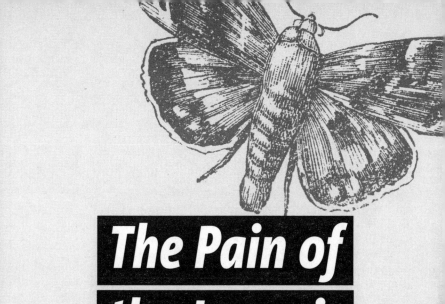

The Pain of the Jump is Nothing

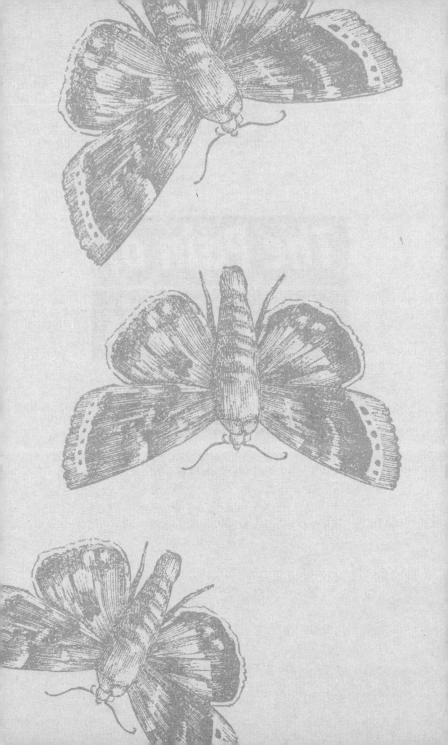

Christina Lamb

War and Ham Sandwiches

In my wardrobe, where most women keep their little black dress, I keep something I call my war bag. In my war bag I keep my flak jacket, my helmets, some boots, and a medical kit. Not with Band-Aid or Tylenol, but with tourniquet ties and Celox powder, which magically clots your blood if you get shot or step on an IED.

I also keep children's toys that my son has given me, or clothes that he's grown out of to give to kids that I might find. It's all part of my strange double life, being a mom and a war correspondent, that sometimes leads to some extreme situations.

In October 2007, for example, when I should have been at a school parents' evening, I was on Benazir Bhutto's bus when it was blown up. Most extreme of all, however, was in June 2006, when I was in Helmand, Afghanistan. We were being told that Afghanistan was a reconstruction project, not a war.

I'd been going to Afghanistan since 1987. It was the first place I went as a foreign correspondent. In those days I didn't really know what a foreign correspondent did or needed, I just knew I wanted to be one.

So I took something called the Flying Coach up to Peshawar in Pakistan, and I had with me a case in which

I had a big bag of wine gums, a copy of Kipling's *Kim*, my lucky pink stuffed rabbit, and a trade bottle of Chanel No. 5 that a friend had given me.

When I got off the Flying Coach in the old city of Peshawar, dusk was just settling, and all I could see were men, most of whom had guns, and everybody seemed to be trying to sell me something.

So I got into a rickshaw, and I asked him to take me to a cheap hotel. He took me to a place called Green's Hotel, which I later discovered was where arms dealers stayed. I discovered this because somebody tried to sell me a Chinese multi-barrel rocket launcher at breakfast (for a very cheap price, apparently).

That first night in the hotel I lay on my mattress, and I looked out of the window, and I could see these mountains silhouetted in the distance. Beyond them lay Afghanistan, and I thought about all the people who had invaded over the centuries: Alexander the Great, Tamerlane, Genghis Khan, Babur, the first Mughal emperor, and at that time, 1987, the Russians.

I never imagined then that I would be back twenty years later covering troops from my own country. But so it was in 2006 that I was embedded with British troops from the Parachute Regiment, which we call the Paras, when they went into Helmand for the first time.

One day we were sent on a hearts and mind patrol to a village called Zumbelay. We set off. There were about forty-five soldiers and me in fifteen vehicles, and when we got near the village we parked outside, and left the vehicles and the big guns and about fifteen soldiers outside. And the rest of us walked in so that we wouldn't look threatening.

It was a hot, sunny day, as it always is in Helmand, and it was sort of picturesque. Everybody was in high spirits, almost as if we were going on a picnic. I was wearing my flak jacket, which has the word "PRESS" in big white letters across the front, which is supposed to indicate that I'm a member of the media, but the British soldiers thought it was very funny to come up and "press" me.

When we got to the village, I noticed that there weren't many elders around, and it was also odd that nobody invited us for tea. Afghans are usually very hospitable.

If I'd been on my own, my antennae would have been raised by that, but I was with the elite of the British Army, so it was their show, not mine.

I did say to them, "There don't seem to be many elders around."

And the commander actually asked someone, and he was told, "Oh, the elders are at the mosque praying."

We went and sat on this muddy bank with the few elders that were there, and the commander said to them, "We've come at the invitation of your government to bring you development."

I couldn't help thinking that that's probably what the Russians had said twenty years earlier.

And then the commander said to the elder, "Are there any Taliban in your village?"

He said, "No."

And then he chatted a little bit, and at the end of the conversation the main elder said to us, "If you go out of the village that way," as opposed to the way we'd come in, "You'll find that there's a bridge over the canal, and you won't need to jump over it."

Well, that seemed rather good, because coming in, when we jumped, I actually fell in and got very muddy, much to the amusement of the soldiers. So we started going the way that he said.

The commander said to me, "Well, that seemed to go well, didn't it?"

I had my notebook out, writing it down.

And literally, as he said that, the first shots rang out, and his radio crackled to life.

It was the guys that we'd left outside with the big guns, and they said, "We've been ambushed."

We stopped to try and understand what was happening, and we could hear these shots going, and within a minute we were under fire, too.

Somebody shouted, "Helmets on! Get down!"

Everybody just ran. And there were all these irrigation ditches, so we jumped into one. As I jumped I dropped my notebook. Now in twenty-eight years of being a foreign correspondent I have never lost a notebook. So I immediately started scrambling back up the ditch to try and get the notebook back.

As I did, an RPG came so close that the whoosh made the hairs on the back of my neck lift. So I left it and went back down. (I sometimes wonder if the Taliban went through that notebook and thought, *These are the secret British plans for Helmand*. My husband says, "They wouldn't be able to read your writing.")

So we stayed in that ditch, and there was all this firing going on, and then somebody shouted, "We've got to get out of the ditch."

I was like, "No. It's fine in the ditch. Everything's going over the top," so I felt quite safe.

But he said, "No. We've got to get out," and they shouted that the Taliban had mortars.

It was scary because there was a kind of earthwork over the top, which made you very exposed as you came out. But literally, as we got out there was suddenly a burst of orange flame, and a mortar landed in the ditch.

We started running, and for the next two and a half hours we were under fire, with Kalashnikov fire, RPGs and bullets sending up clods of earth everywhere. Sometimes it was deafening and blinding. And it was like being in a First World War movie where we were running through these muddy fields, jumping in ditches.

My heart was thudding against my chest, and my mouth was dry because I dropped my water bottle when I dropped my notebook. Helmand in the summer is about 120 Fahrenheit, so it was hot and my breath was coming in these short, rasping pants, like an animal. But every time I thought I couldn't run anymore, the paratroopers shouted at me to keep going.

And to start with I thought, *Okay, it's fine. I'm with the elite of the British Army, the Parachute Regiment. They'll know what to do.*

Then I realized that they were scared, too. In fact, most of them were young enough to be my children, and I realized I'd probably been under much more fire than they had at that point.

And then the sergeant-major, Mick Bolton, said to me, "Can you use a pistol?"

I said, "What do you mean?"

He said, "We're going to probably have to fight for our lives. We'll be pinned down in these ditches. Can you use a pistol?"

We were running, and everywhere there was all this firing going on.

And the one thing that kept me going was I could see in my mind's eye a picture of a little boy with curly hair and big, blue eyes, the color of the sea, my son, Lourenço. I had to get out for him. That Sunday I was supposed to be hosting his seventh birthday party, a football party, and I just kept thinking about that.

I really didn't want to die in that muddy field in Helmand.

We just kept running. We'd run in one direction, and the firing would come from that way. Then we'd run another way, it would come from there too. We'd been totally surrounded.

It was almost as if the Taliban were playing with us, like we were pieces in a game of chess.

Later on I talked to the commander, and he said that he was radioing headquarters and begging them for air support, and they said, "There's nothing available."

He said, "But I've got forty-five people and a journalist. We're all going to get fucking rolled up here."

And they said, "No. There's so much fighting elsewhere that everything's been used up."

So at that point he realized that they would have to fight their way out, and it was pretty impressive how they did it.

The guys we'd left outside with the big guns managed to get out of their ambush.

They came along the ridge at the top, and they could see us down below, and they could see one particular group of about ten to fifteen Taliban. And so they trained their fifty-caliber gun on that group and shot them.

Afterwards the fire support commander said to me rather graphically, "We turned them into pink mist."

So because that group had been taken out, we managed to get onto open hillside, which the army liked better, because then they could see all around. I didn't like it – I preferred being in the ditches. The sergeant major, once we were on the open hillside, said for us to run across the hillside, but with big gaps between us so that they couldn't fix a target.

I didn't like that. I wanted to stand by a soldier.

So he shouted at me, "This isn't fucking Club Med, you know!"

Eventually an Apache helicopter appeared, and the Taliban were scared of the Hellfire missiles, so we managed to get back to our vehicles.

But it wasn't over, because the commander said, "We can't go back to our camp, because there's only one way back, and the Taliban will know that we have to go that way."

He said, "We'll have to go and camp in the desert for the night."

We camped, and we put the vehicles in a protective circle around us.

And I'm not going to lie to you; being in war and surviving is exhilarating. We were all on quite a high, and I couldn't stop talking. In fact we lay on the sand, under all the stars, and I even forgot about the scorpions and the scary camel spiders, which are these sort of Martian-like, transparent spiders in Helmand.

We spent the night there, and then in the early hours of the next morning, an American pilot got in touch and said he could offer air support from his A-10. But he said he'd only got fuel for forty-five minutes, which is about the length of time it would take us to get back to camp.

So we set off and immediately one of the vehicles got stuck in the sand. It took ages to get it out, and meanwhile the clock was ticking. Eventually we got the vehicle out, and we got back to the bridge across from our camp. As we crossed the bridge, the American A-10 was dropping these white flares all around us as cover, so no one could fire at us. It looked like eggs raining down. It was kind of cool.

And afterwards the British commander then said to

him, "Thank you very much for that," in a very British way.

When we got back to camp I thought about what had happened. I realized what had been odd about the village, which was that there were no children. In Afghan villages, kids always come and ask for candy, and that hadn't happened.

This wasn't a reconstruction project. This was war. And when I told my editor what had happened, he gave me five pages to fill, which was unprecedented for a story in the *Sunday Times*. I managed to get back to London just in time for the football party.

I went straight from Heathrow Airport to Tesco's to buy ham and bread to make sandwiches, and then was in a park hosting the party. It was bizarre being there, watching all these six- and seven-year-old boys running around without a care in the world. I was still covered in bruises and thorns from the ambush.

In all my years of being a foreign correspondent at that time, I'd covered wars from Angola to Zimbabwe, from Iraq to the West Bank, but that was the most terrifying experience that I'd had.

Of course, a few weeks later I was on a plane again. I felt that if I hadn't been there to see what happened, nobody would have known.

A few years later the commander got married, and his best man read some of my article out at his wedding speech.

As you know, the British have left Helmand. Now the Taliban are mostly coming back into those places. Zumbelay has become a very notorious Taliban stronghold.

And after having been told that "not a single bullet" would be fired in Afghanistan, the British ended up firing forty-six million bullets in Helmand.

CHRISTINA LAMB is one of Britain's leading foreign correspondents and a bestselling author. She has reported from the world's hotspots, starting with Afghanistan after an unexpected wedding invitation when she was just twenty-one. She traveled with the mujaheddin and was named Young Journalist of the Year. Currently Chief Foreign Correspondent of the *Sunday Times*, she has been named Foreign Correspondent of the Year five times and won the Prix Bayeux. The Queen made her an OBE in 2013. She has written nine books, including *I Am Malala* with Malala Yousafzai. Her most recent book is *Our Bodies, Their Battlefields*, about women in war.

Terrance Flynn

C'est la Vie

It's the middle of the 1980s when I arrive at college. Marquette is a Jesuit Catholic university in Milwaukee, Wisconsin, and my first function is my freshman dorm orientation.

The resident adviser gathers everyone around, and he introduces himself, and looks at us and says, "You guys look really uptight, so I'm gonna give you an icebreaker to help you relax – a joke."

And he says, "You guys know what 'GAY' stands for, right?

"'Got AIDS Yet?'"

And it worked. The ice was broken, everyone's laughing, including me, because I'm thinking, *Okay. I've been in the closet for eighteen years. What's another four? I know the drill.*

But by second semester I started getting this reputation that nobody in college wants: I'm known as a good listener. It's only because I have nothing to add to the conversations, which are all about my friends' love lives. Since I lack one, I just become this repository for all their dating details.

By Valentine's Day I was desperate enough to do something drastic. So I went into my dorm room, I locked the door, and I did the 1980s version of Googling something, which is to dial 411 – the number for information.

I hear this voice pick up, and I realize I'd never come out of the closet to *anyone,* not even a stranger on the phone.

It's too much. I hang up the phone.

But I wait fifteen minutes, I call back, the operator answers – same voice, I think – and I say, "Do you think maybe you could give me the address of a gay bar?"

And there's just this silence. She then quickly mumbles an address and hangs up.

That very night I am standing in the freezing-cold industrial section of Milwaukee, staring at this dimly lit door. The numbers are peeling off, there's no name on it, and I'm thinking, *How can a dump like this possibly be a gay bar named C'est la Vie?*

But I go in, and there's a handful of guys standing around drinking and smoking and doing a bad job pretending to ignore each other. So I join them, you know, *my people* – all ten of us. And I realize that this is not going to be the place where I meet the love of my life. That is, until the door opens and this other guy walks in.

I was so relieved. I remember thinking, *Okay,* because I didn't know gay guys could look like that. I mean this guy, above the neck, he looked like a young Kennedy – he had the strong jaw and the cleft chin, and intelligent blue eyes, and this windswept blond hair, like he'd been sailing or canvassing.

But below the neck, he was all blue-collar realness, you know? He had on these chunky work boots and a factory uniform, and he had the sleeves rolled past these Popeye forearms. And no coat.

No coat in Milwaukee in February is really saying something.

What it said to me was that he probably had a car, and he definitely had a real job, and possibly an apartment nearby.

So he walks over to the bar, and I think there's going to be this stampede to get next to him, but there isn't.

So I do. I go stand next to him. I notice he orders a whiskey, so I order a whiskey (which I hate, but who cares – I would have ordered gasoline if he had).

At some point our elbows make contact, and he doesn't move away, and I don't move away.

And it was the most wonderful male conversation that I'd never had.

That was when I noticed the wonderful smell. I thought I was mistaken at first, but there is no mistaking the smell of chocolate – this guy smelled of *chocolate*. And this bar reeked of Stetson and too much smoking and rancid beer.

So I'm there, and I'm thinking, *This guy is a tough factory guy, and here he has this sweet aura around him. You know, maybe I should just say something to him.*

But all I have is, "Is that you who smells like cookies?" which is weird, so I don't say anything.

But I do smile, and he gives me this look. And it's just pure confidence. There's nothing extra in it. It's the look of someone who knows what he wants to be doing. And what he does is order another round. And he picks up the drinks, looks at me briefly, and then walks away.

I look into the bar mirror, and I see him go give the drink – what I thought was going to be *my* drink – to some other guy in a Brewers cap, and the two of them chat for a while and then they leave together. I feel so stupid because I did not see that coming.

But I go back the next week, and he's there, and the same exact thing happens.

And then the next week, too, the same thing happens again. The only difference is that he gets more efficient at picking people who aren't me and walking out with them.

So during this whole series of rejections, I got to know the bartender, as you do in those situations.

I went up to him, and I said, "What is the deal with that guy?"

And he's like, "Oh, is he your type?"

I said, "Yeah."

He's like, "Well, we call him 'ET' – he's everyone's type, honey, not just yours."

He told me that, actually, the factory guy's type was dark and skinny.

So I thought, *If I can't date him, maybe I can be like him a little bit, at least copy his style.*

I started with the boots. I went to campus, to this surplus store, and I bought these chunky black boots. It changed the way I walked to more of a lumber. Then I bought these tight work shirts. And since the factory guy was muscular, I hit the gym.

Even my friends noticed a difference.

When one of them said to me, "You know, you're not such a good listener after all," I knew I was getting somewhere.

So I go back to the bar, and the bartender is not there for some reason. But there's the factory guy, and he's sitting in the corner, but he looks somehow different. He's drunker than usual, but like most really handsome people it only suits him.

So I went to the bar, and I ordered the two whiskeys. And I turned around just in time to see the factory guy do something that I'd never seen him do before, which is to leave *alone*.

I wasn't even consolation prize material for this guy – to him, I wasn't better than nothing.

I left, and never came back, because I was so afraid I would become like those regulars at C'est la Vie.

College ended, and the eighties ended, and I got my ass out of the closet, moved to New York, and got a job teaching English as a second language in Washington Heights. I got friends and roommates and an apartment and even my first serious boyfriend.

One afternoon I was teaching, and I would try to use the TV to expand my students' vocabulary and comprehension. We would watch current events and get new vocabulary words that were ripped from the headlines.

We are doing this when a news bulletin breaks out of Milwaukee. It shows this guy, and he's got his hands behind his back. He's doing a perp walk, and there is a close-up on his face, and I'm like, *THAT'S HIM! That's the factory guy!*

I said to my class, "I know him. I know that guy!"

But then I had to sit down because of what they showed next.

It was a hazmat team in gas masks, and they were hoisting these blue fifty-five-gallon drums down some steps. The drums were later said to contain acid and the undissolvable remains of Jeffrey Dahmer's love life.

My students struggled to comprehend the story. Everyone knew the term "serial killer," but other words escaped them, like "Rohypnol" and "stench." The words with cognates they got right away, like "dismemberment" and "decapitation."

But the word that brought a chilling silence to the classroom was "cannibalism."

Eleven of Jeffrey Dahmer's seventeen victims spent their last unimaginable moments in number 213 of the Oxford Apartment Building, just a short, ten-minute drive up Wisconsin Avenue from C'est la Vie.

I was feeling nauseous and confused, trying to take in this information. I turned off the TV, canceled class, and decided to walk all the way home to Chelsea.

I had to sweat something out of me.

I was walking for a while, and I thought, *I was right about one thing – that he smelled of chocolate, and not just a little.* He put in eight-hour shifts at the Ambrosia Chocolate factory in downtown Milwaukee before he went out to the bars.

As I am walking down Broadway, I am hot. Mostly my feet, and I notice I am wearing those boots I bought in Milwaukee six years earlier – the ones I got to make myself more rugged, more like him. They are slowing me down, and I don't want to be slowed down, because then I think of how I yearned not just for Jeffrey Dahmer's attention but specifically for an invitation to get in his car and to go to that apartment, where I was sure he would jump-start my love life.

But he didn't choose me.

And it might seem callous, but unlike any of his seventeen victims, I was alive and young and filled with ambition and passion, and all sorts of ideas about the kind of man I wanted to be.

I decided to go to a sporting-goods store. I walked in and bought the first pair of white sneakers I saw. I put them on and paid for them, and I walked out of that store.

I took the laces of those boots, and I tied them together, and threw them into the first garbage can I could find.

I kept walking. And with each block I left them further and further behind.

TERRANCE FLYNN is a writer, teacher, psychotherapist, and contributor to the *Wall Street Journal*. A chapter from his memoir, *Dying to Meet You*, earned a notable-essay citation in *Best American Essays*. The memoir depicts the intertwined journeys of having a baby through surrogacy and undergoing a heart transplant. His fellowships include the MacDowell Colony, PEN Center USA, and SPACE on Ryder Farm. Awards include the Sustainable Arts Promise Award and the Thomas Wilhelmus Award for Nonfiction. His work has been published in *Slice, The Normal School, Creative Nonfiction*, and others. Terrance grew up outside Detroit in an Irish Catholic family. www.terranceflynn.com.

Abbas Mousa

Leaving Baghdad

I was in a van on my way to school, driving through the center of Baghdad. It was one of those vans that had a row of seats behind the driver where you ride backwards. I remember I was sitting behind the driver, and in front of me was my friend. She studied English literature, so we were speaking in English to practice.

As we passed the children's hospital, all of a sudden I felt a wave of heat, followed by an incredible explosion. The force of the explosion sent people flying from their seats. My friend jumped on me and hugged me. I put my arms around her as she cried, but my eyes were fixed on the fire and the smoke behind us.

We were just five minutes away from school, and I was in shock. I couldn't believe that someone drove a car bomb into the children's hospital. How evil can you be to do something like that?

I grew up in Baghdad, Iraq, where car bombs were an everyday occurrence after 2003, but this was the first time I had been mere seconds from being blown up myself.

At that time Baghdad was considered the most dangerous city in the world. My twenty-five-minute ride to school took two hours because of the many checkpoints in the city. We got used to it, but we weren't happy. My mom would hug and kiss us every day before we left for school, because she knew it might be her last hug or kiss.

I always told myself, *I should focus on school, get my degree, and tomorrow will be better than today.* I always hoped for an end to the Sunni and Shia civil war and to see a strong Iraqi military defeat al-Qaeda.

Once I graduated, I got a job, but to get there I had to cross town. One morning, after news of sectarian killings and kidnappings, my mom said the salary the job paid wasn't worth the risk that making the journey posed. So my only choice was to leave Baghdad.

On Thursday, November 23, 2006, I kissed my mom and siblings good-bye. I didn't cry, because I almost never cry. My mom told me to look after myself and be careful.

She hugged me tight, and her eyes started to tear.

I wiped her tears and told her, "I'll be okay, and I'll come visit."

She said, "Don't. I'm okay with you being away and alive. It's better than you being close and always in danger."

My dad dropped me off at the Baghdad airport and, as I was dragging my suitcase, I wondered why it was so heavy. And that's when it hit me – my mom knew I would not be coming back to Baghdad to live, so she had stuffed it with everything I owned.

I stood and looked back to see my city one more time before I flew away.

I arrived in Kurdistan, in northern Iraq, and managed to get a job. Every day after work, I would sit by the square and watch people walking after sunset – *cars driving* after sunset. I remember watching the colors of the traffic lights because they were actually working.

In Baghdad we had a 6:00 p.m. curfew. I never sat out at sunset. *No one* was out at sunset. People here lived normally without the fear of an IED or a car bomb that would take their lives in a second. I would sit and enjoy the peace, but I wasn't very happy because I kept thinking about my family back home and their safety.

Later I got a job offer to work for the US military as a translator. My first challenge was the American accent. In Iraq we studied English starting in elementary school, but we studied the Queen's British English. There were so many words that I couldn't understand, because Americans, when they talk, they swallow letters.

One time a soldier asked me, "Do you want a wadder bodder?"

I was like, "What? What is wadder bodder?"

I couldn't hear the "t"s.

He said, "This."

I was like, "Oh, a *bottle of water*?"

One time when I worked for a unit from Mississippi, I was like, "Oh, my God, *really,* Mississippi?" That was like a whole new language for me.

Being a translator, I would translate documents, paperwork, and meetings between Iraqi military, Iraqi police, local mayors, and top US military commanders, at other times between soldiers and local Iraqi labor.

Living on the base with soldiers, I learned a lot about them. They became my new family. It was a dangerous job, but I felt safe because I was surrounded by armed soldiers. So, if someone would shoot at us, I felt protected, unlike when I lived on the civilian side.

After a year of being away from home, I really missed my family, so I asked to go on vacation during Christmas and New Year's break and was able to go to Baghdad to visit my family and spend time with my mom.

One evening I took a two-mile walk to a nearby restaurant, and, after I ate, I was feeling a bit lazy and full and the sun was setting, so I decided to take the bus. In

Baghdad most buses are these ten-passenger vans, and one pulled over to pick me up. The van was empty, so I sat in the front passenger seat. The driver was listening to really loud music. I didn't care for that. But I told him where I needed to go.

Once we got to my stop, he didn't stop.

I told him, "Hey, you missed my stop, but it's okay, you can drop me off here, I'll walk back."

He said, "I'm sorry, I was distracted by the loud music. I'll turn around for you."

I said, "It's okay, I can walk back," but he insisted on turning around.

At the end of the street, he turned left and then took the highway ramp.

I said, "Where are we going?"

And that's when he gave me the evil face and said, "You'll know once we get there."

With no speed limits on the highway, he was driving at least a hundred miles per hour, and I didn't know what to do.

I looked at him and saw a gun in his hand and calmly asked, "What do you want from me?"

I was afraid. If he knew I worked for the U.S. military, then I would be beheaded, no matter what.

He said, "You'll know once you meet my group."

His answer made me even more scared.

Living in Baghdad, I would hear about kidnappings almost every day in the news, but they never told you what to do if this happened to you.

I thought of hitting him, like what Tom Cruise or Jack Bauer would do. In the movies the lead actor always survives, because it's a movie. In reality a terrorist would just put a bullet in my head or simply crash the van and kill both of us.

The sun had set, and all I could think was, *Will I see another day? Will I see my family again?*

My mom?

He exited the highway, and he was still driving faster than he should but slower than he was before, and all of a sudden I saw an Iraqi military checkpoint on my right.

A voice inside me said, *If you don't survive this now, you might not survive it at all.*

Without thinking, I opened the door, and I screamed, "HELP ME!"

I didn't know if they heard or saw me.

And again that voice said, *The pain of the jump is nothing compared to the pain of being terrified until they behead you.*

It's amazing how much information your brain can process in a matter of seconds. The next thing I knew, I was on the ground, and all I can remember is getting up and running. I don't remember if I rolled. I don't remember feeling any pain. I just ran.

I ran for my life.

I made it to the checkpoint and fell to the ground.

Two soldiers rushed to help me, asking, "What happened, what happened?" and all I could do was point to the street.

I couldn't catch my breath to even speak. But I made it. I survived.

Later I was escorted home by the police, but I knew I couldn't stay. I left Baghdad early the next morning, knowing it would be years before I could ever return.

In July of 2009, I got my special immigrant visa. It's a program that was set up for translators and their families to go to America, because once you worked for the U.S. military, you will forever be an al-Qaeda target. So my family and I were able to come here and become citizens.

My mom was the most excited, because she said, "Now we can finally live, all of us, in one country, in peace."

I was excited about living my American dream. I enrolled in the University of Wisconsin-Milwaukee to get my master's degree, and life was going well for me. But every time I saw a post on Facebook from one of my soldier friends, I felt something was missing. I felt like I should be with them. I was afraid of losing my new, safe home, America, like I had lost Baghdad.

In Baghdad I was weak. I couldn't belong to an entity that could help me stay and defend my city. But in America I am strong.

Now I am a sergeant in the Army National Guard and belong to an organization that can prepare me to defend my adopted country and do my part as a citizen.

Because I know how it feels living under terrorism, and I don't want to ever experience that again.

ABBAS MOUSA emigrated to the United States in 2009 from Iraq through the Special Immigrant Program for Iraqi translators and was granted U.S. citizenship. Since then he joined the Army National Guard, and received a master's degree in summer of 2015 in Economics from the University of Wisconsin-Milwaukee and now works as an Economist for the Department of Commerce and serves with the Washington, DC, Army National Guard. He loves sharing stories from his life in both Iraq and America. Mousa is currently writing his memoir and has a three novel series to work on after finishing his first book.

Maris Blechner

The Value of Words

I used to be a high-school English teacher, and so words are very important to me. Words have a tremendous amount of power, good or bad, and you have to be so careful about the words that you choose. In my life there are certain words that have significance, and that's really the heart of what I want to tell you about.

I met my husband in college, and when we were dating, we found out that each of us had a cousin who had an adopted child, and we both had made a life plan that included adoption.

So when we decided to get married, we knew just what we were going to do. We were going to have a bunch of kids, and then we would absolutely adopt.

Sometimes, though, life does not work out the way you expect. When we first got married, I didn't want to have kids yet – my husband was in school, and I was working, and I loved my work.

Then eventually I was ready, but I couldn't get pregnant. It was really hard. It took a very long time.

Finally I got pregnant. I had a wonderful pregnancy, but the baby had birth defects and died at birth.

Hospitals today are far more sensitive than they used to be when a baby dies. In those days I didn't see the baby. I never held him or said goodbye. My husband and

I named him, and we made arrangements to bury him, because that is what you do.

But there I was in the hospital, devastated. All around me were flowers and balloons and mothers and their babies, and I went home with no baby, back into my neighborhood, surrounded by young couples with children.

It was just awful. I felt so disconnected.

Well, now I wanted to have a baby more than ever, and once again I couldn't get pregnant. So I went back to teaching.

And then one day there was one of those moments – you know, the ones that change the whole rest of your life forever?

The teacher from next door came in, and she said to me, "Maris, I have to leave early because my brother and sister-in-law just adopted a baby from Seattle, and I want to go see the baby."

Well, that was it for me.

I went home, and I said to my husband, "We said we were going to adopt someday anyway. Here's our chance. How about if we find out what that couple did, and maybe we can adopt a baby now?"

He was fine with that, and I did it. I spoke to the sister-in-law, and I spoke to the adoption attorney in Seattle, and six months later we got a call to come and pick up our newborn baby daughter.

It was an incredibly exciting time. We flew to Seattle on a Sunday. The attorney took us to the hospital, and my husband and I were walking down the corridor to get to the big nursery window.

I knew I had to warn him, because I'm the oldest of four, and he's the younger of two and really didn't know anything about babies.

So I said to him, "Listen, newborn babies are not always pretty. In fact, sometimes they're really funny-looking. But it's okay, they get better – just be prepared."

Sure enough, we got to the window of the nursery and there in front of me were five of the ugliest babies I had ever seen. I didn't care – I just wanted to know which one was mine!

The attorney said something to the nurse, and I figured she was going to point out which was our baby. Instead, from the back of the nursery came *another nurse,* carrying a newborn wrapped in a new pink blanket.

That was our baby. And she was the most *beautiful* baby I had ever seen in my life. The next day we brought her home.

Now, I have to tell you that in the months that we were waiting for that phone call I had an opportunity to talk to a surgeon about having a procedure that would maybe help me get pregnant.

I said to the surgeon, "I don't know what to do. We're supposed to adopt a baby."

The surgeon said to me, "Maris, this procedure only works half the time anyway, and if you do get pregnant it won't be for probably a year or more. So have the procedure and go adopt your baby."

Would you like me to tell you the sequence of events?

I had the surgery in September.

We picked up our daughter in November.

I became pregnant in January, and ten months and three weeks after our daughter was born, our son was born.

So now we had two babies.

Now, why am I telling you this? Because of words. Because we never imagined in a million years that we would hear the words that we heard when we entered this new world of having a baby by birth and a baby by adoption. People said really strange things. They were not nice words.

When our son was born, somebody said to me, "Well, aren't you sorry you didn't wait a little longer?"

In other words, why did we bother going to Seattle?

And some were worse than that.

Somebody else said to me, "Well, you're going to give that girl back now, aren't you, now that you have your *own* child?"

Incredible. As though our daughter were any less our own child than our son was.

We ended up adding a third child to our family by adoption. We had had two babies in a year; I didn't want another baby. So we adopted an older child. I wrote a letter and sent an application to a big international adoption agency, and we got a referral for a three-year-old girl from Korea who needed a family.

Now, it's not like today. Today when you get an international referral, you get a photo album, you get a video, you get a file of medical reports to bring to your pediatrician.

Not then. We got a couple of pages of information and one little picture – like a mug shot – of this little girl with a very serious face.

It was enough for us!

I immediately wrote back to that agency and said, "Yup, we'll take her! Absolutely. She's ours," and then we waited for her to come to America.

Well, it was the end of the Vietnam War, and it took a really long time. We ended up going to Kennedy Airport six or seven months later. By coincidence it was a friend of ours who was the volunteer who was bringing her off the plane.

As they were walking toward us, I wasn't really worried about whether I would bond with her or whether having a three-year-old to start was the same as having a newborn. What struck me was that our friend wasn't bringing me some stranger who was just coming into our family – she was bringing us our *daughter* who had *been* our daughter for six months already and was just finally coming home.

Now, there we were, an interesting family. Don't you think somebody didn't say something?

Somebody actually said to me, "Well, Maris, it's obvious that you love all three of your children. But didn't you feel just a little bit different when your son was born? After all, he's your blood."

I would've liked to have the words right then and there to answer people like that and tell them how I felt about my children. But for years I, who loved words, did not know what to say.

And it didn't stop.

Fast-forward twenty-five years. Our three children all grew up great, and they all got married – imagine, three out of three, which is in itself astounding!

And our son, who is our birth child, married a woman who had been adopted as a baby. So we had two adopted daughters and an adopted daughter-in-law, who in fact has truly become our third daughter.

All of them decided they wanted to start a family.

Well, you know what I said. "Don't you want to adopt?"

And in essence, all three women answered me the same way. "Oh, Mom, I want to *have* a baby."

Rightfully so.

And they did. In the course of fifteen months, each of those three women gave birth to a baby girl. So now we had these three incredible, delicious granddaughters –

not genetically related to each other, don't look anything like each other, but they're close cousins. They talk to each other, they laugh with each other, they play with each other, they love each other. And all the rest of that stuff is just details that they don't care about.

Well, don't you think somebody didn't say something to me about them?

Somebody said, "Maris, it's obvious that you love all three of your grandchildren, but didn't you feel just a little bit different when your son's wife had a baby? After all, that one's your blood."

As our kids got bigger, I went back to school. I became a social worker, and I started to do work with an adoption agency. I loved doing adoption work, because I was bringing other people to the place where I was.

Then a bunch of us who did this work together decided that we wanted to open our own adoption agency. We wanted to place babies, but also older children.

Now, obviously, some of the motivation was the good stuff from my own life. But it was more than that. We wanted to make sure that these older kids didn't have to wait so long for a family, and we wanted to do it the best possible way.

And I have to tell you – we did. We opened our own adoption agency, Family Focus, in Queens, and it's still going strong, all these years later.

We had to create it from scratch.

So there we were, sitting around thinking, *Well, what should we say to people who come in the door?*

After all, people come in and sometimes they don't really know what adoption is. We have to be able to explain it to them, so that they can decide if it's even something they want to do.

I was going to be the trainer for those new families,

because I was a teacher. And I already knew in my head what I would say to new people.

"Listen, adoption isn't just when you go to court and a judge signs papers. And it isn't just when a social worker comes to your house and writes a report and you give all this documentation and paperwork. Adoption is different, and it's way more than that."

And that's when I came upon a word – the best word. And actually the word had probably been inside me all those years.

We were doing the planning, and I was talking about my own life. And all of a sudden, it popped right out of my mouth.

I said, "I know what adoption is. It's just a claim you make. You *claim* your child, and it's forever. And that's it."

Everybody in the room picked up on the power of that word right away. And we've been using it in our training ever since.

I'll tell you that all adoptive parents understand it, because what it is saying is that we claim our children exactly the way birth parents claim their birth children.

I'll tell you who else understands it: stepparents. Many stepparents can never go to court to legally adopt their stepchildren, but in their hearts they absolutely claim them, and that's forever, too.

And adoptive parents don't only claim babies.

A woman once came to our agency who wanted to adopt a much older child. She looked in a picture book of children who needed to be adopted, and she saw a teenage boy who really needed a family. He had some learning disabilities, he had some medical issues, but mostly he had had many disappointments in his life.

She liked him. She read his material. She asked if she could meet him.

We introduced them. They got along really well.

She visited with him a long time, until he felt comfortable enough to move into her house. They went to court, and she adopted him.

Two years later I happened to bump into her at a conference.

After we did the whole big hello, I said to her, "So how's Larry?"

She said, "Oh," and she reached into her giant pocketbook and pulled out one of those little plastic photo albums – the kind that new mothers and new grandmothers used to have before everybody put their pictures in a smartphone.

She said, "Look! Larry graduated from high school. Here's his picture. And here he went to the prom – look at his tuxedo! And here he is in his uniform working at McDonald's."

And I realized this was a new mother who had claimed her baby. It didn't matter that he was eighteen years old. He was *her baby,* and she was one happy woman.

So did I ever claim my baby that died, or did I remain forever disconnected? Of course I claimed him. Absolutely. I realized long, long ago that he is every bit as much my child as all the others.

And as far as that ridiculous question, *Can you love a child you didn't create as much as you love your blood child?* I have an answer for that, too, now, and it's really simple:

There's no such thing as "as much as," because love is not measurable. Our children – *all* our children – are claimed by us, and that's it.

What's ours is ours.

And that's my last word.

 **MARIS BLECHNER** is an adoptive and birth parent, a licensed clinical social worker and educator, and a nationally respected trainer and speaker who has spent the last thirty-eight years working for the improvement of adoption and the child -welfare system. One of the founders of Family Focus, the parent-led multiservice adoption agency that she directed for twenty-six years, Maris proudly comes from the citizen-activist child-advocacy community and brings that neighborhood and personal family experience to her professional work. In addition to writing, training, and consulting, she enjoys teaching as an adjunct at the Silberman School of Social Work at Hunter College, New York City.

David Litt

"Have You Met Him Yet?"

In 2008 I was one of those young people who became obsessed with Barack Obama.

I was a senior in college at the time, and after I graduated, I went out to Ohio and worked on his campaign. After the campaign I moved to Washington because, well, hope and change. And two years later the White House actually hired me. They hired me to write speeches.

People would hear about my new job, and they would say, "Wow, you must be really good."

And I'd say, "I don't know. I hope so."

They thought I was pretending to be humble, but I was entirely sincere. It's not that I thought I had no talent whatsoever; it's just that I knew there are more than 300 *million* people in America. And some of them are babies. But a lot of them are adults. It just seemed unlikely that I was the best We the People could do.

So every day I walked through the gates of the White House absolutely sure somebody had made a mistake.

While this was going on, my friends and family were equally sure they now had direct access to the President of the United States.

Like, I'm sitting in my White House office and get a text from my sister that says, HOW COME THE DEPARTMENT OF

106

HOMELAND SECURITY DOESN'T HAVE A MAILING ADDRESS? Even in the best of circumstances, this is a disturbing question to get from a family member. But if you work in the White House, you want to know the answer to this kind of stuff, and I have no idea.

It was like that with everything. Suddenly everyone has a law that only I can get through Congress. Everybody has something wrong with Obamacare that I need to know about.

Mostly, everybody has the same question:

They all want to know "Have you met him yet? Have you met Obama yet?"

I'd say no, I haven't met him yet. And I'd get this look, and it's a look I soon learned means *You may be twenty-four years old and working at the White House, but you're still a disappointment to your family and friends.*

And I have to say, I totally get it. Everybody thinks that the White House is either like the TV show *The West Wing,* where everyone's hanging out with the president, or it's like the TV show *Scandal,* where everyone's having sex with the president. But if you're looking for a Hollywood analogy, the White House is like the Death Star. There are thousands of people running around the hallways, and they're all trying to make sure their little bit of the operation works well, and just because Darth Vader is the public face of the organization doesn't mean that every stormtrooper gets personal one-on-one time.

So I try to explain this whole Death Star thing, and it doesn't work – I still get that disappointed look.

Frankly, nobody's more disappointed than I am. I mean, nobody wants me to meet the president more than I do.

There's two reasons for this. The first is kind of corny, but it's true: I moved to Washington because I thought, *I don't know what it is, but there must be something I can do for my country.* I want to be the kind of person who makes the president of the United States just a little bit better at his job when I'm in the room.

The second reason is: I would really like Barack Obama and I to become best friends.

Now, I'm not saying every White House staffer imagined they would become buddies with the president, I'm just saying none of us ruled it out. You would hear these stories, you know, somebody got a fist bump in the hallway or someone else got invited to play cards on Air Force One. The moral was always the same: any moment could be the moment that changes your life forever.

My first chance at a life-changing moment came in November 2011, when I was asked to write the Thanksgiving video address. I will say up front that if the State of the Union is all the way on one end of the presidential speechwriting spectrum, "Happy Thanksgiving, America!" is kind of on the other. But as far as I was concerned, this was the most important set of words Barack Obama would ever say.

I threw myself into this. I wrote and I rewrote, and I made edits, and I made edits to the edits.

Finally the day of the taping came, and I went to the Diplomatic Reception Room, which is one of the most beautiful rooms in the White House. It has this wraparound mural of nineteenth-century American life. And the advice I always got about working in the White House was "You have to act like you've been there before."

So I'm standing there, trying to act like I've been there before, and the woman behind the camera takes one look at me and goes, "This is your first time here, isn't it?"

And I crack immediately.

I'm like, "Yes, I have never been here before, please help."

She says, "Don't worry." Her name is Hope Hall, she films the president all the time, she's going to take care of everything. All I have to do is wait.

So I wait, and I wait, and I wait and I wait and I wait, and just when I'm wondering, *Is this whole thing a nightmare? Is it a practical joke?*, somebody gets an email on their BlackBerry, and they say, "Okay, he's moving."

There's kind of a crackling in the air, and a minute later President Obama enters the room.

He's standing up, so we all stand up.

He sits down, so we all sit down.

He looks at the camera to start taping when Hope stops him, and she says, "Actually, Mr. President, this is David. This is the first video he's ever written for you."

President Obama looks at me, and he says, "Oh. How's it going, David?"

I had exactly one thought in that moment: *I did not realize we were going to have to answer questions.*

And I have literally no idea what I said after that.

I actually blacked out.

Like I went home for Thanksgiving, and my family was like, "So, have you met him yet?"

And I was like, "Yeah!"

And they were like, "What did he say?"

And I was like, "'How's it going?'"

And they were like, "What did you say?"

And I was like, "I don't know. I blacked out."

And I got that disappointed look . . .

Again, nobody is more disappointed than me. Because if I'm going to be the kind of person who makes the president a little bit better at his job when I'm in the room, I am going to have to deal with questions more complicated than "How's it going?" And at the moment there's no indication I can do it.

But I make a promise to myself. I say, *If I ever get another shot at a life-changing moment, I am not going to let myself down.*

And I didn't know if it would ever happen for me, but in fact it happened just a couple weeks later. I was sitting in my office, and I got a phone call from the chief speechwriter at the time. His name was Jon Favreau.

He said, "Betty White is turning ninety years old, and NBC is doing this special where different famous people wish her a happy birthday in these thirty-second skits, and you're pretty funny, and no one else wants to do it. Want to give it a shot?"

I said, "Absolutely."

And again, I understand: State of the Union is over here, and "Happy birthday, Betty White!" is over there. But this was my Gettysburg Address.

We had one week to make it perfect. Jon and I started by coming up with a joke for the president. We were going to have him fill out a birthday card, and then while he was filling it out, you would hear his voice in a voice-over say:

"Dear Betty, you're so young and full of life, I can't believe you're turning ninety . . . In fact, I don't *believe it. Please send a copy of your long-form birth certificate to 1600 Pennsylvania Avenue, Washington, DC."*

We feel good about the joke, but we still need a birthday card. So I go to the CVS near the White House and I grab a card, but then right when I'm about to leave, I have a stroke of genius. We don't actually need one birthday card, we need *two identical* birthday cards, because we have two different camera angles, and in that second camera angle we don't want anyone to see that the president's already filled his card out.

I'm thinking, *Yes, this is how White House staffers are supposed to feel.* I've saved the day!

So I get identical cards, and I ring it up, and I go back to my office, and I'm feeling really good.

The last thing we need is some way to end the video. What I come up with is we're going to have the president put on headphones and then he'll listen to the theme song from *The Golden Girls,* which is Betty White's most popular show.

I find the perfect pair of headphones – they go over the ear, they'll look great on camera. I listen to the *Golden Girls* theme song on repeat, just to get in the mood.

Finally on Friday I get the call. "Come on over."

Here's what they don't tell you about having a meeting in the Oval Office: When you have a meeting in the Oval Office, you do not just walk into the Oval Office. You wait in this windowless chamber, which is a little like a doctor's office, except instead of last year's *Marie Claire* magazine they have priceless pieces of American art. And instead of a receptionist they have a man with a gun who, in a worst-case scenario, is legally obligated to kill you.

It turns out this little room is the perfect place to second-guess every life choice you have ever made.

So I'm sitting there with Hope Hall, the videographer, and I'm just thinking, *Do I remember how to explain the joke? Do I have both of the birthday cards?*

I check my pants pocket.

Are the headphones still there?

Are the headphones still there?

Are the headphones still there?

I'm on the verge of a nervous breakdown when finally one of the president's aides pokes her head out and says, "Okay, he's ready for you. Go on in."

To my credit, the first time I enter the Oval Office, I do not black out. I can remember this very clearly. Right in front of me, I can see a painting of the Statue of Liberty that was done by Norman Rockwell and that someone has told me is valued at $12 million.

And behind me, out of the corner of my eye, I can see the Emancipation Proclamation.

Not a *photocopy* of the Emancipation Proclamation.

The Emancipation Proclamation.

I can feel the message that this document is sending through the room. And that message is *I'm here because I freed the slaves. What are* you *doing here?*

I look across the desk at the president, and I realize he may also be wondering what I'm doing here.

But I feel great. I've spent an entire week just practicing how to explain this one joke to the president. So I step up, and I open my mouth . . . and what comes out is like I'm trying to ask for directions, but in Spanish. Like, the nouns and the verbs are there, but there's nothing in between them.

I just say, "Betty White video NBC special birthday card . . . *Está bien?*"

President Obama gives me kind of a confused look. Hope Hall, the videographer, jumps in and explains everything and rescues me. But I'm a little concerned, because I am here to show the president how professional I am, and in my professional opinion we are not off to a great start.

Still, I'm not that worried, because I have that second birthday card in my pocket, so I'm going to get a chance to show President Obama how I saved the day. As soon as Hope is finished filming, even I am surprised by how confident I sound when I walk up to the desk. I put my hand down, and I say, "Mr. President, I'm gonna need to take *that* birthday card and replace it with this *identical* birthday card, because we don't want anyone to know you've already written your birthday greeting."

President Obama looks up at me, and he says, "We're filming this from all the way across the room?"

I say, "Yes, that's right."

He says, "So no one's going to see the *inside* of the card."

"Yes. That's right."

"So I can just *pretend* to write in the card. We don't actually need another one?"

"Yes . . . that's right."

And I put the card back in my pocket, and it's strike two.

But I'm not giving up yet, because I made that promise to myself. And besides, I really do feel good about the ending with the headphones. So the moment Hope is done filming her second camera angle, I walk back up to the president, and I reach into my pocket, and I pull out what looks like a hairball made out of wires. I don't really know what's happened. I guess somewhere in that waiting room I have just worried this thing into a hopeless tangle.

And now I don't know what to do, so I just hand the entire thing to the president of the United States.

Now, if you work in the White House, you will hear the phrase "There is no commodity on earth more valuable than a president's time," which I always thought was a cliché. Until. I watched Barack Obama . . . untangle headphones . . . for thirty seconds . . . while looking directly at me.

He untangles and untangles, and when he finishes, he sighs and looks at Hope and just goes, "Shoddy advance work."

He does it in this way that lets you know that (a) he's only joking and also that (b) he is not even a tiny bit joking.

And I'll tell you, my heart just sinks. This was my third chance to make a second first impression on the

THE MOTH | DAVID LITT

president, and I let myself down. All I want to do is get out of the Oval Office.

And President Obama says something like, "Well, would it be funnier if I bob my head in time to the music?" and I say, "Yeah, that would be funnier," but my heart isn't in it. I know I don't belong there. And the president looks into the camera to tape this final scene.

And then suddenly he stops.

And he says, "Well, wait a second. If I'm gonna bob my head in time to the music, I need to know how the music goes. Does anyone here know the *Golden Girls* theme song?"

President Obama looks at Hope, and Hope doesn't say anything.

So I look at Hope, and Hope doesn't say anything.

So President Obama looks at me.

And suddenly I know *exactly* what I can do for my country.

I'm standing there in the Oval Office, with the Emancipation Proclamation right behind me. And I look our commander-in-chief in the eye, and I say:

Bum bum bum bum,
Thank you for being a friend,
Bum bum bum bum,
Traveled down the road and back again,
Something, something,
You're a pal and a confidant,
Bum bum bum bum.

He looks kind of amused, so I keep going.

And if you threw a party,
Invited everyone you knew . . .

And that's when he gives me a look that's like, *Okay, president's time.*

But it works. President Obama bobs his head in time to the music, Betty White gets her card, NBC gets their special.

I leave the Oval Office that day with my head held high, knowing that the president of the United States was just a tiny bit better at his job because I was in the room.

After that people still ask me, "Have you met him yet? Have you met Obama yet?"

And I can finally say, "Yeah, actually, I have."

And then, just to myself, I think, *Not to brag or anything, but technically I'm thankful he's a friend.*

A former speechwriter for President Barack Obama, **DAVID LITT** worked at the White House from 2011 to 2016. In addition to drafting remarks on domestic policy, he was described as the "comic muse for the president" for his work on the annual White House Correspondents' Dinner. Since leaving the White House, he has written for the *Atlantic, Esquire, GQ*, the *New York Times*, and www.brides.com. He is also the author of the *New York Times* bestselling memoir *Thanks, Obama: My Hopey, Changey White House Years*.

Bess Stillman

How to Say It

I know what happens after you die.

I take your family into a quiet room, with Kleenex, and then I say the word "dead." Not "expired" (because you are a person, not milk), and not "passed on," because families always want to believe that means I just transferred you to another hospital.

Dead.

I have to say it.

That's basically all they taught us about how to deliver bad news in medical school. A one-hour lecture.

So we learned by watching our teaching physicians. We were their constant companions in this sort of theater of the bereaved, lurking in doorways and at bedsides and the hospital's ER, waiting to see how soft they made their voices. When did they touch someone on the shoulder? How much medical jargon did they use before getting to the word "dead"? When you train to become a doctor, they don't really teach you about death. They teach you how to prevent it, how to *fight* it, how to *say* it, but not how to *face* it.

So, on one of my first nights as a teaching physician in the emergency room, as we work on the body of a sixteen-year-old boy with eight bullet holes in his chest and abdomen, we are almost angry at his body for not responding to our efforts.

Is he breathing? Is he bleeding? Is his heart beating?

I go to the head of the bed, and I hook him up to a respirator that breathes for him.

We put tubes . . . everywhere. A large-bore IV goes into each arm, an even larger one into his groin, and through that we start pressure-bagging type-O-negative blood, trying to replace what he's lost. I call for another unit of blood, but, no matter how fast we work, we can't work fast enough.

The monitor begins to sound this shrill insect whine meant to alert us that the patient is crashing, which we already know, so it feels less like a warning and more like a rebuke.

Then we lose his blood pressure and his pulse.

But he's sixteen.

So I perform a trauma Hail Mary. I grab a ten-blade scalpel and make a deep incision from the nipple all the way down to the bed. I take the scissors and cut through the intercostal muscles. I take the rib spreaders, push them between the ribs, and crank his chest open.

There's a giant gush of blood and then a moment of stillness, like the second after a lightning strike. Even his blood smells metallic, like ozone.

I reach my hands into his chest, and I put them around his still heart. I begin pumping it for him, feeling for damage. I slide my fingers down the length of his aorta, but it is so riddled with holes that the frayed pieces disintegrate in my hands.

The first time I had to be the one to break that news to a family, I was in my second year of residency. I remember I had to do it in the patient's room, because his adult daughter refused to leave his bedside.

I said, "I'm sorry. He's dead. We did everything we could."

And then I was supposed to step out of the room, give her a few moments alone. But I was paralyzed, rooted to the spot by a sense of failure and loss. When I looked at the bed, I couldn't stop imagining my own father lying in it.

My attending physician must have seen what was going on in my face, because she grabbed me by the arm and she dragged me outside.

She said, "Don't you ever do that again. Don't you *EVER* pretend that grief belongs to you when it doesn't. One day the person you love will be in that bed. But today you say you're sorry, you mean it. Then you have to walk away."

I look up from the sixteen-year-old boy and see that my own audience has formed. They wait to see what I will do next.

I realize that in front of me is a gaping hole, and the boy's family will probably be here very soon, so I turn to the surgery resident, and I say, "Listen, you have to get this kid closed up as fast as you can."

Not ten minutes go by when we hear the sound of a woman demanding to be let in.

We are not ready.

We are shoving tubes and gauze and surgical supplies into giant trash bags. Security is trying to keep her out, but she is a tsunamic force. We barely had this boy closed up and half covered with a sheet when I see her standing in the doorway.

Clearly his mother. And she goes absolutely quiet.

"I'm sorry. He's dead. We did everything we could."

She takes a running leap toward the body. The nurse at the head of the bed sees a large needle still attached to the sutures holding him together and plucks it off the table just before his mother lands on top of his body, trying to protect it with her own.

She starts keening. It's a terrible sound.

I repeat, "I'm sorry. He's dead. We did everything we could."

She slides off his body. I see her touch the boy's fingers to her mouth briefly before holding them against her cheek. I leave the room as soon as the social worker enters, motioning for everybody to follow me out.

I think, *That's what they can learn from watching me: how to walk away.*

And without a moment's break, I go to see the next patient. Because there are forty people in the waiting room who all want immediate attention, and they can't know that I still feel the dead boy's heart in my hands like an anchor.

But I know that if I don't put it down now, I might never remember that this loss doesn't belong to me.

One day that grief will be mine. But not tonight.

BESS STILLMAN is an emergency physician, a wellness consultant, and a writer living in New York City. She is currently at work on a novel. You can find her at www.BessStillman.com, where you can listen to more of her stories, only some of which will make you cry.

Larry Kerr

The Magic of Maggie

In the early autumn of 1969, I was a hot mess.

Not yet twenty-six years old, I was finishing up my second one-year tour in Vietnam. I had been at war for two and a half years altogether at that point, and I had no idea what I was going to do in the future.

I knew exactly what the problem was: there was a girl, Omie, who I should have married and didn't, and that was the whole story at that point.

She was smart, meltingly lovely, strong, and she had a fierce belief in the possibility of occasional magic. I could have married her, and I didn't, and that was it.

I had no idea what to do. I'd come back on active duty to spend a second year in Vietnam. I told myself it was out of a sense of duty, but, looking back, it was more because I hadn't found a place for myself in a very changed America when I went home after the first tour. And here I was at the end of the second year and still didn't know what to do.

Now, this sad tale is not just about me, this is about my mother as well. We raised one another; we practically grew up together. She was a girl when I was born, and then we raised my two younger brothers.

This is a woman who supported me all my life, but when she heard that Omie had married another man, she said, "You stupid boy! You stupid, STUPID boy!," and didn't talk to me for several weeks.

I was a pretty pathetic figure, but this hopelessness, I just had to hold it in, because I couldn't show it to the world. I led the Kontum MIKE Force, comprised of some six hundred Montagnard tribesmen and seventeen Green Berets, and our job was to be the cavalry when Special Forces camps along the border areas came under siege. And so they expected me to be steady, to be serious, and I presented as steely and as hard-faced as I could to the world. I guess I was probably off-putting enough that nobody in the gang noticed when I got a letter.

Some of you may not know what a letter is – it's what we did before Snapchat and Twitter and email and so forth – and it came on paper. I got a letter from the girl, Omie.

She said, "I'm divorced."

Period.

Bang.

She said, "I thought I would be traveling, perhaps, in Southeast Asia, probably at the end of October."

Well, that happened to be just when my tour ended, and I sorted it out that she had been talking to my mother.

Well, I went into military precision mode: I started by getting a car and driver in Bangkok, where we were going to meet.

The way she put it, "Why not, let's just meet in Bangkok," as if, you know, two people who knew each other vaguely would go to the Oriental Hotel on the other side of the world to have some tea.

But I knew this was serious for her, and so I wanted to make everything just right. The timing was the crucial element, because this was a woman who hadn't had, in the years I had known her, ten dollars in her purse. And I knew if she managed somehow to buy this ticket to Bangkok, she was gonna arrive broke, and so I had to be there.

So planning the timing was meticulous. I figured out how long it would take, I added one day for every movement – every time I had to change planes, every time I had to walk across the street – I added a day. I was gonna get there four days early as my target, and then I threw in another *three* days.

Look, I'm playing for my life here.

And then very quickly we get to the middle of October, and the fellow who's relieving me has reported for duty. I've signed over the equipment and the weapons to him, we've shaken hands, it's essentially done. But I don't get out the door quite fast enough when a message comes in and says one of our posts on the Laotian border has come under siege and we have to go do our part to save them.

I could have left, but in truth none of my guys expected me to, because the new guy didn't even know everyone's names yet. You can't expect him to march off to war when he's just in these "hey, you" sorts of relationships with his men.

So I put down my packed bags and went back to the war. We went up to the camp. It was an ugly bit of business – they were being shelled by heavy mortars and artillery, and we pushed back the forward observers, the eyes and ears of the artillery, and then we went after the guns themselves, and eventually it was all over.

And I had a day left.

But I rushed to an airplane without being on the manifest, against the rules, and got down to Saigon, and I had one day to find a way to Bangkok.

It was five days till the next commercial flights went across, and three days until the embassy courier flight went to Bangkok.

At the end of a long and very frustrating day, arguably the darkest day of my life, a guy said, "Captain, you can't

get there by the twenty-eighth, even if you hijack an airplane."

I felt like I couldn't breathe. I felt like I'd somehow
been hit with something, and so I went to the Special
Forces club. The bar there was open seven days a week,
twenty-four hours a day, for eight years all in all, and I
went there, and I had a lot of money in my jeans. So I
drank good Scotch, and after three scotches, generously
poured, it came to me. I could fix this.

I was going to drink myself to death in that bar.

I told myself, *You're not leaving here until they carry
you out dead.* And just as I had started into that mode, in
through the door came Maggie Raye, the patron saint of
the Green Berets.

Now, some of you may not know who Martha Raye is,
or was. She was born in 1916. By 1921, when she was
only five, she already was a headliner in vaudeville. She
made her first movie in 1934, then made twenty-five
more of them, three times with Bob Hope. But in my
favorite movie, *Monsieur Verdoux,* she played with Charlie Chaplin; she acted him right off the screen throughout the entire movie, and he was the director and the
producer!

Maggie and I had known each other since the beginning of that second tour of mine, and we had a good relationship. We had shared common interests – we liked
good coffee and vodka and movies – and we had spent a
lot of time talking.

Well, she walked in, surveyed her domain there. Maggie had been in Vietnam six months a year for seven
years, and it wasn't to do shows, and it wasn't to promote
herself or her career or anything. She came and largely
just hung around with the guys, with the Green Berets.
She was our cheerleader, she was our confidante.

Well, she walked in, and then she looked at me, and she sat down and ordered a drink and gave me a huge stage frown, tapped my hand, and said, "Larry, what's wrong?"

I said, "Maggie, I've screwed up my whole life. There's one girl, she's gonna be in Bangkok, I'm not gonna be able to get there, I don't know what I'm gonna do. I just ruined everything, I've just completely fouled this whole thing up.

"She's gonna arrive in Bangkok, she's gonna be broke, she's gonna wait a day, maybe two, and then she's gonna have to go home."

And Maggie thought about it, and she said, "Larry, are you *sure* that this girl is that important? Because there are an awful lot of ways to have fun in this world without, you know, just inventing yourself all over again."

I said, "No, Maggie, she's absolutely the girl I want, the girl I need, the girl I want to marry. This is everything, she's it."

And she gave me another pause, and then she said, "We'll fix this. We're going to go tomorrow and see the head of the Seventh Air Force" – that's a four-star general – "and we'll get you a ride to get into Bangkok on time."

And so I went to my room and slept a little bit. I woke up, and ten minutes later the adrenaline in me had burned off all the hangover, and I was ready for the day.

I marched out to meet Maggie, and off we went to see the head of the Seventh Air Force. We walked into the building at Tan Son Nhut Air Base that said HEADQUARTERS, SEVENTH AIR FORCE, went through the door, and there were signs that said EXECUTIVE SUITES THIS DIRECTION. We went in the opposite direction. Maggie understood that the real head of the Seventh

Air Force was *not* the four-star general who got in the pictures, it was the senior noncommissioned officer who really ran the place: Command Master Sergeant Francis Patrick Mahoney.

Mahoney operated in a huge bay of busy people doing busy and important work in a sort of Plexiglas cube; that was his office, so he could see in every direction. I was left to sit outside.

Maggie is received like royalty.

Her gesticulations get wilder and wilder, and she's pointing over her shoulder at me. But Mahoney's head is slowly turning this way, and what was a smile has turned to an *Oh, my God.*

And the issue is in real doubt, I can tell, because Maggie cries.

(Maggie only cried on cue – she was pulling out all the stops.)

This goes on for some time. I'm fidgeting, trying to look professional, and I'm finally called in.

He looks at me like I was something the dog dragged in and says, "Captain, we'd be glad to give you a hand with this problem. Be at Marker 102 at midnight tonight, and we'll get you to Bangkok on time."

Well, I must have given him six thank-you-very-muches.

I ran out to see Marker 102. (A marker's just a circle on the ground with a number painted on it; it's a meeting place.)

I rushed back to my room, packed my bag, and with a flashlight I went onto a very dark, very dimly lit, eerily quiet air force base. I was having some questions about which way to turn when I got to the headquarters, but then I saw there was a light shining, and it seemed to be in about the right direction, so I walked to the light.

That light was right over Marker 102. It's in a war zone, we're on an air base, it's dark everywhere except where I'm standing.

I felt like Bogart in *Casablanca*.

But along comes a major right at the crack of midnight, grabs my arm, and says, "You're Kerr?"

I say, "Yes, sir."

And we go to the general's Learjet. *Eh!?* There's a lieutenant colonel flying, the general's personal pilot, this major is a copilot, and there's a senior enlisted guy in the back who's a crew chief and an occasional steward.

Moments later we're moving toward altitude in the general's plane, I'm leaning back drinking some of the general's booze. Now, the surreal is part of the actual fabric of war, and I was at the end of any ability to generate any disbelief about anything. But this was strange even for Vietnam, and Maggie's mojo was sensational.

So I landed, got my way to Bangkok. I had enough time for a few hours' sleep, to get nice and clean and spiffy, and go to the airport to meet this woman. It was a big green room, cement blocks. It's a palace now, that airport, but back then it was very basic. The gates emptied into the hall from a distance, and all of us waiting to see people were kept behind the lines at some distance off.

So I'm peering very carefully to see her and, for reasons that she's never been able to justify, she's about the last person off the plane.

I look for her, and finally there she is.

She can't see me yet, but I can see her. Her eyes are shining, her face is shining, she's ready for adventure, she's thrilled to be there.

She's thrilled about making a new life with me.

A year later I married her. (Not as dumb as I look.) And forty-six years later, when I go to pick her up at a ferry stop or a train or an airport, I run through a mental catalog of my visions of her, and it always stops – *bang* – on that picture of her back in Bangkok in 1969, and the face I look for and the face I find is that same 1969 face.

Dark eyes glistening, face shining, ready for an adventure.

LARRY KERR served in the U.S. Army from 1964 to 1974. After graduating Infantry Officer Candidate School, he completed two Vietnam tours, first as a 101st Airborne platoon leader, then as an A-team leader with the 5th Special Forces. Larry retired from his twenty-five-year career as a foreign service officer in 2004. He and Omie, also a Foreign Service officer, had postings around the world, but settled on Bainbridge Island near daughter Margot. Daughter Katie and grandchildren Juliet and Luke live in Raleigh, North Carolina. Larry authored *Captain Billy and the Lunatic*, a book of poems based on his Vietnam experience.

This Place is Bold, This Place is Brave

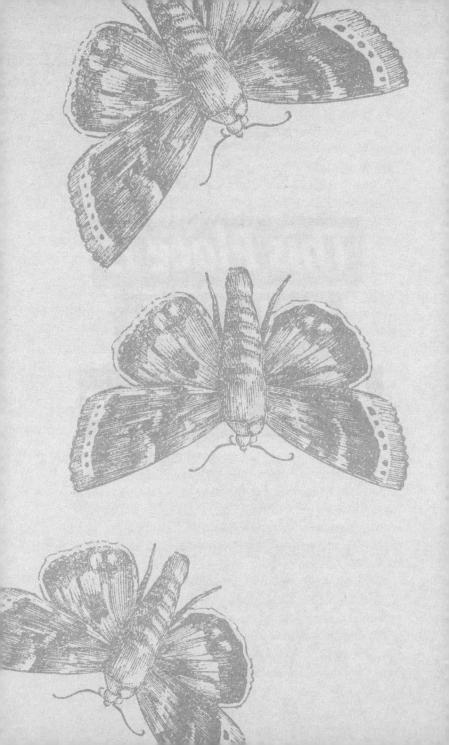

Rosanne Cash

Until the Real You Shows Up

When I was a kid, my dad brought me to New York City many times. He loved the city, and so did I.

We always stayed at the Plaza, and we took carriage rides in the park. We had dinners at Trader Vic's and ice cream at Rumpelmayer's. We went to the last remaining automat in the city. We saw Lauren Bacall on Broadway. I spent many happy afternoons shopping at Bonwit Teller.

It was a city of magic and wonder.

When I was fifteen years old, he took me to Greenwich Village to a hippie shop that made custom leather and suede jackets, and he had me fitted for a green suede jacket. I stood in front of that full-length mirror in the shop, and I looked out at Bleecker Street, and I looked back at myself in the mirror, and I thought, *That's the real me. I belong here. This is my city.*

It seemed a long way from where I was growing up in Southern California, but I kept it right here at the edge of my dreams.

And the jacket still fits.

Kind of. Almost.

Twenty years later I was living in Nashville, and I had just come off a really big record called *King's Record Shop*. It had four number-one singles on one album. It was the first time a woman had ever done that. And it was a very sexist industry in Nashville at that time, so it was a big deal. I garnered a lot of respect and even leverage with my record company.

So I asked them if I might produce the next record myself, and they were sufficiently impressed with me that they said yes. They thought that I would repeat the prior formula for the successful record, but I decided to go another way. I wanted to make something that was the real me.

I made this dark, spare, lyrically troubling, acoustic-based record that I called *Interiors*. It was an apt title for this dark, reflective record.

I finished it, and I was so proud of it. I thought, *This is the most authentic thing I've ever done. This is the* real *me*.

I was in the studio, waiting to play it for the head of the record company for the very first time. I was so proud.

He came in, and he sat down at the recording console. We played the album, start to finish.

He didn't say a word in between songs, and I thought, *He's speechless with the sheer beauty of this record. He's stunned into silence.*

As the last note faded away, he turned to me and he said, "We can't do anything with this. What were you thinking? Radio is not going to play this."

I was taken aback momentarily, but then I went straight to *It's the little minds who don't get the masterpieces right at the beginning. He'll come around.*

When he left the studio, I turned to the engineer and I said, "He's wrong. I'm going to prove him wrong."

Well, he was right.

Radio wouldn't play it. The marketing department at the record label dropped it after a few weeks. They wanted nothing to do with it.

I was devastated. It turns out they didn't want the real me. They wanted the successful me.

I was somewhat heartened by the reviews. There was a review in *Rolling Stone* that said it was a deeply troubling record – but they gave me four stars. The *Village Voice* said it was a divorce record.

It turns out they were also right, and the next year I got divorced.

It was then that I started to think about New York. It was still right here. And it wasn't long before I packed the green jacket and moved to the city. That was 1991.

Far from being the city of magic and wonder of my youth – Bonwit Teller was closed, the automat was gone – everything fell apart in my life in the most spectacular way. An unscrupulous subleaser scammed me out of a year's rent. I was mugged in the Jack and Jill Deli on Carmine Street. A homeless guy threw a rock and hit me square in the back of the head.

But the worst part was that my kids weren't doing well. My three-year-old daughter in particular was very anxious. She was so anxious that I had to go to nursery school with her and sit there all day long so that she would feel comfortable enough to stay.

It was mind-numbing. They had a musician come in once a week to nursery school to play songs for the kids, songs like [*singing*] "Peanut, peanut butter. Jelly!"

I would sit there, glazed over. One day he came in, and he couldn't get his guitar tuned, and I felt my old self kind of rising up in me, the musician self who knew something about something that was going on.

I said, "It's your D string, if you'll just turn your D string, you'll get in tune."

He looked up at me as if to say, *Who the hell are you? You're just some mom who goes to nursery school.*

The truth is, I was thinking the same exact thing.

Not long after that, I got on the subway. I got out in midtown, walked up the stairs to the sidewalk, into a torrential downpour, which I had not expected. I reached in my handbag to get some money so I could go into a deli and buy a cheap umbrella.

I had left my wallet at home.

And I realized at that same moment that I had also just used my last subway token.

So I was standing there, drenched, penniless, humiliated, looking at a really long, wet walk home.

At that moment my cell phone rang. So I hoisted my early-nineties five-pound cell phone out of my handbag and said very miserably, "Hello?"

And this cheerful voice on the other end said, "Rosanne! Hello, it's Al Gore."

"Mr. Vice President, hello. How are you? Nice to hear from you."

He said, "I know it's last-minute, but I'm in the city. I'm at the Regency. I wondered if you had time for lunch. I wanted to ask you if you'd perform for my environmental group as we head off to South America. It was so great at the conference you did the last time, you know. Do you have time to come over and talk about it, do a few songs at that conference?"

I thought quickly, *Could I walk to the Regency and get there before mid-afternoon without looking as if I had drowned?*

I could not.

I briefly considered asking the vice president to meet me on the street and pay for my taxi. I thought it ... might be inappropriate.

So I made up an excuse to avoid having lunch with the vice president of the United States to talk about saving the planet.

I hung up, and it was then that it hit me: this was my New York.

This was the New York that would kick your ass until the real you showed up, because it wanted the real you, and it would keep at you until it got it.

This was the New York that would give you humiliation in one hand and a tremendous gift in the other, and you had to take them both – you couldn't have one without the other.

This was the New York I wanted and didn't even know.

This was the New York where you would stand penniless, drenched, with the vice president of the United States on the line.

Some weeks later I got in a taxi.

As the taxi driver pulled away from the curb, without even looking at me, very matter-of-factly, he said, "Rosanne Cash . . . I reviewed *Interiors* for *Rolling Stone*."

And there it was again. My New York. My taxi driver who wrote these words that I had clung to, that meant so much to me, about a project that meant so much to me. And here we were in our New York together.

And then he glanced at me in the rearview mirror, and he shook his head, and he said, "It should have been the lead review."

ROSANNE CASH is one of America's preeminent singer/songwriters. She has released fifteen albums, earned four Grammy Awards and eleven nominations, and had twenty-one Top 40 hits, including eleven number-one singles. She has written four books, including bestselling memoir, *Composed*. Cash has collaborated with Carnegie Hall, Lincoln Center, San Francisco Jazz, Minnesota Orchestra, and the Library of Congress. She won the 2012 SAG/AFTRA Lifetime Achievement Award for Sound Recordings and the 2014 Smithsonian Ingenuity Award in the Performing Arts. Her album *The River and the Thread* garnered worldwide acclaim and three Grammys. Her latest album, *She Remembers Everything*, was released in 2018.

Victor Levenstein

Surviving Comrade Stalin

There was a hard knock at the door in the middle of the night. I saw three men in military uniforms. One of them, the KGB major, handed me a warrant for my arrest.

It was Moscow, the Soviet Union, May of 1944, and I was twenty-one years old.

They put me in a black passenger car, and after a short ride we arrived at the large iron gates at Lubyanka Street. The gate slid open, the car drove inside the prison yard, and I heard the rattle of the gate closing behind me.

Just a few yards from the street, and I found myself in a completely different world. Growing up in the Soviet Union, I knew that parallel to our world there was another mysterious and dreadful world where people were disappearing from our life, and among them my father.

Both my parents had been arrested seven years earlier. My mom came back after a year and a half in a KGB jail. My father was sent far north above the polar circle to a labor camp.

Many years later I learned that this camp had killed him with cold, hunger, and overwork.

So, sitting in the back seat of the car, I was thinking, *Well, it's my turn.*

They put me in a tiny cell with no windows. They called it a box. The box was a meter by a meter and a half. I don't know how long they kept me there. All sense of time was lost. Hours, maybe days.

I had a feeling that they had buried me in this box, this grave, for the rest of my life.

But then a prison guard led me to a large room. A huge portrait of Stalin hung on the wall, and sitting under the portrait was a puny man in a KGB uniform with a pale, ratlike face.

He announced to me, "You have been arrested as a participant in an anti-Soviet terrorist group."

"Terrorist?"

I didn't understand what he's talking about. I was confused.

"What does it mean, terrorist?" I asked.

He said, "It means that you nasty little snakes were planning to kill Comrade Stalin."

A chill ran through my body. It was the Soviet Union. I knew that they could arrest me for any reason they wanted, but planning to kill Stalin was absurd.

It was scary. It meant big trouble – the death penalty.

I understood that the "nasty little snakes" he was referring to were my friends and myself. Several friends had been arrested recently. Some of them were my buddies from elementary school. We grew up together; we were very close. It was a company of really bright kids. There was no TV – we read a lot and discussed books.

In spite of the censorship in the Soviet Union, books by authors like Jack London, Hemingway, and Steinbeck were published in translation, because the KGB considered the authors critics of the capitalist reality.

We read these books and saw a very attractive picture of the Western world.

Freedom.

Writers were free to criticize. People were free to speak, to travel, to do whatever they wanted – to change their profession, go to Spain and watch bullfights.

Not like in our country.

The officer started asking questions:

"What kind of anti-Soviet conversation was taking place in your company?"

"Who participated in the anti-Soviet conversation?"

"Who expressed anti-Soviet views in your presence?"

"Did *you* express your anti-Soviet views?"

"Did you *have* anti-Soviet views?"

There was nothing like this going on, and I denied everything. But the questioning continued the whole night.

In the morning I was brought back to my box. Sleeping in the daytime in the prison was strictly prohibited. The guard watched me through the peephole in the door and kept me awake.

The next night I was back to questioning. One interrogator, then two. They showed me testimonies of my friends who had already confessed and implicated me. They turned on a powerful, very bright lamp and directed it at me.

They cursed me.

They humiliated me.

They threatened me.

The officer would put his finger up to the back of my head. "Here our KGB bullet will enter your damn enemy skull. Here it will come out. We will grind you into the dust. We will erase you."

This went on night after night, with sleepless days in the box.

My feet were swollen, my eyes were irritated.

I was so exhausted from the sleeplessness that from time to time my head would dive forward and down, and the officer would kick me with the toe of his boot to keep me awake.

Finally I stopped thinking clearly. I couldn't concentrate. Everything was in a fog. And on the sixth sleepless night, that was it. I couldn't take it anymore.

I didn't care. I just wanted this torture to end.

And when my interrogator said, "Have you participated in this anti-Soviet conversation?"

I said, "Yes, I did."

"Do you accept being a member of this anti-Soviet group?"

And I said, "Yes, I do."

But the interrogation didn't stop. Now they wanted me to confess in planning to kill Stalin. And here, I don't know how, but I found the strength to resist. Maybe in my subconscious the idea stuck that this confession would bring my death.

They transferred me to a regular prison cell, and the interrogation continued for nine months. But I never confessed to planning to kill Stalin.

Then one day I was sentenced. It was not like an American court with a big chamber and a judge and a jury.

I was led to a small room without a window.

The KGB manager was sitting at a small desk. He handed me a piece of paper. It was my verdict – the Resolution of the Special Board of the KGB. I was convicted as a member of an anti-Soviet group and for anti-Soviet agitation.

I was sentenced to a labor camp for five years.

As you can see, I survived the five years.

As soon as my term ended, I was sent to Siberia in exile for life.

Then, four years later, friendly cosmic forces intervened in my life.

Stalin croaked.

He died, and my exile ended.

I came back to Moscow, completed my education, married Dora, the girl I fell in love with. Our son, Matvey, was born. Little by little we built a decent life by Soviet Union standards.

But as soon as the door for immigration opened slightly, we applied and emigrated to the United States. I was fifty-seven years old at the time. My wife was fifty-four. Not the best time to start a new life in a new country! But I always remembered the years behind barbed wire and the humiliation I suffered under the KGB interrogation.

I knew we had to go.

Many years later, when the Soviet Union collapsed and in Russia the KGB files became open for victims, I finally found the reason I was arrested.

It happened to be that this company of independently thinking young people was under suspicion and surveillance, so my friend's apartment was bugged. Using the recordings of our conversations, the KGB fabricated this plot about Stalin's assassination.

Why? To prove the importance of the KGB. To prove that the watchful eye of the KGB never sleeps. Thirteen young people were arrested so dear Comrade Stalin could sleep peacefully. They made seven confess to this nonsense about killing Stalin. They didn't have any proof, but it didn't matter. They had the confessions, and it was enough for sentencing.

Three young and healthy gifted guys didn't come back from the camps – the camps killed them. The camps took long years of life from others who survived.

I am ninety-four now, and I am the only survivor of those boys, who in faraway Moscow were reading Hemingway and Steinbeck, dreaming about freedom, and paid a heavy price for daring to think.

I live in the United States now, and I have come to realize that this life is the life we all dreamed about.

Life in freedom.

VICTOR LEVENSTEIN was born in the Soviet Union in 1922. Arrested at age twenty-one, he spent nine years in prisons, labor camps, and exile until Stalin's death. He emigrated to the United States in 1980 and, at age fifty-eight, started a successful career in Columbus, Ohio, designing mining machinery. After retiring in 2003, Victor wrote and published two books in Russian and one in English: *Thirteen Nasty Little Snakes: The Case of Stalin's "Assassins."* He lives in Columbus with his wife of sixty-three years, Dora. His son, Matvey, and daughter-in-law, Lisa Yuskavage, are artists in New York.

Vin Shambry

Outdoor Camp

When I was a kid, I never cried – I never had time to.

I was always put in adult situations. Like the time when I was twelve. My mother abruptly woke us up in the middle of the night, tears streaming down her face, her mouth filled with blood from being punched repeatedly.

We knew that it was time to flee from him, and from that day on we were homeless and on the streets.

I was the man in charge. My four-year-old sister and I would wait down the street in a park while my mother scoped out the shelters. But those places always had social workers and police, which meant we might get taken away from her. So most of the time, we'd sleep under a tree in a park.

Living under trees was only hard for the first couple of weeks. It was early fall, so it wasn't too cold yet. At that time of year, all we really needed was a layer of cardboard underneath us, a blanket we all shared, and plastic on top of it.

We had a routine all worked out: free breakfast at school, showers at the local swimming pool, then we'd walk around with a shopping cart until dark. We knew exactly when the police would patrol the parks, and when they were done with their rounds, we could safely crawl under the tree without being seen.

It was all right, until we found *the* tree.

It was this beautiful fifty-foot pine tree. Once you settled yourself in near the trunk, you were immediately hidden by its branches. The tree itself became a wonderland of a home. The dirt was smoothed over by all the Portland rain. It felt good – good enough for us to relax a little, and sometimes sleep.

I lay back and looked up through the branches of this tree that I called home. I looked at my mom and sister, amazed at how peacefully they could sleep here, not a care in the world when their eyes were closed. I admired it, imagining how wonderful their dreams must be. But me? I had to protect them no matter what. As the only man in the tree, it was my duty, so I never dreamed.

But that night when I watched over them, I thought, with mixed emotions, about what I was about to embark on the next week with all the Portland public-school sixth-graders – Outdoor School, a five-day environmental school at a sleepaway camp in the forest.

We'd been hearing about it since kindergarten: no classrooms, just outdoor learning around fires, and s'mores for a whole week. But best of all, I'd get to have my *own bed,* with clean sheets and a pillow!

The day I leave for Outdoor School is hard for me.

I tell my mom, "Now, look, if you're going to walk me to the bus, you have got to leave our shopping cart with all of our stuff behind the market so nobody sees us."

She agrees. My little sister is holding my backpack, which is as big as she is. She's always trying to help.

I give my mom and sister a big hug, and I hop on the bus.

The conversation on the bus with the other sixth-graders is around who will be the first to cry of homesickness, and they say that at the end everybody cries, because you're so sad that it's over.

Cry? What for? This is the opportunity of a lifetime: a bed for a week, clean sheets, hot food at every meal. Nothing to cry about here.

We got there, and we were bombarded by cool sixteen-year-old counselors, who actually wanted to hang out with us. They had been waiting here. They gave us each a necklace made out of a slice of tree trunk, with our name on it, and we all had the opportunity to run and jump in the river if we wanted to.

All the other kids just ran and did it, without even worrying about their clothes. I really wanted to. But I only had two pairs of pants and two pairs of underwear and no quarters for the Laundromat. Matter of fact, I didn't even know if they *had* a Laundromat.

So I went to the counselor, and I asked him. He told me that they would wash and dry my clothes for me, and I didn't have to worry about it, so it was okay to run and jump in the river.

I felt taken care of. At Outdoor School I didn't have a care in the world.

As the week went on, I forgot about my family and the struggles we faced; I forgot about the struggles they were probably facing right now while I was away. I liked not thinking about how hard everything was. For the first moment in my life, I felt like a kid.

The high point of Outdoor School was the competitive game of tug-of-war. Now ten of us would represent our school to pull as hard as we could against the other rival middle schools.

I knew that this was my opportunity to shine.

The teacher came up to us and said, "All right, kids, raise your hand if you want to go on the front line and pull as hard as you can."

Nobody raised their hand, so I did.

She said, "Go ahead. You pull as hard as you can."

I approached the tape to get ready to take my position in the muddy area where the competition was taking place. Then I looked down at my shoes.

These are my only pair of shoes, and they're actually Nikes, which gives me just enough credibility at school that the kids don't know I'm homeless. And now they're going to get really dirty, and I'm going to have to wear them home like that.

They're patent leather – white-and-red Deion Sanders Nikes that I got as a gift from a girl at school whose dad worked for Nike – and I know that next week the kids are going to see my dirty shoes and know that my family has no money. But this opportunity is too great for me to worry about adult things, like trying to find a place to wash and dry my shoes. So I don't hesitate for long.

I grab that rope in my hands. My feet begin to sink in the mud, giving me the proper leverage I need to pull for my team.

Before the whistle blows, I look in the eyes of the kids from the rival school. They're taunting me, saying that I'm not strong enough, and blowing kisses at me.

I tilt my head up to the sky, and I thank whoever gave me this gift to just be a kid for five days.

The whistle blows. I pull with all my might for my team. I hear grunting and screaming, and suddenly it's over, and we won!

All the kids are running toward me, picking me up in the air, telling me that I was strong, that I belonged.

The last night of Outdoor School, we sat around listening to counselors tell stories like they do. And one story I will never forget.

It was a story from long ago about how all the animals sought shelter from the worst of a storm. Some of them went into the cliffs, and some of them went into the caves, but in the end the mice were left with nowhere to go. So what they did was they sought shelter in the mighty pine trees. To this day, if you look at a pine cone, you can still see what looks like their tails sticking out from the bottom.

Hearing that story, I start to cry. After a while I could tell that all the kids have noticed that I'm crying, and they're all whispering.

But in that moment I do not care. I am too overwhelmed with emotion to be embarrassed. I look around at this wonderful place and my new friends, yet I can't help but think that I've deserted my family in *our* tree.

I had deserted them this whole time, and I only just realized it. My tears were coming from a place of gratitude for this awesome week, but also from the realization that my family needed me, and I'm the man in charge.

I'm supposed to push the shopping cart with all our stuff.

I'm supposed to find the cardboard for us to sleep on.

I'm supposed to protect my mom and sister.

There was a storm coming, and I wasn't there to stay awake.

But for five whole days, I got to be a kid.

They said that at the end of Outdoor School everybody cries, and in the end I did, too.

VIN SHAMBRY is a performing artist and a native of Portland, Oregon. Vin has worked on Broadway and toured the country in numerous national tours and at the Edinburgh fringe festival in Scotland. For more about Vin, see his website www.vinshambry.com

Emma Gordon

I Know It by Heart

I'm standing in the conference room of an immigration law firm reading the asylum cases that are framed on the wall and keeping one eye on my boyfriend, who's pacing. Six months ago I didn't even know this man, and now I am clutching his deportation notice with both hands.

Two lawyers come in, and as the whole story unfolds, I'm taking notes furiously.

One of the lawyers asks, "Did you love her?"

And without hesitation he says, "I loved her very much."

She says, "Good, because now we just have to prove it."

I write that down – *"Prove love for ex-wife"* – and circle it.

We had met in a dive bar in Brooklyn. There were flames painted on the outside. I walked in, and I saw a guy.

He's got messy hair, a big coat, he's holding a beer. He sees me, lowers his beer, and says, "Oh, wow."

I go directly to the bar, but I can feel the coat hovering behind me. He offers to buy me a drink, and I sense the hint of an accent.

I try to find somewhere else to sit, but there isn't one, so when I walk back, he greets me with open arms and says, "They always come back!"

He was relentless, making jokes and talking, but it was impossible to ignore him because he was just so free. So I gave in, and we talked for hours.

At one point our bodies stopped facing the bar and started facing each other. I asked him about a scar that he had on his forehead, and his face changed like I had unlocked something, and I kissed him.

Actually, I threw myself at his mouth, and he stopped me and said, "That's not how you kiss."

And I didn't have a second to process the criticism before he said, "*This* is how you kiss." He started over by my ear, and he dragged his lips over my cheeks and then kissed me, and I burst into tears. I wasn't sure if I was crying because I hadn't been kissed in a really long time or if I had just never been kissed like that before.

He came home with me that night, and as I was about to take off my clothes, I asked him, "Um, what's your name again?"

"Csaba."

I made him say it slowly. "Like someone is chubby."

I went to the bathroom, and I came back, and my bedroom was covered in Post-it notes that said *"Csaba."*

Csaba on the wall.

Csaba on the lamp.

Everywhere Csaba.

We stayed up all night talking and fooling around like teenagers until the dawn got us. He fell asleep, but I stayed awake, holding this man that I had just met and connecting the freckles on his back like I was tracing a constellation, but a new one, ours.

Exactly one week later, I looked at him and the words just fell out: "I love you."

He looked at me and he said, "I love you, too."

And that was that.

Csaba is from Hungary. I am from Australia. When I meet Americans, the question is always *Where are you from?*

But when I meet foreigners, the question is *How are you here?*

The response is either a mishmash of words, visas, green cards, renewals, O-1, H-1, J-1 ... or silence. And the silence means *I don't want to talk about it. I can't talk about it. It's all I think about.*

Csaba was the latter. When I met Csaba, I already had my green card and he had nothing. He was out of status.

He had been married to an American girl years before, but they'd gotten divorced. And he did get a green card in the mail, but they'd made a mistake, and his name was on it but the face was of an Asian lady. The letter said that if the information on the card is incorrect, send it back, and he did.

And that's the last thing he ever heard from immigration.

By the time I met Csaba, he had been out of status for years. He couldn't travel.

No driver's license, get paid in cash. Don't get arrested, no red flags. And you can't go home, not unless you want to stay there and not come back.

In those first few months when we were together, we tossed around the idea of having a lawyer look at the case, like maybe there was something that could be done. But it cost hundreds, and we never had it, and we thought, *Let's just cross that bridge when we come to it.*

And then the bridge came to us.

I came home, and he was sitting on the couch staring at the wall, and he didn't speak or turn. He just held up a piece of paper, 'Letter of Removal'. Csaba had to appear in deportation court and plead his case or leave the country within sixty days or be deported.

I read that notice over and over, staring at that word "Removal," trying to imagine my life without this man that I had just met six months earlier, and the air left the room.

We barely spoke that night. We showered holding hands. We slept molded to one another.

That brought us to the lawyer's office. In order to keep Csaba in the country, and for us to be together, we had to prove that, even though his marriage had ended in divorce, it had been real, which meant finding evidence that he had loved her, finding evidence that my new boyfriend had loved an elementary-school teacher from New Jersey.

The first time I saw Csaba in a suit was in his wedding photos. We hadn't even celebrated an anniversary, but in those photos my boyfriend looked good. I pored over photos of wedding invitations, searched for insurance records. I called their dentist, anything I could to prove their relationship.

The entire time I did so as the anonymous detective and not the new girlfriend, because we both knew that it would muddy the case. But it also gave me this sense of remove, until one day I couldn't avoid it anymore and I had to go to the source. I muted the TV, I sat down next to him, and I asked how they met, and if he knew right away, and how he proposed.

He took a deep breath, and he told me about the barbecue that they met at and how they fell fast. The proposal was simple, nothing special. I focused on taking notes.

"Did you guys write love letters to each other like we do?"

Please say no.

"Did you keep any?"

Please say yes.

Every time it stung, I just applied more pressure, more emails, more phone calls, more research, until the filing deadline came, and I packed everything up and sent it to the lawyers, and the case was filed. I had spent weeks reaching into his heart and plucking at his heartstrings, and now all there was to do was wait.

But wait with who? I knew that this could take years, and Csaba was no longer the free and playful guy from the bar that night. I had stopped feeling like I was in our relationship, and I felt like a third wheel in theirs. It was like I looked at him and I could see in his mind that he had already started packing.

I wanted to shake him and say, *Why are you giving up? Don't you want to stay here with me?*

Before the court date, there was an interview, and in place of his ex-wife, who couldn't be there, her parents went to vouch for their former son-in-law.

Csaba and I took the subway in, and we walked to Federal Plaza, but we stopped a few blocks short, and I said it so he didn't have to. "They probably shouldn't see me."

That was the plan. It was the right thing to do. It was my idea. But in that moment I wanted him to grab my hand and take me anyway. Make a scene like in a John Hughes movie.

But he said, "Go home. I'll see you in the afternoon."

When I saw him, he said it had gone fine, but he didn't want to talk about it, and he was different. It was like a spark was back, and it hit me: I had spent so much time, worked so hard to prove this love to the court, maybe I had proven it *too* well to him. Maybe *our* love story was just a small part of their *bigger* love story.

And I thought, *Oh, I could really get hurt here.*

But the truth was that I loved him – I'd never loved anyone as much as I loved him – and I wanted him to be free.

On the day of the court hearing, we met our lawyer in the lobby, and she was wearing a waistcoat that had little embroidered cowboy boots on it. If she wasn't the smart-est woman I'd ever met, I would have panicked. I sat up in the back and watched Csaba stand before the judge.

I knew that I had done so much to get him to that point, but it wasn't me standing up there, it was him, standing up for his life and his loves and his mistakes and his future. I saw a strength that I hadn't seen before, and that guy, *that guy*, looked great in a suit.

I prayed that it was going to go quick. Whatever the outcome, make it quick. The judge went over the box of relationship that we had given him, and there was a little bit of back-and-forth, and it *was* quick.

He looked up long enough to say, "Welcome to Amer-ica," and then he called the next case.

Csaba turned to me, and he smiled, and I knew that he was back.

It took a while for it to sink in that it was over, that we weren't being torn apart. We were just us. And a sparkle had gone, but we had uncovered something even better.

These days Csaba prefers to sleep molded to one another like we used to, but I can't. I'm not a snuggler.

But I made him a deal. "I'll lay my hand on your back."

I don't have to trace the constellation anymore. I know it by heart.

EMMA GORDON is a creative professional and teaching artist. A graduate of the Neighborhood Playhouse School of the Theatre in New York, she has performed on stage, TV, and film. She has voiced ad campaigns including Outback Steakhouse, Qantas, Marriott, and Philips. She combines her skills as a performer, writer, and illustrator with her passion for science to create arts-infused science curriculum for kids. She founded Science Baby Playshops (www.sciencebabyplayshops.com), which teaches science through story and play. Emma was born and raised in Sydney. After traveling extensively, she settled in New York with her husband, Csaba, and their two sons.

Ann Daniels

Living in the Extreme

My story starts on a warm August day in 1995. I was at home playing with my eighteen-month-old triplets, and I was given an advert asking for ordinary women to apply to be part of a North Pole expedition.

Now, I had no experience. But something in this advert spoke to me. I knew my marriage was ending, and I had a bleak future, but there was hope in there.

I thought, *Well, they're asking for ordinary women, and I'm definitely that.*

It didn't occur to me at the time that I should have some outdoor experience or at least have spent a night in a tent.

It said "ordinary." I was a mother of triplets. If I could do that, I could do anything, surely. And so I sent an application form off with seventy-five pounds that I actually couldn't afford, and I wondered if I'd ever hear back.

But I did. A thick brown envelope arrived on my doormat with a kit list and instructions to report to an old farmhouse in Dartmoor, where the selection was to take place.

Well, I owned nothing on this kit list. I couldn't afford to buy anything. So I made a few calls to some military friends of mine, and within three days I had everything I needed from my feet to my head. It was all this sort of drab olive-green color, so I didn't ask where it came from! I could go now.

I turned up on Dartmoor, and I walked into the barn. Over two hundred women had applied, and I saw them all in their outdoor kit – bright colors, all from specialist outdoor shops – and I'm in my drab green army kit.

I stood out.

The weekend started with a talk on the Arctic, and then we were marched out on Dartmoor.

It was hell, I hated it. It was cold, it was rainy.

We walked for mile upon mile upon mile. After an hour I was in so much pain I didn't know what to do with myself. But I kept going, just putting one foot in front of the other. That's all I could do.

When it got dark, and it was still raining, I literally sobbed with the pain, and all I could think was, *Take me home, take me home.*

What was I *doing* here?

We finished. I got to the end, and I was just going to leave it – this was not for me at all.

But then the media came down, and they interviewed everybody, but particularly me – mother of triplets – and after every interview they said to me, "What will it be like to be part of this expedition? What will it be like to go to the North Pole?"

And somewhere along those interviews, I suddenly caught the dream. This was my *chance in a lifetime* to do something.

But I was crap.

So I had two choices. I'd give it up or I'd give it *everything*.

Well, I wasn't going to give it up.

So I went home, and I spent the next nine months on my own, with three babies, training. When they slept in the afternoon, I was in the garden, running around, doing military-style circuits. Friends taught me how to read a map and pack a rucksack. I went back in nine months' time, and this time I was ready.

For days they put us through our paces, and the selectors tested our emotional and physical strength to the limit. We were subjected to many military-style drills and marches for hours across the moor.

At the end of it all, I was chosen. I'd made it! It was the biggest achievement of my life.

This expedition, it was a relay – five teams of four women went in relay format to the North Pole. So I actually never went the whole way. I did the first leg. Just seventeen days, and then the next team took over from us.

But it was here I fell in love with the Arctic Ocean. It was beautiful, the ice and the sounds were amazing. The expedition was just fantastic. I'd found, at the age of thirty, what I was meant to do with my life.

So I came back. Five women from that expedition, we got together and skied all the way across Antarctica, and we became the first British women's team to ski to the South Pole.

I then began to guide expeditions in the Arctic, but a big dream was still in me – I wanted to go the whole way, to the very top of the world. So I spoke to Caroline Hamilton and Pom Oliver, my polar colleagues, and asked them to join me. At first they said no. Very few expeditions had gone the whole way to the North Pole, and no women's team had made it, not the whole way. But I persuaded them, and eventually they agreed that we'd have a go – three women against the fierce Arctic Ocean.

We had to raise thousands of pounds for our kit, our food, our support team, and the complicated logistics of working in the high Arctic. But the hardest thing that we had to get beforehand was insurance.

It's not your average holiday insurance, is it?

Who would insure a group of unknown women, especially a mother? We thought *I* would be the sticking point. The bad press that the insurance company would get if it went wrong.

We were sitting in a posh office in Canary Wharf at yet another insurance company. We could see them turning off. Suddenly, unfortunately, Pom mentioned I was a mother, and we just thought, *Oh, God, Pom, that's it! No chance.*

One of the guys looked at us and went, "What, one of you has got children?"

"Yes, yes, yes, sorry."

He said, "Well, actually that changes things," and they had a big conversation, and they decided that they *would* give us insurance, because I was sure to come back for my children.

So we got it. The last piece of the jigsaw puzzle. We were going to make this happen.

I couldn't have done any of this without my parents. They moved into my home, and they looked after my children, who were excited to be with Granny and Granddad. The hardest moment was when we said goodbye at the airport, and I saw them being really brave, trying not to cry. That was a bit of a gut wrench.

We flew from London to the high Arctic, and then we took a Twin Otter airplane up to the very last piece of land, Ward Hunt Island.

It's five hundred miles of ice and snow to the pole from there. You need to ski, hauling sledges across the Arctic Ocean to the North Pole. We had in our sledges everything we needed for the expedition: our food, our clothing, our kit, and enough fuel to melt water.

As the plane took off, we were terrified. It was terrible terrain and really cold. There was no person for thousands of miles. All we had connecting us to the outside world was a satellite phone. The nearest airplane was two days away in good weather. It was sincerely up to us to make this journey. We just had to make that first step.

I'd been on the first leg of the relay and thought I knew what to expect, but this expedition was worse than any I had ever encountered. For the first twenty-seven days, the temperatures were between minus forty-four and minus sixty-nine degrees Fahrenheit on the thermometer. With wind chill we were simply surviving. Our sledges were too heavy – they were about twice our own body weight – and it took all three of us to haul one sledge over every ridge as we moved forward.

It was debilitating and so slow. And in the beginning we all got frostbite.

I can remember skiing at the front. I had frostbite on my middle toe and my little toe, and a little bit on my big toe, and I could feel it getting worse. But I couldn't call a halt to the team to warm it, because we were so far behind schedule. We had endured three storms, breaking ice, backwards drift, and the worst ice conditions I'd ever encountered. We would never get there if we stopped.

I can remember thinking, *Oh, God, okay, I can't feel my middle toe. Well, oh hell, who needs a middle toe? I can live without a middle toe.*

And a little toe . . . well, yeah, I can live without a little toe.

I can't live without a big toe. If it starts to go for that, that's it.

We were literally bargaining with bits of our bodies in order to make this happen.

I found on the ice that when I could think about things, I missed the children terribly. I could go about fourteen days, fifteen days – that seemed to be the limit before it affected my morale.

Pom and Caroline were really good. They would give me time with the satellite phone and the precious batteries. I'd call, and the kids were so excited to tell me about everything they were doing and how great it all was. They chattered, and I listened, and when I put the phone down, I was filled with them again, and I could keep going.

If I had trouble with frostbite, Pom was the worst. All her toes were frostbitten, and after forty-seven days we had a resupply plane that came in to give us new food and fuel, and Pom had to leave.

I never thought about getting on that plane, even though the chances of us getting to the pole were so slim. On day thirty-seven of the expedition, before Pom left, we'd gone just sixty-nine miles of the five hundred. We'd gone a few more in the next ten days, but we still had over three hundred miles to go. It was impossible. But we weren't going to give in.

It was now just me and Caroline. And although we missed Pom, when she left, we began to use her as our motivation. "We'll do this for Pom. We'll do another hour for her."

We became one driving force. We swam through open water, we skied across thin ice. We added hours to our days. Because we were walking across the Arctic Ocean, the ice moved constantly – always against us. So some nights we would get into our frozen sleeping bags that we would have to break, and as we slept, we would drift backwards.

Those were the tough nights. But eventually, after eighty grueling days, we knew we had two hours left. We were literally feet from the pole, and we thought, *This is it, this is it.*

We pinpointed the North Pole with a GPS. The ice moves on the ocean so fast that, while the North Pole is a fixed place, it feels like it's moving as the ice moves you this way and that.

You have no concept that you're moving, so it feels like the North Pole is running away from you.

We got the GPS out and zigzagged this way and that, and we couldn't pinpoint it. As quickly as we were getting there, the ice was moving.

"We can't be the first women to go thirteen feet from the Pole!"

We stood there on a piece of ice, not sure what to do. We could almost hear the planes. And we looked at the GPS and the numbers and, as we looked, it started to count upwards.

We watched it moving and moving, and that piece of ice, as we stood still, moved up to the magical ninety degrees north.

We got it.

I planted the Union Jack, we sang the national anthem, and I asked Caroline if she would take a picture of me holding a photo of my children, because I felt they were there with me. I could never have made the sacrifices without them inside my very soul.

ANN DANIELS is one of Britain's leading explorers. She was the first woman to ski to the North and South Poles as part of all-woman teams in 2002. Experiencing minus fifty degrees Celsius temperatures, she has sledge-hauled over three thousand miles in inhospitable environments, completed over ten Arctic expeditions, and survived more than four hundred days on the ice. Ann has worked with NASA, ESA, NOAA, and the University of Washington to help scientists understand the fragile polar icescape and how this affects our planet. www.anndaniels.com.

George Dawes Green

The Haunted Freezer

I used to play a lot of poker at the house of my oldest friend, Wanda Bullard, on St. Simons island off the coast of Georgia.

I loved those nights. I would pull up in Wanda's driveway and look through her dining-room window, and I could see her in there setting up for poker. She'd be cleaning the cat food off the dining-room table and then cleaning the cats off the dining-room table, and then setting out her lucky Chinese coins, and lucky sharks' teeth, and lucky bottle caps, and her lucky ashtray from South of the Border.

When she became intent, she would always put her tongue like this, so even though she was sixty years old, she looked a little like Charlie Brown from the comics.

My friend Larry would be there in his black cowboy hat and his hooded cobra eyes, shuffling and reshuffling the deck.

And I loved these people.

I'd go into that house of junk, and Wanda would just light up and say, "Well, hello there!"

And she'd give me a hug, which was always a little awkward, because she came up to about here on me [*gestures to his chest*].

She'd been a teacher for forty years. Her students loved her. *Everybody* loved Wanda, because she was so kind and generous.

I recognized those qualities, but what really drew me to Wanda was her mean streak. You'd give that girl a glass of bourbon and the insults would start to fly. In fact, these poker nights were just orgies of insults. All of us – me, my ninety-year-old mother who would sometimes come by, and Larry and Wanda – would just sit there all night and play poker and insult each other.

Wanda would say, "You're a weasel! Your hand is pitiful! And you're especially ugly tonight."

I would say, "Larry, you look like a cobra."

Larry would say, "George, you look like a New York pimp in that getup."

And Wanda would say, "I can't show ya this hand right now. But when I do show it to you, I promise you you'll remember it for the rest of your life – your *sorry life!*"

And guarding this little circle of insults was a ring of just pure blissful chaos. Wanda's cats – she had six cats, and all night long they'd be jumping up and down from the table and scattering the poker pot. She had these two big ugly hound dogs that would be howling all night, anytime anybody ever came by. And there were always strange people coming in and out of that house.

There was one particular character named Frankie Stump. Frankie was a drunk, and a good ol' boy, and he loved to hunt.

Actually, he loved to drunk-hunt. One day he shot a deer out at the Sea Palms Golf Club on Sunday afternoon, from the window of his pickup truck while he was stopped at Frederica Road at a red light. He pulled over, and he got out, and he field-dressed that deer right there on the fairway in front of all these astonished golfers.

And one day he had a big freezer delivered to Wanda's house. He just gives her the freezer, chock-full of venison, which we thought was kind of generous. But there was one friend of ours, Miss Lucy Mayo, who did not care for Frankie Stump. She was a tiny woman, and she was one of those people who are always aware of the invisible world all around her. She was aware of the doings of ghosts and demons and angels. And she hated Frankie Stump, and she said there was nothing generous about Frankie giving us that freezer. She said, "He can't eat all them critters he's killin', and he wants to say that the meat doesn't go to waste, so he gives you that freezer so he can keep up the slaughter. But it's just an excuse. That freezer is full of the spirits of all of those deer he's murdered and it will bring a curse on this house, and it's an abomination."

And she was rolling on about this while we were trying to play poker, until Wanda couldn't take it anymore, and she said, "I don't care! Shut up and play!"

And then it was Christmas.

This was just a couple of Christmases ago. Larry got Wanda one of those singing Santa Clauses that you get in Kmart, and I got Wanda one of those singing trophy fish. She really loved all that crap. Lucy Mayo got her one of those Roombas, you know? One of those robotic vacuum cleaners? And that was bouncing around all Christmas Day in the kitchen, and the cats were all hissing at it, and the dogs were barking at the cats, and the fish was up on the wall singing away, and Wanda was saying, "I OWN this hand, put your money in the pot, put YOUR MONEY IN, you little cowards!"

And it was just about the best Christmas ever.

I remember one time I went outside to make a call, and as I was coming back in, I looked in through the window, and I saw Larry and my mom and Wanda sitting there, and I began to think maybe I was just too attached to these people. So I told myself that nothing lasts forever. I reminded myself that I might well come here one day and Larry would be gone, and my mom would be gone, and Wanda would be gone, and the house would be empty. I told myself these things as a way to inoculate myself against future grief, and I did succeed in making myself really sad for about ten minutes, until we started playing poker again.

And then the poker was just so amazing that after everybody else was gone, Larry and Wanda and I stayed there and kept playing poker and laughing – we played all night.

We couldn't stop: we played till *5:00 p.m. the next day*.

And after twenty-four hours of poker, I staggered out of that house, and my eyeballs were rattling around inside my skull, and Wanda shouted after me, "You're a quitter!"

Then a few months passed, and Larry went into the pantry to get something. He happened to look down, and he noticed that when Lucy Mayo had plugged in the Roomba home base she had unplugged the freezer.

She had done that on Christmas Day, and now it was the end of February.

Larry called me and Wanda in, and he pointed at the freezer and said solemnly, "Don't ever open this. *Ever*."

The next day Wanda hired a couple of neighbor kids to come over and haul the freezer out.

Three kids showed up – I guess it shoulda been four – because Wanda and me and my mother and Larry were sitting in the dining room playing poker, and the kids were back in the pantry getting the freezer. In between was the kitchen, where the pets hung out and molested each other, and we were playing.

Then we heard this terrible crash.

And then a moment's silence.

Then one of the neighbor boys came streaking through the kitchen and ran right past us. His face was white as a sheet, and he was screaming and running for the front door. His two friends were right behind him, and they were throwing chairs out of the way and clawing at each other just to get past each other, to get out, to get *out of that house.*

And then the dogs showed up – the dogs came running past, and you could see the whites of their eyes. They were horrified, and they were running for the door.

Then the cats emerged, and they were just little dark streaks.

One of them jumped on the table and slid all the way across, and everything – the bourbon, the coins, the lucky sharks' teeth, *everything* – went flying, and the cat shot out of there.

And we were just sitting around staring at each other blinking, wondering what was going on.

And then it hit.

The smell.

Because those neighbor kids had dropped the freezer, and everything had come out, and God knows what kind of meats were in there, but they were all rotten.

And I can't describe to you the smell. All I can say is that, wherever that smell was, you had to be elsewhere.

And so we got out of there, and I may have lost a little dignity, because I think I might have elbowed past my ninety-year-old mother in my haste to get out.

But then we were out, and we were alive. We rounded up the animals, and we brought them over to the neighbor's house. And then we decided that we were gonna go back. We were going to put scarves on our faces like masks, and go rushing in there, and grab the freezer, and get it out of there.

So we wrapped these scarves around our faces, and we walked back, and as we came around the corner of the house we could see Lucy Mayo standing at the front door knocking, but a little puzzled because the front door was open, which it never was because the pets would get out. But the pets weren't around, and nobody else was around, and she was sniffing the air and getting that smell of death. And you could just see that she was putting together this narrative, this terrible narrative, about a burglary gone bad and the murders, and all her friends in there dead.

And then she heard our footsteps, and she wheeled around and saw arrayed before her seven masked banditos. Or maybe they were the spirits of Frankie's murdered deer.

She was just so terrified, but then Wanda started to laugh. And she leaned up against the house, and she sank down into a crouch, and she just became a ball of laughter.

And then all of us were laughing. Even the neighbor kids were on their asses laughing. Even Lucy Mayo, who had no idea what was going on, couldn't help but laugh, because this was one of those moments – those astonishing moments at Wanda's house – that happened all the time, thousands of times.

Until last summer when Larry suddenly died. And then my mom died, and then Wanda died, within a few months of each other – one-two-three. So it's all as foretold, everybody's gone, and that house is empty.

I was just there a few months ago, and the sermon that I told myself about how I had to be prepared for this darkness? That sermon was useless, because I wasn't prepared at all.

Because when the invisible world strikes, we're hopeless.

And I shouldn't have even wasted my time with this sermon. I should have just gone back in that house and spent every minute I could playing poker with my friends and taking their money and listening to the insults of my beloved Wanda.

GEORGE DAWES GREEN is the founder of The Moth and an internationally celebrated author. His first novel, *The Caveman's Valentine*, won the Edgar Award and became a film starring Samuel L. Jackson. *The Juror* was an international bestseller in more than twenty languages and was the basis for the movie starring Demi Moore and Alec Baldwin. His novel *Ravens* was also an international bestseller and chosen as a Best Book of the Year by the *LA times*, the *Wall Street Journal*, the London *Daily Mail*, and more. Mr. Green divides his time between New York City and Savannah, Georgia.

Fatou Wurie

When the Heart Is Full

My mother always says, "If you don't know where you're going, know from where you come."

I was at a point in my life where I didn't feel connected to my roots, and I certainly didn't know where I was going. So after several years of living abroad, I decided to return to my home country of Sierra Leone and move back in with my mother.

I was particularly excited to see my grandmother. She had raised me up until age three. She was the matriarch of our family.

She was this amazing human being. She was bold and vivacious. She was the glue that held our family together. And so when I finally made it to Sierra Leone, the first person I went to see was her.

I remember driving up to her house, where I had grown up, and it didn't look as big as I remembered it.

And there was my grandmother, standing by the doorway, and *she* didn't look as big as I remembered *her*. She was looking a little frail.

But it didn't matter. I ran to her embrace and just hugged her and held her and inhaled her scent.

I was finally home.

I spent that weekend with my grandmother and cousins and aunts. We were catching up; we were cooking and eating and laughing.

They reminded me that my name isn't pronounced fa-toooo. It's Fah-TOO.

You know, learn to say your name!

I also learned that my last name had roots, had ancestry, had place.

It was really good to be with my family. My cousins and I were getting to know each other again. They told me that my grandmother hadn't been her usual self lately, that she wasn't as lively or as outgoing as she had been; she was a little more withdrawn.

So one afternoon I went to my grandmother's room, and I lay beside her, and I said, "Grandma, what's wrong? Everyone says you're not as jovial. You're a little quiet. What's going on?"

She simply turned to me and said, "Fatou, when the heart is full, it cannot speak."

In that moment I remembered that my grandmother had endured eleven years of civil war; she had lost her husband, my grandfather, to the war; she had lost her only two sons, my two uncles, to the war; and most recently she had lost her eldest daughter, my aunt.

I could feel the sadness in her, and I knew she was tired. I edged closer to her, once again inhaling her scent and just being with her.

A couple of days later, my mother and I returned from my grandmother's village to the capital city, Freetown, where my mother lived.

And listen, my mom and I were getting reacquainted with one another. When you haven't lived with your parents for a while, then go back to their house, it can be challenging.

My mother was not feeling me. She didn't appreciate that my nose was pierced and I didn't have hair – I was bald.

Apparently I was really loud.

She would say things like, "This is not the daughter I raised."

And I'd be like, "But, Mommy, this is who I *am*. I'm independent. Accept me."

We would be just back and forth, back and forth. It was awkward. But every Sunday we would have dinner together, and we tried to get to know one another and understand each other.

One Sunday we were having our usual mother–daughter dinner when I got a call from one of my aunts.

I picked up the phone, and my aunt said, "Grandma *Don-Go*."

I could feel my mother looking at me, worriedly, and so I turned to her and said, "Mommy, Grandma *Don-Go*."

Grandma is gone.

My mother quickly stood up from the table, and said, "Okay, go to the spare bedroom, open the second drawer, pack everything that you see in there, pack your bags, and let's go."

And so that's what I did. I went to the spare bedroom, I opened the second drawer, and I found all this white material – linen, chiffon, cotton – and I recognized that my mother had been preparing for this day when her mother would go.

I quickly packed everything that I saw in a bag, and in twenty minutes my mother and I were on our way to my grandmother's house.

The only thing I really remember from that night is how bright the moon was when we pulled up to my grandmother's house, how it lit up the entire street, which was usually filled with life and joy and noise. But that night it was so quiet.

We arrived, and the minute we entered my grand-mother's house, my mother dropped her bags to the ground and let out a howl that could only come from the depths of her being.

Her mother, my grandmother, was gone.

My aunts rushed to my mother's side, and she sobbed in their arms. I just stood there and watched.

My aunts took my mother towards my grandmother's room, and some of my aunts went in, and then my mother went in. But as I was about to enter my grandmother's room, one of my older aunts came and shut the door in front of me.

I was confused.

I said, "Auntie, what's going on? I want to go inside. Mommy is inside. I want to participate in washing Grandma's body. This is the most intimate and important part of our tradition. Why did you close the door?"

My aunt just looked at me and said, "Fatou, I cannot let you in that room. You're not a society woman."

I knew what she meant. She meant that I hadn't gone through *bondo*. *Bondo* is what we know as female genital mutilation or circumcision.

I hadn't gone through *bondo* because my grandmother was a Chief Sowie – a *sowie* is a female leader who does the initiating of young girls into the society of *bondo*. And she had decided that my sisters and I would be the first girls in our family and in our community not to go through *bondo*.

But her decision meant that I was now on the other side of the door. I could not enter.

I saw that my aunt would not relent. And for the first time since coming home, I felt like an outsider. I had to walk away, trying not to make a scene. But I was a little sad and disappointed.

The next day was my grandmother's funeral, and in the morning the entire community came to pay their final respects.

They had washed my grandmother's body and laid her in the center of her living room. She looked so regal and beautiful and at peace, wrapped in white.

I went to her bedroom and sat for a moment, trying to feel her presence, perhaps for the last time.

I was lost in my thoughts when seven young girls, no older than ten, all rushed into the room, wearing big, colorful skirts. They were decked out in white clay masks, and they had so much energy – they were the happiest people at the funeral. And for the moment there, they lightened the mood, and so I just watched them play.

A couple of minutes later, one of my older aunts walked into the room and said to the girls, "Hush. Get yourselves together. We have to go."

I turned to my aunt and said, "Auntie, what's going on? We're about to bury Grandma. Where are you going?"

She said, "Listen, in order to bury your grandmother, we need to take these girls to the bush and initiate them so that Grandma can rest in peace."

What could I say to that? My grandmother was a Chief Sowie. In our culture, in order for her to rest in peace, these seven young girls must go to the bush and be initiated. And I wanted my grandmother, who I loved so much, to rest in peace.

So what could I do? In that moment I recognized that I really didn't have any say or power in that space. And so, even though I stood there silently and watched as my aunt took the seven young girls away to the bush, it did not feel right.

A couple of hours later, I was told that we were ready to bury my grandmother, and so I walked outside with the entire community. My mother, as per the ritual, walked toward my grandmother for the last time and sprayed perfume on her body, turned her back, and walked away. I stood there with everyone else and watched as they hoisted my grandmother to her grave.

And in that moment I realized something about the place I come from:

It's strong.

It's bold.

It's brave.

This is the place that my grandmother came from, and my grandmother, a *sowie,* a chief in this society, had made the decision to give me this gift of *not* going through *bondo.* A gift that allows me so many different choices. A gift I would want for those seven girls. For every girl, really.

Her decision meant that wherever I decide to go in this world, whatever I decide to do in this world, I will be a different kind of girl and have a completely different life. A different life that I can pass on to the next generation of women in my family.

FATOU WURIE has a decade of international development experience, focusing on African women's health and gender equality. Fatou consults with UNICEF HQ and served as Africa Regional Advocacy Lead for the MamaYe Campaign to end maternal mortality. Fatou founded the Survivor Dream Project, which builds psychosocial services for Sierra Leonean women and youth. An Abshire-Inamori (Ethical Leadership) Fellow and the first African Governance Initiative Scholar at the Blavatnik School of Government, Fatou was the first woman of color to lead the University of Oxford Women in Politics Society. Fatou speaks at diaspora workshops for humanitarian action and mobilization across Europe.

Michael Such

Waiting to Go

I was standing on the Millennium Bridge in the centre of London. It was 2:00 a.m.

It was quiet. I could hear the water sloshing below me and the traffic in the distance.

It was dark, but it's never *really* dark at night in London. I could see the lights of the buildings beside the river, St. Paul's to my right – grand and majestic – and the Tate – large and brutal – to my left.

And it was late summer, but it was getting cold. I was anxious and agitated and leaning against the railing of the bridge.

I remember this moment. It's frozen in my mind, because I wanted it to be my *last* moment.

I thought I had just completely failed my exams at the end of the first year of university. I was feeling isolated, not part of the crowd. I was still a virgin, and I thought my whole life had been a failure.

I was always anxious and unhappy as a child. I remember crying in the playground at some simple game because someone might possibly get hurt. And I remember, after they showed one of those child safety videos, being terrified of child snatchers, and anxious about walking to my friend's house in our small Suffolk village.

I remember lying on my bed on Saturday afternoons feeling listless and lost and in a low mood, but not knowing how to get out of it. I remember being picked on and called out for being awkward and ill-fitting, and unable to stand up for myself at school.

And my escape from that was always the approval of the teachers. For all of my frailties of mind and scattered decision-making, I was always intelligent and obedient enough to draw praise from adults, and maybe that's what damned me.

And so at eighteen I moved to London to study Physics at Imperial College. To understand the universe, even as I little understood my own mind and my own emotions. I was hopeful for a change, for the new setting to break my old habits.

And things did improve that year. I made a new set of friends. I went out more. I learned a lot, gained a larger measure of independence. But the borders of my anxiety still remained jagged, and they still held me back from things big and small, like finding love ... and stupid, simple stuff. For instance, I remember lying on my bed in halls and hearing my sink gurgle, and a strange sewer smell filling the room, and thinking, *I should really go and tell someone and get that fixed.* And then being maddeningly terrified about the idea of that conversation, and then thinking I'll do it next week, and then the next, and then never.

Delay had always been my way of dealing with my anxiety, and it leached into the other areas of my life. But delay isn't a very good response when you are in your first year, studying theoretical physics and have a lot of work to do and no one to tell you to do it. And with that delay came a tide of self-hatred which gradually swallowed me whole.

As I got towards the end of the year, I couldn't see a way out, and I started to think about killing myself.

As I got closer to the exams, that feeling of dread grew, and I started planning. I decided I would jump. I thought it would be simple, quick and clean. I picked the Millennium Bridge because I knew it would be quiet at night, and I was embarrassed and afraid of getting caught in the moment – more embarrassed and afraid somehow than the dying itself.

The exams came, and I thought they didn't go well. My friends began to drift off at the end of the year. I didn't plan any big farewells, but maybe there was some more poise in my goodbyes. And maybe they knew something was up. I would occasionally drop out of social events or seem down, but I never reached out and asked for help.

And so I finally reached what I planned to be my last day. It was a Sunday. I don't remember a lot about it. I remember cleaning my room and trying to leave things neat and tidy for when I was gone. I remember procrastinating on cleaning my room, and playing video games.

I think it's very difficult to really live any day as your last, because your mind can't comprehend the idea of not existing, of nothingness, and you catch yourself thinking, *I'll do that next week*.

Finally I closed up my room. I walked from my halls near Edgware Road to the Millennium Bridge in the centre of London.

I picked a route which was self-consciously poetic, past Hyde Park, past Buckingham Palace lit up in lights, past St. James's. And as I walked I was filled with a mix of abject terror and determination. In my mind I was on an almost sacred quest to eliminate a problem from the world, namely me. My depression has often told me that I'm a terrible person who does terrible things even if other people can't see it.

But beneath that, there were doubts still bubbling.

I reached the bridge.

I walked onto the bridge.

Then I delayed, growing anxious, my stomach churning between living and dying, holding onto the railing, looking out when people passed, trying to look normal and casual.

Eventually I walked to one side of the bridge and, after a few false starts, I ran across the width of the bridge, my boots clanking on the metal.

I reached for the railing and pushed myself up, my hips hitting the metal.

I tipped over and felt my feet kicking free.

And then a frozen moment, which I can still see. I'm airborne and feeling a strange sensation of weightlessness.

I'm looking down at the water and I'm thinking, *Oh fuck, I've really done it.*

That weird sick feeling that something you thought about, and imagined or had seen on TV is really happening to you right now.

I had an almost resigned acceptance of it. Maybe this was the wrong decision, but it was happening.

I hit the water with a hard slap, and I plunged deep down into the Thames.

I found myself kicking up and swimming. I'd learned to swim from an early age – Saturday morning lessons followed by greasy spoon sessions with my dad. But I wasn't supposed to do this now. I had told myself that I would be knocked out, but even if I wasn't I would hold tight and let myself drown. But my body made another decision.

And then I was floating on my back down the Thames, another frozen moment. I could see the lights peeking over the embankment. I was very cold, wet through into my boots, and I was trying to decide what to do next.

I thought about letting go and trying to drown, but I realized I didn't have the commitment for that.

And a thought passes through my mind, *Fuck it, I'll just live*.

I roll onto my front, and as the current pushes me along, I see the Blackfriars Bridge coming up. I manage to catch myself on the support, and see a ladder further down in the water, and latch onto that and haul myself out of the muddy water.

I'm standing on the embankment.

It's 3:00 a.m.

I'm soaked through.

I'm feeling angry that I'm still alive. I'm feeling kind of lost about what to do next, so I decide the only thing I know to do is to walk back to halls and as I walk I try and process what's just happened. The specter of dying seems to have resized the idea of failing exams, and I'm thinking maybe I'll stick around for a while longer.

Suddenly I'm confronting the idea of having a future, of having to deal with the next year of living, and maybe even sixty years of living I might likely have. The thought terrifies me.

I'm still embarrassed I've done this and I'm still alive. And I'm comforted to discover that London is exactly the kind of city which you can walk through in the middle of the night soaking wet, dressed in all black, and no one will pay attention to you. I sneak back into halls and I go to bed.

It's been eleven years since that night. And, if I'm being honest, I'm still anxious, still lonely. I still struggle with stupid stuff like phoning the council to order more liners for your food waste bin. And there's still a part of me which tells me that I'm a terrible person and didn't deserve to survive.

But when I look back on that night I realize my suicidal, depressed brain made a lot of predictions which my life has varied from immensely, in good and bad ways. Four years later I graduated from Imperial with a first in Physics.

I watched *Waiting for Godot* recently, and reflecting on the story these lines stick with me:

Estragon says to Vladimir, "I can't go on like this."

To which Vladimir replies, "That's what you think."

MICHAEL SUCH was raised in rural England and moved to London to study physics. After university he walked from London to Milan. Since then he has worked as a data analyst. Michael directed the improvised road trip movie *Open Roads* as part of the Camden Fringe 2018 and helps organise The Smoke international LARP festival in London. Although still suffering from depression, he is alive and in therapy.

On the Other Side of That Wall

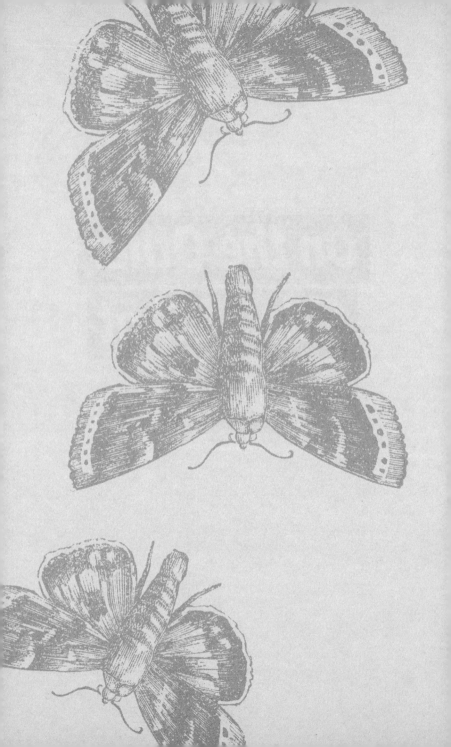

Barbara Collins Bowie

The Freedom Riders and Me

My brother and I were born and raised in Jackson, Mississippi, during Jim Crow. In 1961 my brother got involved with Martin Luther King and the civil rights movement. He became a Freedom Rider. At that time I had no idea what a Freedom Rider was.

I was only thirteen, but my brother was nineteen, and this became a very serious movement for him. The Freedom Riders were involved in the integration of the interstate transportation system across the South. And wherever there were the Colored Only and White Only signs in the bus stations and in bathrooms and restaurants, they would challenge them.

This was very dangerous for them, because the Ku Klux Klan did not want this to happen. So they were getting beat up and arrested. They got hosed down. The buses they rode got bombed.

I loved my brother, and I always wanted to do everything he did. But I was too young for all that, so my friends and I got involved by doing sit-ins locally. Now, this was fun for us, because it gave us the opportunity to walk into restaurants and shops that we had never been in before.

For instance, there was a restaurant in our neighborhood that we used to go to almost every day after school.

On one side it said COLORED ONLY, on the other side it said WHITES ONLY.

Well, the colored side was kind of small. It had a counter and a couple of booths and a jukebox – we could put a nickel in there and hear our music.

If we wanted to get something to eat, there was a window with a doorbell, and we could order sodas, and hot dogs and French fries on paper plates.

But as you were standing at the window, you could see into the other side. It was big, with lots of round tables covered in beautiful white tablecloths and place settings. White people were seated and being served dinner.

And this was just how it *was*.

Like when my mother would take us shopping for school clothes, before we left the house, she'd say, "Barbara, go use the bathroom."

I was like, "Mama, I already used the—"

"Go use the bathroom *again*."

I didn't understand that, until one day we were downtown in a store. She had picked out a few items. I had to use the bathroom, and she got very upset with me because she had to put those things back. We had to leave that store and go to a side street where there were colored businesses, use the bathroom, go back to the store, and start over again.

And while we were in the store, she had to know my sizes, because they would not allow us to try on clothes or shoes, and so if we bought something that was too small or too big, they would not allow us to bring it back.

When we left the store, Mama would grab my hand, and I'd say, "Mama, I'm a big girl, you don't have—"

"Shut up, gal."

When a white person would approach us, Mama would pull me off the sidewalk into the street to let them pass by – they didn't want to brush up against us.

So I *did* understand what was going on, and how we were being treated, and that it was wrong.

But I didn't understand what the civil rights movement or the Freedom Riders could do about it.

This was our life. This was how it was. This was what we accepted, you know?

One day several years later, I was walking home from downtown with my friends, and as I was coming up my street, people sitting out on their porches started yelling, "Barbara, Barbara, you need to get home! Your mom got sick, and she was taken to the hospital!"

I'm like, "Hospital?" We never went to the hospital! Mama always had home remedies.

I ran home, and I tried to find someone to take me. But I couldn't find anyone, so I ran to the hospital.

When I got there, Mama was sitting in the waiting room of the emergency room with the friend who had brought her there, and she was very distraught. She looked like she was going to pass out. She was clammy, and she had a cold paper towel on her head.

She said, "I'm trying to keep from vomiting again."

Her friend told me, "She vomited a washpan-ful of blood."

I'm like, *I can't believe that. A washpan is big.*

So I said, "Well, how long have you guys been here?"

And he said, "We've been here since two o'clock."

I looked, and it was about five thirty.

So I went up to the desk, and I said, "You know, my mama's been here since two. She needs to see the doctor. She needs to lie down."

The young lady said, very rudely, "We don't have a bed for your mother, and there are other people here who need to see the doctor first."

All I could do was go and sit down and wait with them.

As I'm sitting there, I'm seeing people being called up to see the doctor. Now, some of them might have been there before me, but most of them came in after, but they were being called first.

They were all white.

So about nine thirty or so, they called Mama.

I was glad. I thought, *She can lie down, and she'll see the doctor.*

So we're waiting in the treatment room for the doctor, and the nurse came in with a wheelchair.

She said, "I'm sorry. We're going to have to put your mother outside the door for a while, because we have someone else who needs to see the doctor."

I was like, "No. My mama's been here since two o'clock. She needs to see the doctor."

Well, I was a teenager, so they ignored me. But when they went to get her up, she vomited, and she almost filled that room with blood. So now nurses and doctors were coming from everywhere. She needed blood transfusions. They took her up to the fifth floor.

We went looking for her, and, as I was passing by a treatment room, I heard a burst of laughter coming out.

I looked through the little crack in the door, at the doctors and nurses, and I said, "That's where Mama is," because no matter what was going on, even if she was sick, Mama always had something funny to say or do to make you laugh.

We were waiting to go in and see her, but the doctor came out, and he said, "It's very late. We're trying to get her admitted. Why don't you all go home and come back tomorrow?"

I didn't want to leave. I wanted to see Mama. I wanted to hug Mama.

I wanted to say "I love you," because we were a family who never said that to one another. I never remembered saying that to my mama.

But he wouldn't let us in, so we left.

The next morning we came back, and she was critical. We were outside her room again, waiting to go in and see her and say "I love you."

The doctor came out, and he said, "We're preparing your mother for surgery," so we couldn't go in.

When they rolled her out on the stretcher, I could see just a glimpse of her face between their bodies. Her eyes were swollen and red with tears, and I got this big, hard ball right in the middle of my chest.

We went down to the second floor to wait for her to come out of surgery, and we waited and waited.

Finally the doctor came out, and he said, "I'm sorry. Your mother didn't make it."

That ball in my chest just burst out of me.

I started screaming, "You let my mama die! YOU LET MY MAMA DIE!"

I cried, and I cried, and I cried.

I cried for *days*.

But it was at that moment that I realized what that civil rights movement was all about.

I realized why my brother and the Freedom Riders were challenging the COLORED ONLY and WHITE ONLY signs, why they were riding the buses, and why we were doing sit-ins and protests.

Because this was our struggle, this was our fight.

This movement was about equality and freedom.

This was a fight for life and death.

Born in 1947 in Jackson, Mississippi, **BARBARA COLLINS BOWIE**, endured the oppression of those times. Barbara got involved with the civil-rights movement inspired by her brother, Freedom Rider Jesse James Davis. Barbara became a licensed nurse in 1969, later becoming a licensed social worker and published writer. She established the Bowie Foundation "Arts in Focus" after-school program, devoted to helping youth use art as an alternative to negative behavior. The Dr. Bowie Scholarship Foundation, named for her late husband, Dr. Jesse Bowie, has provided over twenty years of arts programs, community events, scholarships, and more in Bexar and surrounding counties.

Leland Melvin

A Moment in Silence

I peered into a five-million-gallon pool; submerged thirty-five feet below the surface was a replica of the International Space Station and a space shuttle. I was training as an ASCAN (yeah, "ASS-CAN" . . . that's NASA-speak for "astronaut candidate"). We were simulating working in space.

I'm in a suit that looks like a cross between the Michelin man and the Pillsbury Doughboy. I'm on the deck, and they start to lower me down into the pool.

At about twenty feet, I realize that the two-dollar block of styrofoam that should be in my helmet is missing. It's what you use to clear your ears by pressing your nose against it.

I go down another five feet, and I tell the test director to turn up the volume in the headset. From that point on, I hear nothing but static. I think, *There's probably a kink in the communication cable or some malfunction in the control center,* and then I'm getting pulled up out of the pool.

I arrive on the deck. The technician walks over to me, he pops off my helmet, and the flight surgeon walks towards me. He's actually moving his lips, but I don't hear anything. He gets closer, and he touches my right ear with his index finger, and I can feel blood streaming down the side of my face.

At this point I realize I am completely deaf.

They take me to the showers; my head starts spinning violently, and I throw up. They rush me to the emergency room, and they put me under so they can do emergency surgery to figure out what happened. As I wake up from the anesthesia, I see the three faces of my surgeons, and they don't look happy.

They don't know what happened. They couldn't find the smoking gun as to what caused me to lose my hearing. From that point on, I can still talk, but we're communicating with yellow legal pads as they write things to me.

They write, *"We couldn't find what happened."*

But the note I really remember is, *"You will never fly in space."*

As I lie in the hospital bed thinking about these things, totally depressed, a friend writes me a note, and it says, *"Remember what Janette said."*

And then I think back to four days before this accident. I was in Lynchburg, Virginia, my hometown. My parents were having their thirty-fifth wedding anniversary, and my cousin was there with a friend of hers, Janette. Janette called herself a prophetess, and I'd never heard that term before.

But she said to me, "Leland, I don't know you, but something's going to happen to you. No one's going to know why it happened. You'll be healed of this, you will fly in space, and you will share this with the world."

I was like, "Oh ... okay. Thank you, thanks for that information."

I was in top physical condition. I had just come back from Russia, where I'd been working with the cosmonauts and helping the first crew get to the International Space Station.

I had gone from being at the top the world, an astronaut candidate, to not being able to hear a bomb drop.

That note reminding me to remember what Janette said was the only hope I had to hold on to.

My hearing slowly comes back. NASA's trying to figure out what to do with me, because the doctors say I'm medically disqualified. So they put me in the robotics branch, which is a pretty benign branch, because all the training you do is on a computer screen, so you can't damage anything. After I'd been doing that job for a little while, they asked me to go to Washington, DC, to work in education, because NASA is starting the Educator Astronaut Program. We're going to get kids to nominate their teachers to become astronauts.

Around that same time, there was excitement because the space shuttle *Columbia* was launching into space.

I was driving from DC to Lynchburg, Virginia, on Highway 66 when I got the phone call from my education boss, who was new to NASA, and she said, "Leland, what does it mean when the countdown clock starts counting *up*?"

I did an illegal U-turn on 66 and turned the radio on, and there were eyewitness accounts of large pieces of debris falling over the West Texas sky. I knew my friends were all dead.

I rushed back to NASA headquarters.

I was dispatched out to Washington, Virginia, which is about two hours outside DC, to console the parents of David Brown, who was on that mission. As astronauts we take care of our families when there's a tragedy.

I get to the door, I go in, I hug David's mom, Dottie, and we're both crying. She takes me over to her husband, Judge Brown, who's in a wheelchair. And he looks up at me with the same sparkling blue eyes that David had, and they were full of tears.

He says to me, "Leland, my son is gone. There is nothing you can do to bring him back. But the biggest tragedy would be if we don't continue to fly in space to honor their legacy."

I'm thinking, *How can I honor their legacy if I'm medically disqualified to fly in space?*

We started flying around the country to the different memorial services to honor our fallen heroes. We took the NASA jet with the families, and on every takeoff and landing there was a gentleman sitting beside me. He was the head of all the flight surgeons.

Every descent, as I squeezed my nose to clear, I saw him writing notes in a little black book.

When we got back to DC, he called me into his office, and he said, "Leland, I've been watching you, and even though your hearing isn't a hundred percent in either ear, you are still able to clear your ears and handle the air pressure of flight. I think you will be able to fly in space, and I believe in you. Here's a waiver for you to fly in space."

I was like, "Really?!"

I took this waiver back to Houston to the flight surgeons, and it was like one of those get-out-of-jail-free cards. I handed it to them, and I got assigned to a flight soon after that.

So I was finally sitting in the space shuttle *Atlantis* before launch.

The solid rocket boosters light.

Three.

   Two.

      One.

         Liftoff!

We're now careening off the planet into the cosmos. At two and a half minutes, the boosters jettison and the ride gets much smoother. Six minutes later I'm undoing my seat belt and I'm floating in space.

I float over to the window and look out and see the Caribbean. I know maybe seven variations of the color blue – cerulean, azure, indigo, turquoise, light navy, dark navy, medium navy – but I need twenty more hues to describe what I see below me.

We arrive at the space station, and the commander invites us over to the Russian segment to have a meal.

She says, "You guys bring the rehydrated vegetables from the shuttle, we'll have the meat."

So we float over with a bag of vegetables. We get to the Russian segment, the *Zarya,* which means "sunrise" in Russian, and it's like I'm in my mother's home.

The smell of meat getting heated up. Their beef and barley, our green beans with almonds, all being shared with people that we used to fight against – the Russians and the Germans. As we broke bread at seventeen thousand five hundred miles per hour, going around the planet every ninety minutes, seeing a sunrise and a sunset every forty-five, I thought about the people I'm now trusting with my life.

African-American, Asian-American, French, German, Russian, the first female commander of the International Space Station. Floating food to each other's mouths.

All while listening to Sade's "Smooth Operator."

This was the moment. This was when my brain cognitively shifted and I felt connected with everyone on the planet.

I thought about my race – the human race – as we connected and worked together.

I thought about what Janette had said: "You will fly in space, and you will share this with the world."

I thought about David Brown's father, and I thought about the *Columbia* crew.

I thought, *We did something good. We did honor their legacy.*

Before becoming an astronaut, **LELAND MELVIN** played professional football with the Detroit Lions and the Dallas Cowboys. He has traveled off-planet twice on the space shuttle *Atlantis* to help build the International Space Station. Upon hanging up his space boots, he led NASA Education and co-chaired the White House's Federal Coordination in STEM Education Task Force, developing the nation's five-year STEM education plan. After twenty-four years with NASA as a researcher, astronaut, and senior executive service leader, he shares his life story as an athlete, astronaut, scientist, engineer, photographer, and musician to inspire the next generation to pursue STEM careers.

Jon Bennett

Curses

I grew up on a little farm in the middle of rural South Australia, with my three older brothers and my mum and my dad. It was a pig farm, and it was one of those pig farms where the pigs are in these tiny pens.

When I was six years old, I woke up in the middle of the night, and I snuck up to the pig shed, and I set free all of the pigs. I ran back to my bedroom, and I jumped into bed.

This wasn't some sort of animal-liberation thing. I was only six years old. I wanted to wake up and look out the window and see pigs on the tractor, pigs walking into the kitchen where a pig was doing the dishes.

I wanted to see pigs *everywhere*.

But instead I awoke to my dad shaking me, and he took me out to the pig shed.

And none of the pigs had moved.

Dad said, "See? They *want* to be here. I hope you've learned something."

That's the sort of thing that my dad would say all the time: "I hope you've learned something."

My dad was this very dominant man, a very serious, stern, proud, and impatient man.

When my brothers and I grew up, we had to work on the pig farm with him, and my dad was the kind of man who had to have a hand in everything we did.

You know that kind of man: you're doing the dishes, and Dad pushes you out of the way and starts doing the dishes to show you the *proper* way to do it.

And he was everything in my life in this tiny little community where we grew up in South Australia.

But Dad wasn't just a pig farmer, he was also my schoolteacher. And I don't mean *a* teacher at my school, I mean *my* teacher. So I saw him every single day at school.

But Dad wasn't just a schoolteacher either. He was also my bus driver. So he'd pick us up from our house, drop me off at school, teach me all day, and then I'd work with him on the pig farm after he dropped me off at home.

So I saw him every single day, from the morning until the nighttime.

On Sundays my family and I would go to church.

Dad was the minister at the local church.

So all I had were Saturdays. And when you grow up on the farm in rural South Australia, all you do on Saturdays is play sports.

Dad was my football coach, my basketball coach, and my tennis coach.

He was everything in my life, this very serious, stern, proud, and impatient man.

My dad was also a man who had never said a swear word in his entire life.

And even as little kids, we'd say, "How is this possible, Dad? How is this possible you've never said a swear word?"

He had the same answer every time: "There are other words you can use, and there's no need for that language."

I'm not kidding. I've seen him walk around the back of the car at nighttime and hit his shin so hard on the tow bar of the car that he dropped to his knees, looked up at the moon, raised his fists, and yelled, "CURSES!"

Like a *Scooby-Doo* villain, he yells, "Curses!" This is the only word that my dad uses.

The other thing he did instead of swearing is just yell out his feelings.

So he'd be out working on the farm, and we'd hear this scream of "I'm ANGRY!"

"I'm annoyed! I'm UPSET!"

That's what he does instead of swearing.

When I turned eighteen years old, I decided that farm life wasn't for me, and I moved to the city and started going to university. I was studying the arts, and I became a vegetarian.

Around this time my second-oldest brother moved to a place called Kangaroo Island. Kangaroo Island is off the coast of South Australia. It's this beautiful, natural wonderland.

My dad loves Kangaroo Island. He's never been anywhere else in the world, never even gotten on a plane. And he's got the same excuse for not traveling anywhere, and that's "Why do I need to go anywhere? Kangaroo Island is right there."

I would say to him, "Look, you know, Dad, I've been to Japan and places like that."

He said, "I've seen Japanese people on Kangaroo Island. Why do I need to go anywhere else?"

He loves Kangaroo Island so much that he goes to visit my brother every single weekend. He visits him so much that he managed to get a job on Kangaroo Island as the minister at the local church on Sundays. He takes another job after church on Sunday going hunting with farmers, hunting these wild pigs, which are one of the only introduced species on Kangaroo Island.

I go to visit my brother when I'm eighteen years old, and we go to church in the morning.

My dad does the service, and then after church my dad says to me, "Do you want to come hunting with me?"

I say, "Uh, no, I don't. I don't need to do that."

He says, "Do you just want to come and check it out? It's in this beautiful national park."

And I say, "Okay, that's sounds fun," and so Dad and I drive to this national park.

There's a big shed out in the front. I walk into the shed, and there are all these hunters and farmers loading up trucks with guns and then driving off through this national park, hunting these wild pigs.

Dad says again, "Are you sure you don't want to come hunting with me?"

I say, "Oh, no, no, no, I don't need to do that."

He says, "Okay, I'll organize for a ride back for you, but before we do, can you help me load up this truck with guns?" and Dad hands me a gun.

Now, I don't know if you've ever held a gun before.

(We're in America, you're probably all packing right now.)

But I feel the weight of this gun, and I feel a sense of power, and this weird feeling, like *Oh, yeah, I want to shoot something. Let's* shoot *something. I want to go hunting.*

So I tell my Dad I'll go, and Dad says, "Great."

We load up this truck with guns, and then Dad and I drive off through this national park. We park the truck, and it's just Dad and me hunting the wild pigs. After about three hours, Dad shoots six wild pigs.

I shoot none. I enjoy looking through the scope at things far away. I like jumping out from bushes and pretending to shoot things and going "Pow, pow, pow!" I'm having a really good time.

Dad keeps thinking I'm going to shoot something, when I'm not, I'm just looking through my scope.

He's getting very annoyed, and I know this because he's screaming, "I'm annoyed!"

He says, "Look, do you want to shoot something?"

I say, "No, Dad, I'm having a really good time. I feel like I'm in *Predator* or something like that!"

By this time I've put mud under my eyes like a soldier.

He says, "No, I'm going to find you something to shoot."

He disappears off through these trees, and he comes back about ten minutes later, and he whispers, "I found you something."

I follow him, and he tells me to look through my scope, and I look, and I see a pig, and it is a big pig. As it lies down, I see a bunch of little babies come up and start suckling at its teats. I'm looking at this mother pig through my scope, and Dad whispers in my ear, "It's easy."

I say, "I know it's easy, Dad, but this is a bit fucked, don't you think?"

And he says, "There's no need for that language."

Dad whispers again, "It's easy. You're helping. This pig is a nuisance. They ruin the local flora and fauna. They ruin the environment for the local animals. You're *helping*. You can do this."

I look at this pig, and I say to Dad, "Do I have to shoot the babies as well?"

He goes, "No, just shoot the mum. They'll die on their own."

And again he says, "You're helping, these are pests. You're helping, you can do this."

I sit looking at this pig for what feels like forever, and I think, *I* can *do this*.

I get the pig's head in my sights, I close my eyes and pull the trigger.

When I open my eyes, I see Dad's back in front of me, and I see him drop to the right.

And I have just shot Dad in the back.

He swings around as he grabs himself by the shoulder. Blood starts coming out from between his fingers. He looks at me.

His eyes are wide, and he just says, "YOU FUCKING SHOT ME!"

That's the first time he's ever said a swear word. He just unleashes this tirade of abuses.

"You effing shot me! I am effing dead! Do you know where we are? We are in the middle of nowhere. I am effing dead. You have effing killed me!"

And as he's doing this, I sit in shock, and I drop the gun to the ground. I stare at Dad, and secretly, in the back of my brain, I want to go, *There's no need for that language*.

But I don't. I don't say anything.

And Dad just continues, "I can't believe it's you. Out of all of my sons, *you're* the one who kills me. The *vegetarian*, the *city boy*."

He pulls out his phone, and he throws it at me and says, "Call Mum. Call Mum. Tell her you've killed me and I'm dead."

I get his phone, and I dial emergency (I'm not an idiot).

I say, "Uh, I've just shot my dad."

And they say, "Where are you?"

"Kangaroo Island."

And they say, "We need you to be a bit more specific than that."

"I don't know where, there's a national park. There are trees here. People go hunting here."

And they say, "We think we know where you are. There's a property about a kilometer away. Do you think you can get him to this property?"

I say, "Yeah, he seems okay."

I hang up from them, and I tell Dad, "We've got to get to this property."

He says, "Give me your jumper, your sweater."

I take off my sweater, and he uses the sleeve to stuff into the bullet hole. I put my arm around him and hold the jumper into his chest as I carry him back to where we've parked the truck. I put him in the passenger side. I run around to the driver's side.

I start the truck up, but I can't drive a stick shift. And this is a big old truck with one these gearshifts on the steering wheel. I grind it into gear, and we bounce forward and stop.

Dad screams in pain. I start it up again, I grind it into a different gear, and we bounce forward and stop again.

Dad screams again, and says, "Get out!"

I get out of the truck, and I walk around to the passenger side as Dad slides along the seat (leaving a trail of blood across the back of the seat) and drives *himself* to this property. Now, on the emergency line all they've told me is to make sure that Dad stays awake, which is good, *now that he's driving.*

And finally we get to the property. By the time we get there, Dad's gone this bluey-gray color.

The helicopter is there to pick us up, and Dad gets loaded by the ambulance people out of the truck and into the back of the helicopter. I get on the helicopter with Dad, and we get flown to the hospital for free (thanks to Australia's health system).

Dad is in surgery for quite a while, and all I remember next is my mum walking out.

She says, "He's going to be okay. He's lost his collarbone, and he had very little blood left in his body when he got here, but he's going to be okay. Do you want to go and visit him?"

I say, "No," because I just can't.

Mum says, "It's okay," as she counsels me through what has happened.

Eventually I go into my dad's hospital room. He's lying in the bed, sort of strapped up.

We lock eyes, and he says . . . "I hope you've learned something."

And I did learn something.

I've never touched another gun.

Years later I'll learn that Dad has almost been shot about twelve times from different mates because he gets so impatient that he often jumps in front of people as they're about to shoot.

And you know what? I think my *dad* learned something that day.

Sometimes there *is* a need for that kind of language.

JON BENNETT began his comedy career in his homeland of Australia and, fourteen years later, is known as one of the most prolific storyteller/comedians, touring the world with eight-hour-long individual comedy shows. He has won awards such as Funniest Show Award on the London Fringe, Critics Choice Award for Best Solo Show at the Orlando Fringe, and a Golden Gibbo Award nomination at the Melbourne International Comedy Festival. He has performed at prestigious festivals, including the Edinburgh Fringe and Just For Laughs in Montreal. www.jonbennettcomedy.com.

D. Parvaz

Bearing Witness

In the summer of 2013, I was in Cairo, Egypt. I was on assignment for Al Jazeera, covering a major political upheaval. The president at the time, a guy named Mohamed Morsi, who was affiliated with the Muslim Brotherhood, had been deposed and jailed in what his supporters said was a military coup.

So, in protest, they set up these sit-ins in the city. It was a hot, crazy summer – really tense. And by the middle of August, the government finally did what they'd been threatening to do, which is to clear the sit-ins. But they did so with unabated violence.

They started shooting at people in the sit-ins and the surrounding neighborhoods at around seven in the morning and didn't stop until well into the night, until pretty much everybody was either dead or arrested.

I've never seen anything like it. It was a massacre in broad daylight in a capital city of roughly twenty million.

So the next day I went to a mosque where maybe two hundred or so of those bodies were being kept. A lot of them were badly burned, and there were blocks of ice on top of them. There were family members going in and out of this mosque, trying to identify their loved ones.

It was intensely chaotic and emotional.

I am with a producer who works in the local bureau and can translate Arabic for me. We walk outside and start talking to a woman who says that her husband is among the dead. She's shaking and in shock, and she's describing her last phone conversation with her husband, which ended when the shooting started.

She describes him as an engineer who was unarmed and the father of her four children. My colleague is translating, and I'm not even looking up. I'm just in my notebook, furiously writing, not wanting to miss a detail.

And then my colleague stops translating while the woman is still talking, and I look up at him. And the look on my face is like, *Dude, what?*

He leans in and whispers, "Um, now would be a good time for you to put an arm around her."

This makes my little reporter's brain totally short-circuit, because I am *not* a touchy-feely person. I don't hug you for you to tell me your story; that is not how it works.

But the look on his face was clear: *Get over yourself and be human. Now. Put your arm around her.*

So I robotically lift my arm, and the second my hand touches her, she collapses into my chest. She's a tiny woman. And she sinks into me and starts sobbing as she's holding on to me. I'm still holding my pen and paper. And it hits me hard that this woman doesn't care what kind of reporter I am or what my stupid little rules are.

She wants me to register what is happening to her on the worst day of her life.

She wants me to bear witness.

I should have known better, and in fact I *did* know better.

Two years prior to that, in the spring of 2011, was the start of the uprising in Syria, what is now the civil war. I was sitting in the newsroom in Al Jazeera's headquarters in Qatar, watching grainy YouTube footage of unarmed civilians being mowed down by the Syrian military.

At the same time, we had a government spokesperson on our airwaves claiming that this wasn't really happening – it was a distortion of the truth; there was a conspiracy. We couldn't confirm any of this, because they'd already shut down our bureau in Damascus and they weren't issuing journalist visas.

So what to do? Well, I'm a multinational. I have an Iranian passport. So my boss agreed to deploy me to Syria, where I wouldn't need a visa to enter, just to see what's going on.

I fly into Damascus, and unfortunately for me, at this point the Syrian authorities have already become super paranoid.

So they go through my luggage and find a satellite phone, which is not a big deal. If you travel in that part of the world, you know that outside of major cities you don't really have cell-phone coverage. You can buy a satellite phone at any shopping mall; it's not spy gear.

But this was enough for them to get suspicious. So they strip-searched me and found my American passport in the pocket of my jeans. In this passport was a stamp from Al Jazeera, who sponsored my visa for Qatar – it's what I needed to re-enter the country.

This escalated things.

They took me into a tiny office and sat me between two guys on a couch. There were all these other guys on their computers, chain-smoking and banging out some kind of report on me.

When the report was done, the two guys sitting on either side of me got up and strapped on a bunch of guns. They peeled me from the couch, and they led me to the parking garage under the airport. They sat me between them in the back seat, with another armed man in the front seat, and drove off into the night.

We pulled into a compound. There were three or four checkpoints to get into this compound, so I assumed it was some sort of government building. They pulled me out of the car by my hair and threw me in front of a desk in a dimly lit portable office.

There were all these men yelling at me, and I looked down and saw that I was standing in a considerable amount of somebody else's blood.

They processed me for some kind of arrest, blindfolded me, handcuffed me, and took me to an interrogation with a man who told me to call him Firas.

Nothing I said was accepted by Firas: that I was a reporter, that I wasn't part of some conspiracy. He didn't even believe that I didn't speak Arabic. So I realized very quickly that truth had no currency there. They handcuffed me again, blindfolded me, and threw me into a cell.

I took off the blindfold and saw that I was in a cell that was covered in blood – so much that I didn't know where to stand or lean. So I kind of squatted in the corner and tried to wrap my head around the hell that I was in.

An hour or two later, a guy comes to the door and he yells out my father's name, which is also printed in my Iranian passport. He yells out "Fayrouz!" He can't tell the difference between my name and my father's name, I guess. So I get up, and he blindfolds me and handcuffs me.

I thought that I was being taken to another interrogation, but he took me outside into a courtyard and slammed me up against a wall. I could hear people being tortured a few feet away from me. I could hear the guards, the Mukhābarāt, joking and laughing, and I could smell their cigarettes.

They were acting like regular employees on a coffee break. And I stood against that wall and I thought to myself, *They're going to kill me.* And worse than that thought –

believe it or not – worse than dying was the thought of dying like that, which is to say alone, because I was alone.

I couldn't locate the humanity in the people around me, and I knew that I was going to be an anonymous body. If I was lucky, they would throw me in a ditch, and my father, whose name was being called out in that place, would never have any peace: he'd never know what had happened to me.

I've never felt so alone in my life.

So after about twenty minutes of shivering against this wall and waiting to be shot in the head, I get pulled off and taken back inside.

I kept thinking, *Well, okay. They didn't kill me* now, *but they* are *going to kill me, because why, why, why would they let a reporter not cover a street protest but see and hear all of this and live?*

Of course *I'm going to write about it.*

I'm going to die – they're going to kill me was on a pretty tight loop in my head as they threw me back in the cell.

I can hear people being tortured inside the compound. The voices echo and come and go and blend in.

And then there's one voice that stands out, and I can't exactly figure out why, except that he sounded obscenely young. He sounded like a kid, like a teenager – a boy.

And I could tell that there was more than one person hurting him, and he was just howling; he was swearing he didn't know things. He was swearing to God he hadn't done anything wrong. He was calling out to God; he was calling out to his mother.

I couldn't take it anymore after a while. It was brutal. So I put my hands up to my ears just to try to block it out.

But the second I did that, I felt such shame, because I realized that this kid was at his own, far worse, version of the wall. He was alone.

He was *dying* alone.

That's what was happening.

And so I pulled my hands down to do what I could, which was to hear him.

I couldn't call out to him to say, *I hear you. You're not alone.*

I couldn't identify him.

I didn't know his name.

I couldn't contact his family.

I couldn't do anything.

All I had was the ability to bear witness in that fashion.

The kid was choking on his own blood in his own country, and nobody was going to know. I felt bearing witness to his suffering was the least I could do.

So I listened to him for a while, and every scream was excruciating. It was like a hole was being cut inside me with every one of them.

And then, rather abruptly, his voice stopped.

A couple of days later, the Syrians decided that maybe it wasn't a good idea for them to permanently disappear an Iranian citizen, because they have a good relationship with the Iranian government. So they sent me to Iran via extraordinary rendition for additional questioning for a couple of weeks at another prison there.

And, much to my surprise, eventually the Iranian authorities freed me and sent me back to my family.

I needed time off, but I didn't need to go to a spa and breathe alpine air.

What I needed was to work, because not being busy and not working meant the wall was always there. I could feel it, and I wanted to push against that feeling. I couldn't wait to get back to work.

The second I could, I flung myself into my job, taking every assignment. If they didn't give me an assignment,

I would fight for one: Egypt, Libya, nuclear meltdown in Japan, it didn't matter. I was doing it.

And I succeeded a little too well in pushing back against that wall and that feeling. And what I did in doing so was create distance between myself and the things I was reporting on, the people I was reporting on.

So when that woman in Egypt fell into my chest and started crying, she destroyed that distance – she entirely eradicated it.

I was back at the wall, and the boy's voice was in my head.

But, as painful as it was, I realized that it was necessary for me to bear witness fully to what was happening to someone beyond the couple of paragraphs they might actually get in a story.

As much as some stories will leave a mark, sometimes that's just what it takes.

D. PARVAZ is based in Washington, DC, where she covers U.S. foreign policy. She previously worked at Al Jazeera based out of New York and Qatar, focusing on conflict, democracy, and human rights in the Middle East and North Africa. Prior to moving overseas, she worked at several U.S.-based newspapers covering local and national news.

Dan Kennedy

And How Does That Make You Feel?

A few months ago, I walk into a party in New York and there's this guy who I've seen at a lot of different events. He's a therapist, and I always go over to him and say hello, because I gravitate towards therapists at parties. (I actually, sadly, consider this progress.)

I say hello, and we talk for maybe five minutes, and I feel better. Every time I see this guy and say hello to him, I'm in a better mood. I think to myself, *Maybe I should have a better plan for my mental health than just bumping into this guy at parties.*

And then I think, *Maybe I should go back to therapy.*

I don't really want to go back to therapy, because I was in therapy for years; I got the tools I needed to go off and not have to do it anymore, and it came to a really clean end. I don't take that for granted, because I hear a lot of people talk about therapy, and they never quite know when it should end, you know?

It's like, "Do you think you're ready for it to end?"

"I don't know. Do *you* think *I'm* thinking *I'm* ready for it to end, because *you* think *I* thought that?"

This can go on for years. So I really need to think about it before I get back in that situation.

Back in 1998 my life wasn't going super hot. By that I mean I was working at a nine-to-five job that I hated. I was in a terrible relationship – great person, things were just on a downhill slide for a long time, largely helped by me, I'm sure.

Also, I wasn't doing anything that I loved. My idea of writing, which is something I *said* I wanted to do, was to go to restaurants after my nine-to-five job and drink lots of midpriced cocktails and eat really bad appetizers and talk about how "I'm probably a genius," you know? Which is not really the hallmark of genius, ironically enough.

I had this group of friends, and their lives all seemed to get *better* as time went on. Not in any necessarily big, flashy way, but their apartments got nicer, their relationships got stronger, their jobs got better, they got promoted, they did more interesting things.

I was sort of living backwards. As time went by, my apartments got smaller and worse. And my relationships . . . they ended.

I thought, *Well, maybe I should find out what's up with these guys.*

The one thing they all had in common is they talked to this guy named Milton.

I thought, *Hmm . . . maybe I should talk to Milton.*

So I asked, "Would it be weird if I talked to Milton?"

They said, "It wouldn't be weird at all. You should call him up."

So I get an appointment – I'm going to see him Fridays at six thirty. Great.

I meet him. He looks like a real southern gentleman out of another era. He's tall. He's lanky. He's an older guy – gray hair, wears suits – real dapper dresser.

And so we start this thing.

I like the fact that he's not a therapist – he's a licensed social worker, a counselor, which really fits with my nuts-and-bolts approach to this, like, I'm not going to be lying on a Mies van der Rohe daybed, mumbling about luxury problems, clearly. This is right up my alley.

He has this special sort of method. It largely involves making jokes about me. I get the point *through his humor.*

I talk to him about things. I tell him whatever I'm going through. For instance, I never know how to say no; I would always just say yes.

So if I'm out to dinner with somebody that I can tell is trouble and they ask, "Do you want to be in a relationship?"

I'm like, "Yes, yes. Even though I'm not nuts about being at dinner with you, let's give this one to three years."

Or, "Would you like this job for this salary?"

I'd think, *How the hell am I going to live on that in New York City?*

But I'd *say,* "Yes. Thank you very much. That'll be fine."

I was telling Milton about this one time, and he goes, "Oh, well, have you ever read *A Thousand Times No*?

I'm thinking, *Oh, God. Here comes the cheesy self-help-book assignment.*

But I want to be *willing* and get my life together and all that shit, so I'm like, "Oh, gosh, you know, I haven't read that, but I'm willing to get a copy and check that out. I will definitely buy one."

All the while, thinking, *No.*

He goes, "Oh, hang on, I think I've got a copy in the other room."

I say, "All right, great."

He comes back with this eight-and-a-half-by-eleven sheet of paper, and it just says "no" a thousand times on it.

AND HOW DOES THAT MAKE YOU FEEL?

He's like, "Thought this was pretty funny."

And I thought, *I think I like this dude. This is gonna work.*

I was telling him something about a terrible week I had, and I was saying, "You know, this isn't going great. My job sucks," blah, blah, blah.

And he goes, "How many beers did you have this week?"

I say, "Oh, wait a minute. Are you saying there's, like, a link between my drinking and things not going well for me?"

He leans back, and he says, "Well, you're part Irish, your last name's Kennedy, and all your heroes are writers, so let's just keep an eye on it."

"I get what you're saying there."

And it planted this seed, you know? His humor planted a seed.

I had been writing things. They were terrible. They were mostly not commercially viable things, very short things on the Internet.

For instance, I wrote a piece called "Reject Riddles by Depressives."

And "What I Would've Said to Sylvia Plath, Had I Been Her Boyfriend."

You know, gems like that.

Occasionally I would get emails from junior editors at publishers, and I would tell him about that. "Today this junior editor at a publisher emailed me, and it kind of made me feel like I'm doing something!"

And he says, "Oh, they're rolling out the red carpet for you, young man!"

But the most awkward thing is that he taught me to cry, apropos of nothing.

He says, "You know, sometimes when things get painful, what I do is I put on some sad music. I get a towel or a handkerchief, and I sit down on the couch, and I let the feelings come. And then you move on."

I was like, *Okay . . . that's great for you. But I will never be using that, by the way.*

He started getting into stand-up comedy at age sixty-five, which made for a weird relationship sometimes, because you'd finish this session where you're talking about all this stuff, and then he would go, "Well, you know, I'm afraid we're out of time, but if you've got five minutes, I'd like to show you this DVD of the set I did at Caroline's on Tuesday!"

You'd literally be standing in the living room after talking about all this really intimate stuff, and then you'd watch the DVD and be like, "That's a good joke, I guess, but it's a little weird, sir. I should go now."

I should also mention that one of the ways I start to realize that I'm getting close to somebody is if I find myself thinking about their death a lot.

I know most folks probably just look at the beautiful person across the table and go, "I care about you. You're very special to me."

I, on the other hand, just get quiet and start imagining them dead and how sad I'll be when that happens.

So, needless to say, Valentine's Day is a pretty loaded holiday for me. It's a sort of long, morose, quiet day where I'm envisioning someone I love's funeral and getting depressed.

So the day after Valentine's Day, I get there early. I think, *I want to be on time for this. It's probably going to be a little bit loaded after this sick holiday that people have.*

I buzz the door. But Milton's not answering. It's a little bit weird.

I buzz it again. He's still not answering.

I wait five minutes, buzz, no answer.

Call him on his cell phone. He's not answering.

I think, *Hmm, this is* really *weird.*

I'm like, *Well, I've got to take some kind of action.*

He always taught me that time is finite and you have to always take action. That's what keeps you from getting sad and stagnant.

So I think, *Ring it again? I guess that's action.*

I ring it again. Nothing's happening.

Then suddenly the cleaning lady comes running down, and she goes, "Come quick. It's Milton. Come quick," and then she leaves the building.

I go, "Oh, shit."

I didn't sign up for any of this. This is terrible.

But I go in. I run up the stairs, and I'm thinking, *I don't know what I'm running into,* but I just keep reminding myself what he said to me: "Always move forward. Always choose activity.'"

Milton always said, "When you go forward, you'll be able to intuitively handle what used to baffle you."

I get up there. I look around. I call his name.

And then suddenly I see him. He's in his bathrobe still, and I'm like, *That's really weird.* I mean, that's not normal for him at all.

I go, "Milton! Milton!"

I call his name, and he doesn't respond.

I run up to him, and I feel him.

And I say, "Oh, my God. He's dead."

He's just left. It's that simple. He's gone, but he left his body here.

I don't know what to do. Who do you call?

The police? It seems a little silly.

An ambulance? It's too late for that.

I think, *Well, just call 911. They'll intuitively know how to handle this.*

So I call them and ask, "Who do you send for something like this?"

They say, "We'll send an ambulance and the medical examiner."

"Okay, all right, cool."

So that's handled.

In the ten minutes it takes them to get there, I sit and say goodbye. I'm thinking about how much better my life has gotten over the years because of this man. I've stopped drinking. I'm in a better relationship, one that I'm still in years later.

I've been doing my writing. I have a book contract, and my first book is coming out in just a few months.

I realize I'll be dedicating it to him.

I'm thinking of all my friends' lives that he's touched and changed. It's amazing.

And then I think about how he said, "Days are finite. We only have so many."

And I look at him, and I think, *You certainly drove that home in this session, sir.*

The medical examiner comes, and I say one final goodbye, and I take off.

For the first few days, I am numb. I don't really feel anything, and this kind of surprises me.

But a week later I'm in the apartment and something's happening.

I'm thinking, *He's not coming back. There are not going to be any more Friday nights at six thirty. He's totally gone.*

And I'm like, *Oh, no. I'm having feelings.*

But okay. All right, right, right. He told me what to do.

I go into the bathroom. I get a towel.

I sit on the edge of the couch.

Oh, right, right – music. You have to put on sad, classical music.

I don't have any sad classic music. I look through my CDs, and it's all pretty much punk rock.

So I'm like, *I'm gonna put on Black Flag or Fear and weep violently, and that's going to be more disturbing than what I'm going through.*

But my girlfriend had this one CD. I never saw the point of it. It's this guy who just plays his cello, and it goes on forever in the key of like "D-sad." It's the grimmest notes.

I think, Now *I know why this man made his record.*

I put it in the CD player.

I get my towel.

I sit.

The feelings come.

I feel them.

And then I move forward.

DAN KENNEDY hosts The Moth podcast and is a longtime Moth performer. He is the author of *Loser Goes First, Rock On* (a *Times of London* Book of the Year, series rights bought by HBO), and *American Spirit: A Novel* (*Publishers Weekly* starred review). His stories have appeared in *GQ, McSweeney's*, and print anthologies. Kennedy lives in New York and has served on the judging committees of the Writers Guild of America East "Made in New York" Fellowship Program and the PEN America Jean Stein Grant for Literary Oral History.

Beth Nielsen Chapman

Seven Shades of Blue

I was newly married and living in Alabama when my first record came out. My husband, Ernest, and I were really excited. I'd been planning on this since I was eleven.

Unfortunately, its debut coincided with the dawn of the disco era, and I was a singer/songwriter, so it was a total flop.

I had lovely reviews, but they basically said, "Too bad she didn't put this out five years ago."

Shortly thereafter I lost my record deal, I got dropped from my publisher, and I found out I was pregnant, all in the same week.

I was like, *Great. Let's shelve the whole singer/song-writer dream. Tried that. The world didn't want me. Next!*

I gave birth to this beautiful baby boy and threw myself into motherhood. In the absence of songwriting, all my creativity came out sideways. I started painting and baking bread, and I even started making these cool little heads out of Play-Doh.

My husband was looking at me out of the corner of his eye thinking, *Surely she'll snap out of it and start writing again.*

I was like, "No, I'm having a great time!"

One night around three in the morning, he came up behind me. I was sitting at the kitchen table trying to get this Play-Doh nose *just right.*

I felt his hands on my shoulders, and he leaned in and said, "Honey, it's time to start writing songs again."

But I was like, "No, no, no, no, no."

I was totally in denial.

But a couple of days later, we went and saw this movie called *Coal Miner's Daughter,* and it was about the life of Loretta Lynn.

And there was Loretta planting vegetables with at least four of her children climbing all over her and writing a hit song at the same time.

I came out of that movie theater, and I said, *I know, I am totally being a baby about this songwriting thing.* So I decided to get back to it.

I started writing songs again as I had done in the past, bouncing them off my husband, Ernest, playing him stuff as I was working on it.

I'd say, "Here's another one, honey."

I'd play him these songs, and he'd say, "Yeah, you just keep on doing that. Just keep on, write more."

He didn't say anything bad or good. He was very kind.

Then one day I played him a song called "Five Minutes." As I finished it, I looked up, and he was just beaming.

He said, "That's it. *You're back.* That's a hit. That's fantastic."

I said, "Really?"

He said, "Absolutely. And by Friday you're going to send a tape with that song on it to these three people in Nashville, Tennessee."

I said, "Oh, no. I'm just doing this for fun."

He goes, "Oh, yes. You're going to do that by Friday . . . or I'm going to start smoking again."

So I had no choice.

But the good news is, I got a great response, and within six months we were packing up our then five-year-old little boy and moving to Nashville, Tennessee. It was an amazing, terrifying, wonderful, roller-coaster ride of rejection and excitement and meeting people. And finally I started getting a little traction.

During those early years, I would always play my songs for Ernest before I let them leave the house, because he had great suggestions. He wasn't a songwriter, but he was kind of a song doctor.

Late at night after the kid was asleep, we'd pour a little Grand Marnier and he'd say, "What you got?," and I'd play him what I was working on.

So one night I played him this song. It was really just a part of the song – just a verse and a chorus. It referred to our honeymoon.

It was an unusual song for me to write at that time. It was kind of from my life, but then it wasn't, because there were a couple of other lines that were very mysterious and sad. There was one line that went:

In the hollow of your shoulder,
There's a tide pool of my tears,
Where the waves came crashing over,
And the shoreline disappears.

And then the chorus seemed to be talking about the immediacy of life and the preciousness of time, and it said:

We hold it all for a little while, don't we?
Kiss the dice,
Taste the rain,
Like little knives upon our tongue.

He looked at me like, *Wow.*

And I just thought, *Okay, good, he's liking this one.*

He goes, "No, you don't understand. This is your *defining moment* as a songwriter, this is you on another level."

Now, his favorite songwriter was Bob Dylan, and he looked at me and he said, "Bob Dylan *wishes* he could write this."

And I was like, "Okay, honey. That's great. Really? Wow."

But then for the foreseeable future, he pestered me relentlessly about finishing this song.

I'd say, "Here's a new song, honey."

And he'd say, "Yeah, that's great. What's going on with that Bob Dylan song? What's happening with that?"

But there was so much going on in our lives at that point, and the following spring I started having some real success. Enough success, in fact, that my husband could quit his job, start up our own publishing company, and be a full-time Mr. Mom.

I was just getting ready to put out a record with Warner Brothers and going on tour. Willie Nelson had just hit number one with a song I wrote. And that song, "Five Minutes," had just gone to number one for Lorrie Morgan. It was crazy, and the phone was ringing, and I'd wake up every morning and couldn't believe this was all happening.

And right in the middle of that, out of nowhere, Ernest was diagnosed with a very rare form of lymphoma. When we found out about it, unfortunately, it was pretty deeply advanced.

The doctor basically said, "You probably have about six weeks, and you need to just go have some fun and skip the chemo and get your affairs in order."

I remember us driving home bewildered thinking, *This is definitely a bad dream.* Thank goodness our son was at a friend's house, so we climbed into bed, and we took turns holding each other and sobbing for I don't know how many hours.

Somewhere in the late afternoon, I bolted up and I said, "What day is today?"

And I realized that that evening, like an hour from then, I was meant to be singing at a huge black-tie event for Warner Brothers Records.

To make it worse, I was supposed to be singing a song I had written for my husband when we first met, the story of how we met, and it was a song called "All I Have."

I said, "Ernest, I have to call and cancel. I can't do it, there's no way. I mean, look at me. I'm a mess."

And he said, "Listen, the only reason that you'd cancel now would be for something like 'My husband has cancer.' And I'm not ready for us to tell the world that. Why don't we just get dressed and go? Let's walk into a world where I don't have cancer and hang out for a couple hours, and we'll come back here and we'll deal with all this later."

Somehow he talked me into it. I remember being in a surreal, altered state. It was an amazing evening, and I did pretty well, except halfway through the song I was looking down and he was beaming up at me in his beautiful tuxedo. He looked so healthy, and all of a sudden I thought, *Whoa,* and I remembered what we were going through.

I don't know what words came out of my mouth. There was a completely new second verse written in some language from another planet, and then, thank God, I got back on board at the chorus. But in the end it was good that we went, because what else were we going to do? We were in shock.

The next morning, though, we were reading the newspaper and there was an article about the event. It mentioned that there had been somebody in attendance who had left the event and suddenly died of a coronary.

That was incredibly impactful to Ernest.

He looked up at me, and he said, "Wait a minute. Nobody can tell me when I'm going to die. I'm not going do this with an expiration date stamped on me. We're going to do this, and we're going to do it right. I'm going to stay here and fight to live and be in this world as long as I can, whatever it takes."

And that's what he did. And instead of six weeks, we had eighteen months together.

It was an incredible period of time. There were friends, and love, and support, and terrible days of surgeries and chemo, and all the best, and all the worst, and an incredible constant of the present moment that we could appreciate on a level we would've never been able to before.

It was amazing and wondrous, but mostly – it sucked.

And the day came when the outcome was obvious – we weren't going to be able to turn it around.

And so Ernest went from using all his energy to fight to live, and he shifted in the most beautiful, graceful way into "How do I learn to die?"

We came to the point where we were having *those* conversations, and he said, "Look, I want you to take my ashes to the Gulf of Mexico," in the spot where we went fishing on our honeymoon, "and I want you to know that when you walk out to any body of water on earth, you'll feel me there with you."

We finished talking about some other practical stuff, and then he said, "Now, there's just this one more thing, and this is really important."

And I'm like, "What?"

"Well, it's that matter of the Dylan song. What's going on with that song? Did you finish it?"

I said, "Are you *kidding me*? I can't believe you're ask-ing me to do that."

(I had a bit of a fit.)

He said, "You know, I don't have that much time, so maybe you want to work on it this afternoon?"

He was relentless about this song.

I said, "Um, excuse me, my husband's dying, I'm a little *busy* right now. But yeah, maybe I'll get around to it."

He said, "Look . . ."

I said, "No. No," and I got up, and I stomped out of the room and headed for the other end of the house.

And he's calling down the hall, "Consider it my dying wish!"

Somehow, by some grace of God – because by the time I got to the other end of the hall, I was fuming – I started to form this idea in my mind of what it would be.

I started writing it down. I was all like, *I'll show that guy.*

I stomped back into the room, sat down on the edge of the bed, and got really still.

I sang,

So let 'em turn my soul
Seven shades of blue.
And with the ocean's roll, baby,
I will wave to you.
And the birds will sing my laughter,
And the whales will steal my song.
But I'll be happy ever after,
And the world will get along.

He had tears in his eyes, and he said, "That's perfect."

And I said, "Oh, thank God."

But then he goes, "Except for one word."

And I'm like, *Seriously? You're going to critique my song now?*

He said, "It's just this one word that's not quite accurate. See, I don't really know that I'm going to be happy ever after. But I'm pretty sure I can promise you that I'll be okay. So you can say, 'I'll be *okay* forever after, and the world will get along.' How about that, honey? What do you think?"

I said, "Fine."

I was just glad to be done with it.

So the year following Ernest's death was a big blur. I was more the "frozen widow" than the "grieving widow," pressing ahead feeling no need to cry, in a kind of standoff with grief, while my son was very much grieving and turning thirteen. I had too much to do to possibly do anything about this giant boulder of grief that I was carting around with me like a ball and chain.

People would ask, "How are you doing?"

And I'd say, "I'm fine."

I definitely wasn't falling apart enough for them. But I was just putting one foot in front of the other.

I finished a lot of songs, and I was getting ready to go into the studio with Rodney Crowell, who's one of my heroes – a great songwriter, great artist, great producer, and a great friend. He was a great friend of my husband as well. So I was in good hands.

We go into the studio. Day one I get behind the microphone, everything's great. I start singing the song. The Dylan song. That was the first one to get down.

By then it was called "Seven Shades of Blue." I started singing it, and I was fine. But when I got to the line " In the hollow of your shoulder, there's a tide pool of my tears, where the waves came crashing over, and the shoreline disappears," and I just stopped.

All of a sudden, the tumblers fell into place and I realized that I had written those lines *two years* ago, a year
before he was diagnosed. And the day he was diagnosed,
I actually lived those lines. I mean, when we came home
from the doctor's office and we held each other, I felt like
I had literally cried a tide pool of tears into the hollow of
his shoulder.

It just stunned me, and it cracked me open completely,
releasing all the sorrow and sadness that I'd been holding
back, and at the same time I had this feeling of wonder
and grace.

Who does that? Who writes for themselves ahead of
time?

Unfortunately, that opened the floodgates, and I started
sobbing, and I could not stop sobbing for the rest of the
day. And all these really expensive musicians – first-class
musicians – standing around waiting for me to pull it
together.

And the studio's two thousand dollars a day, and I said,
"Rodney, we've got to cancel. We've got to cancel, and I'll
come back in a week."

And he says, "Oh, no. We're going to wait this out. I
don't care how long it takes. Take your time. I'm going to
wait for the performance that's on the other side of that
wall of tears."

And that's the performance that's on the record today.

I can hear in my voice, even now when I listen to it, the
sound of the calm after the storm.

The sound of somebody who has been through the
worst and finds themselves in a place where they can
sing, "'I'll be okay forever after, and the world will get
along.'"

Twice Grammy-nominated, Nashville-based singer/songwriter **BETH NIELSEN CHAPMAN** has released thirteen solo albums and written seven number-one hits. Her work is diverse, from singing in nine languages on *Prism* (2007) to *The Mighty Sky* (2012), a Grammy-nominated astronomy album for kids. *Sand and Water*, written in the wake of her husband's death, was performed by Elton John to honor Princess Diana. *Hearts of Glass* was named one of 2018's 10 Best Roots Records. A breast-cancer survivor and environmentalist, Beth teaches workshops internationally, inspiring others to blossom into their creative lives. In 2016, Beth was inducted into the Songwriters Hall of Fame.

Warren Macdonald

A Crushing Connection

I spent my entire adult life searching. Searching for meaning, wondering why it is that we're even alive. And I say my entire *adult* life because that hasn't always been the case.

I grew up in the western suburbs of Melbourne and I can tell you that the only searching that was going on was for the next party, and the only question, "Are we drinking beer, or bourbon and coke?"

This all changed at eighteen years old. I was taken on a four-day Outward Bound-style hike. And I'm embarrassed, really embarrassed, to tell you that I actually hated it. That hike almost broke me. I wasn't in good enough shape, and at the end of each day I just felt beaten and weak and incompetent.

There was only one consolation. On the last night we got sent out alone. Those of you familiar with Outward Bound will know about the solo. We got sent out with no sleeping bags, no food (save for a bag of flour), no water and a box of matches.

And you had to survive the night.

Now, a lot of the other guys that were on this course couldn't make it; they scurried back to the main camp during the night. But that night I fell into my element. I discovered this peace that came from knowing you could take everything away and I would be okay. And that night I felt this *connection*. I was overcome by this connection and for one of the first times in my life I actually felt at home.

For the next decade, I drifted in and out of that feeling, chasing that connection down, with periods of being lost where I would switch back to my old ways. And April 1997 found me once again lost.

Whenever I'd had that feeling before, I did what I had always done – I reached for my backpack and my hiking boots.

I'd heard about an island called Hinchinbrook Island, off the Queensland coast in the northeast of Australia. What I'd heard about Hinchinbrook Island was that it was this amazing wilderness island.

To get across you have to catch a ferryboat. It takes a couple of hours. And when I say ferryboat, for those of you who have cruised the Greek islands, forget thousands of passengers, I'm talking a boat that can hold twelve people max.

And so I catch the ferryboat across and I start hiking. And at the end of the first day I come to a beach, and I meet a guy who introduces himself as Geert Van Keulen, a Dutchman. Geert tells me his plan is to climb to the top of the island's tallest peak, Mount Bowen.

I've got to tell you, when you look across from the mainland at Hinchinbrook Island, Mount Bowen dominates, absolutely dominates. And so, as soon as Geert started telling me about his plan, I didn't really have to wait for him to ask me. I knew I was in.

I'm all over this.

We break camp first thing the next morning and we start making our way up the side of Mount Bowen. Now there's something that I should point out. There's no trail to the top of Mount Bowen, alright, we're on a wilderness island. So the way you get to the top is you follow a creek bed up. And you bushwhack and you boulder hop, and this is what we did all day.

We found a place to set up camp for the night and strung up a tarpaulin in case it rained. We were kind of tough hiking guys – we were way beyond tents. We set the tarpaulin up and cooked dinner. Geert had just gotten into his sleeping bag.

I was just about to climb into mine when I realized, *Hang on a minute, before I do that . . . I need to use a bathroom.*

If you've ever spent much time in the backcountry you'll know that it's not really a good idea to go and take a leak into a creek that's your water supply, especially when you're coming back down the same way in a couple of days.

So, I figured, you know what, the best way for me to move far enough away from this creek is I should make my way to the other side. I should mention the creek at this point is literally just a trickle running down the center. On the other side is a steep rock wall about twelve or fourteen foot high and I thought, *That's perfect, I can scramble up over that.*

So, I make my way across and, as luck would have it, I found a crack. I got one hand in that crack. I got my left hand up as high as I could. Got my other hand in the crack, put my right foot up against the wall.

And as I pulled up, the world literally gave way.

A refrigerator-sized piece of rock broke loose from the rock wall and absolutely slammed me back down into that creek bed. And I'm talking *slammed*. I was instantly in this world of pain. I screamed out.

Geert came running across to be greeted by the scene of me pinned from the hips down underneath this huge piece of rock and things got pretty frantic at that point, right? I can't even begin to describe what that pain felt like, this incredible weight just grinding, grinding down into my legs.

And there's only one thing going through my mind: *I need this thing off me. I need it off me right now.*

So, I'm pushing at it. Geert jumps in beside me. We are both pushing at this thing with all our might. I feel like I'm going to tear myself in half. But nothing's happening.

When something really serious happens, there's only two ways that things are going to go. You're either going to freak. Or things are going to get crystal clear. And, luckily for me, things became crystal clear.

I took charge. I told Geert what he needed to do. We tried a series of levers to lift the rock.

It didn't work.

We tried using a wedge-shaped stone driven by another stone as a hammer to try and lift it that way.

Didn't work.

Nothing worked.

Just when I thought things couldn't get any worse, I felt the first few drops of rain.

Now, I'm in a creek bed. Those drops turned into a torrential downpour, and within forty-five minutes I had water swirling around my hips. Within an hour and a half I had a raging, flooding creek up around my waist. Things got desperate. Geert started to build a dam.

I'm starting to think about my new backpack and whether it has the same kind of construction as my previous one, which had a frame made out of aluminum tubing. I'm thinking, *If it has, I can take that and stretch it out and use that as a snorkel when the water goes over my head.* I'm convinced the water is going over my head, because I can see by the high-water mark on the wall beside me that it's gone over my head before.

But, as suddenly as it started, the rain stopped. And gradually over the next couple of hours the water level started to subside. But we still had a problem: I was still stuck underneath a one-ton piece of rock. I spent the longest night of my life before we decided that Geert would hike out in the morning. That was the only way that I was coming out, for him to hike out and organize a rescue.

As the sun came up the next morning, I watched Geert pack his things. He packed some things for me, too. We put them in a plastic bag, and slung it over my shoulders around my neck, in case the water came up again while he was gone.

I have never felt so lonely as I did when I hugged this guy goodbye and watched him turn around and hike back down off that mountain, because I knew I was going to be there for at least another twenty-four hours on my own.

He's got to make it back down to the beach where we'd met the day before. He's then got to hike back along the beach to where the ferryboat dropped us off. The ferryboat then only comes in once a day, right?

I knew I was staring down the barrel of my ultimate test.

After he went I did the only thing that I could do and I settled in to wait and to think. I thought about all the people that I would probably never see again. I actually wrote letters to some of those people. I wrote letters to my mum and dad. I got angry. I got really angry. I wondered why I couldn't be happy staying at home, watching TV and mowing the lawn on a Sunday afternoon like a lot of my friends that I grew up with. Why couldn't I be satisfied with that? Why did I always have to be traveling around the world, chasing, looking for something, searching?

And then I remembered: *the connection*. Chasing the connection.

Then I thought, *Great. How's this? Is this connected enough for ya? They're going to find you out here in a couple of days dead under this rock.* And then I pulled myself out from that trough and psyched myself up. You know, *You've got to hang in there, you're going to get through this.*

And I rode that roller-coaster ride all day and all of the next night. By the next morning I thought I was hallucinating when I saw a red pool around my right foot. The way I was trapped I could actually see my right foot.

I thought, *This is interesting, it's a little late now to start bleeding.*

And then I saw why. I saw a nipper of a freshwater crayfish pop up out of the water. And I couldn't believe it!

I thought, *You OPPORTUNISTIC BASTARD! How dare you take on a guy that's stuck under a refrigerator-sized piece of rock like that?* I couldn't believe the cheek of that guy, and I spent the next couple of hours trying to kill him with a long stick.

Now, as this was happening I was starting to think that I was in some kind of David Lynch movie. Because just when I thought that it couldn't get any more bizarre, I felt a sting in my groin. And then another sting. And I started swatting ants.

I looked down and realized that I had quite a few ants running all over me.

And then I noticed to my horror a trail that led back to a now-exposed nest that was behind this refrigerator-sized piece of rock I was now underneath.

I realized that these guys were actually looking for a new home.

And I freaked. I just *freaked.* I had visions because by now I'm starting to lose it and I knew that I couldn't let myself go to sleep. I thought if I went to sleep now, I might not wake up. And I had visions of these ants getting into my ears and my eyes and it was like a horror movie.

I remembered that in my first aid kit I had a tube of bug goop. I prayed that Geert had put that first aid kit in the plastic bag around my neck, and he had. I pulled out that goop and, I'm telling you, I just rubbed it all over my face, all over my head, all over my clothes. I rubbed it into my eyes. I didn't care how much it stung, I just covered myself in the stuff and hoped that it would work. And eventually I drifted off.

I woke up to the sound of a helicopter. And I don't think I've ever been so happy to see another human being as the paramedic made his way towards me and started to stabilize me. Two more guys came down and they spent the next two and a half hours lifting this rock off me before they winched me into a helicopter and sped me straight to Cairns Base Hospital.

I woke up the following afternoon into a whole new world. I woke up minus both legs, amputated at mid-thigh.

And so began my new life. I had to learn how to do everything again. I had to learn how to use a wheelchair. I had to learn how to use prosthetic legs.

But at the same time I was driven by this purpose. The clarity that had come to me under the rock was still with me. And so I pushed, pushed, pushed to reclaim all these different parts of my life.

But there was one burning question tucked away in the back of my mind, and that was, *This is great, but am I ever going to feel that connection again? Am I ever going to experience a wild place? Experience nature on its own terms? Is there any way that that can happen?*

I eventually discovered that you can put fat wheels – mountain bike wheels – onto a wheelchair.

I said, "Where do I get them?"

I started "hiking". I'd just hiked five miles and had my first swim in a water hole in a river – my first swim outside of a swimming pool – and this light bulb went off and I thought, *If I can do this already, I wonder if I could climb a mountain. I wonder if a guy with no legs could climb a mountain?*

I got this picture of a mountain in Tasmania that I'd climbed twice before called Cradle Mountain. It had taken me about five hours round trip. I thought, *D'you know what? There is only one way to find out.*

So, I started training and, a couple of months later, just ten months after losing both legs, I set out from the parking lot and over the course of two and a half days I wheeled, I dragged, I scraped – I crawled on my guts at times – until I got to sit on top of Cradle Mountain. And, I've got to tell you, sitting on top of that mountain I got completely overwhelmed with emotion. I felt like I'd gotten hit by a semi-trailer-load of emotions. Everything came flooding back at me – the accident, the rescue, the months and months of rehabilitation. Everything that I'd lost.

But in that moment, I also realized that I might have lost my legs, but I'd gained so much more.

The thing that most overwhelmed me was that feeling of being connected again. And that I'd actually found my way home.

WARREN MACDONALD
has faced obstacles most
people cannot imagine.
Having lost both legs
from a freak accident
while hiking off the coast
of Australia, Macdonald
decided that his injuries
wouldn't slow him down;
rather, they would propel
him to new heights. Just
ten months later, Warren climbed Tasmania's Cradle Mountain
and later summited both Mount Kilimanjaro and El Capitan.
Warren works with innovative, forward-thinking organizations
looking to foster a shift in perception, inspiring audiences to
turn obstacles into opportunities. He has been featured in the
Discovery Channel's *I Shouldn't Be Alive, Larry King Live,* and *The
Oprah Winfrey Show*.

It's Messy, But It Works

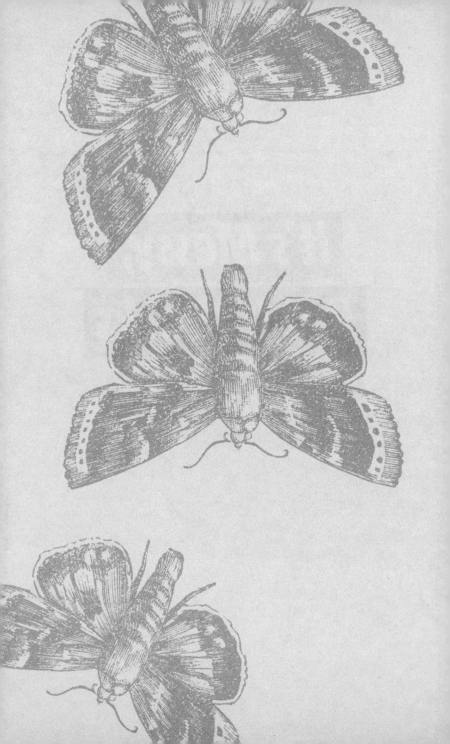

Andrew Solomon

My Post-Nuclear Family

When I was a small child, my mother used to say some-times, "The love you have for your children is unlike any other feeling in the world, and people who don't have children never get to know what it's like."

I took it as the greatest compliment that she so loved my brother and me, and loved being our mother, that she thought so highly of that emotional experience.

When I was growing up, there was an article in *Time* magazine about homosexuality which said, "It is a pathetic little second-rate substitute for reality, a pitiable flight from life. As such, it deserves no glamorization, no rationalization, and, above all, no pretense that it is any-thing but a pernicious sickness."

Living in that world, I was sad as I began to think that I might be gay.

When I was a teenager, my mother would say, "The love you have for your children is unlike any other feeling in the world, and people who don't have children never get to know what it's like."

And that made me intensely anxious.

I thought, *I think I'm gay, but I want to have children. But I think I'm gay, but I want to have children.*

I felt myself banging back and forth. At some point I decided that children were the primary thing and that I was going to change. I read an ad in the back of *New York* magazine for sexual-surrogacy therapy, and I went for a kind of training to transform myself into somebody else.

It was a very peculiar experience. It involved doing so-called exercises with women who were not exactly prostitutes but who were also not exactly anything else. My particular favorite was a buxom, blond southern woman, who eventually admitted to me that she was really a necrophiliac and had taken this job after she got into trouble down at the morgue. I made progress; I got over my fear of sex with women.

But when I was in my early twenties, I decided that this was not all going as planned and that I really was gay.

I told people that I was.

And my mother said, "The love you have for your children is unlike any other feeling in the world. And if you don't have children, you'll never get to know what it's like."

Having first been touched and then been made anxious, I was now made angry by this statement, and I said, "I'm gay, and I'm not going to have children, and I am who I am, and I want you to stop saying that."

Years afterwards, in 2001, I met John, who is the love of my life. And shortly after we met, he told me that he had been a sperm donor for some lesbian friends.

I said, "You have children?"

And he said, "No. *They* have children, and I was the donor for them."

A few weeks later, we were out at the Minnesota State Fair, and we ran into Tammy and Laura and their toddler, Oliver. I looked at them with fascination, and I thought, *How amazing that Tammy and Laura are gay and they have a child, and that John is gay and in some sense at least has a child.*

Oliver had been told that he should call John "Donor Dad." Having a rough time pronouncing that, he came up with "Doughnut Dad."

So I looked at them all, and I thought, *There's Doughnut Dad. There's his moms. There's me. Who are we all to one another?*

A year later John told me that Tammy and Laura had asked him to be a donor again, and they produced Lucy.

So now there were two of these children, and we knew them a little bit and saw them from time to time and were warmly disposed toward them. And John said he'd promised to be in their lives when they were grown up if they particularly wanted him to be.

The idea of having children in some unusual arrangement was not entirely novel to me. I had some years earlier been at a dinner with my closest friend from college, Blaine, who lived in Texas and had recently separated from her husband.

When I asked if she had any regrets, she said, "Only about not being a mother."

I said, and meant it, "You'd be the best mother in the world. And if you ever decided that you wanted to have a child, I'd be so honored to be the father."

I assumed that it was just a statement in passing, since she was beautiful and beloved and had lines of men eager to court her. But on my fortieth birthday she appeared in New York for a surprise party that John and my father and stepmother had organized. We went out to dinner the next day and realized that we really did want to follow through with this plan.

I wasn't ready to tell John right away. When I did tell him, he was angry about it.

I said, "John, how can you be angry at me? You have Oliver and Lucy, and now there'll be this other arrangement."

He said, "I was a *donor* for Oliver and Lucy, and you're setting out to have a child of whom you will be the *acknowledged father* and who will have your last name."

We struggled with it for quite a while.

And then John, whose kindness usually carries the day, said, "If this is what you really need to do, then go ahead and do it."

Soon thereafter he asked me to marry him.

It was 2006, and gay marriage was pretty new. I had never been a big fan of gay marriage. I thought everyone should have the right to marry, though it didn't particularly preoccupy me. But, after he proposed, we began planning a wedding. I thought he had gone along with what I wanted to do and I would go along with what he wanted to do.

We ended up getting married in the English countryside, and we had a beautiful wedding. I found that, though our commitment had seemed to me to be permanent and declared and established before that, the experience of having hundreds of friends gathered together, witnessing our love, shored it up and strengthened it and gave it a new depth and resonance I had never imagined nor anticipated.

I found the fact that we were celebrating our love in a ceremony that echoed, in some sense, the one my parents had had, and the ones my grandparents had had, and the ones that presumably went back generation upon generation, exalted the feeling between us, and it was very joyful.

Blaine was there, three months pregnant with our child, and John ventured that we had had the first gay shotgun wedding.

So six months later, our daughter, Little Blaine, was born. I was in the room when she was delivered, and I was the first person to hold her. Blaine by now had a partner, Richard, who was also to be a significant part of the picture.

I had such a disorienting feeling of suddenly being changed.

I thought, *I'm a father now. I'm a father.*

It was as though someone had told me that I was still myself and also a shooting star.

I held her. And I then had to go down into the basement of the hospital to sign the certificate for her birth, where, given that Blaine and I were not married, I was advised to get a paternity test before I signed for any love child.

I said, "You have no idea the planning that was behind this."

John held her, and we all were enraptured, as one is by the birth of children, because it's so much stranger than even intergalactic travel that someone wasn't there and now all of a sudden she is.

But when John and I got back to New York, I kept feeling as though I was being highly supportive of something *Blaine* had done, rather than as though it were something *I* had done. And yet I found myself thinking of this child all the time.

John fell in love with Little Blaine. He fell in love with Big Blaine. We were all in love with one another. We were trying to understand how everything fit together.

Sometime later I said to John, "Don't you think it would be nice for us to have a child also, a sibling for Little Blaine, whom she might love to have in her life and who might grow up in our house all the time?"

John did not think that would be lovely. And so we had a year in which I kept saying how wonderful it would be and acting as the cheerleader for the cause. And through that year John kept resisting and being unsure.

Finally my birthday rolled around again, and he said, "Your present is upstairs."

We went upstairs, and there was an antique cradle tied up with a bow.

He said, "If it's a boy, can we name him George, after my grandpa?"

We then had to figure out how we were going to produce such a child.

So we found an egg donor, and we began the process of trying to find a surrogate.

We got together with Tammy and Laura and Oliver and Lucy one night, and Laura said to John, "You gave us our children, and I'll never be able to thank you enough for that. But I could show you how much you mean to us by being your surrogate."

She offered to carry our child.

She got pregnant on the second IVF protocol. And nine months after that, George was born. We called Big Blaine and Little Blaine and everyone else in our circle. And we held him and we wondered at him.

Then we came home, and we sent out birth announcements. The announcement included a picture of John and me holding George.

Many friends said, "I loved that picture. I hung it on my refrigerator."

But one of John's cousins wrote back and said, "Your lifestyle is against our Christian values. We wish to have no further contact."

I thought that world, the *Time* magazine world of my childhood, was still there and still going strong. And it made me very sad.

But meanwhile we had spent many, many hours with

Tammy and Laura and Oliver and Lucy through that whole pregnancy, and we had all fallen in love – I think again, anew, more deeply – with one another.

And when Oliver and Lucy learned that Little Blaine called us "Daddy and Papa John," they said they'd like to call us Daddy and Papa, too.

I suddenly found that, in contemplating two children, we seemed to have four.

In the period that followed that, I kept thinking about the angry cousin and what she'd said.

I thought, *It's not really a question of our kind of love being as good as, or better than, or less good than anyone else's love. It's simply another kind of love that we found as six parents of four children in three states.*

And I thought that, just as species diversity is essential to keep the planet functional, so there's a need for a diversity of love to sustain the ecosphere of kindness, and that anyone who rejected any bit of the love in the world was acting from a position of folly.

About six months ago, we went to a game park, and I climbed up with George on a stand, from which you could view some animals below.

I held his hand, and I said, "We're going to go back down the steps now. Go very carefully."

I took one step, and I slipped, and I fell all the way down the flight of stairs, pulling him along behind me.

I remember when it happened thinking that I really didn't care whether I had broken my arm or my leg, as long as I hadn't injured my child. It turned out that I hadn't.

When I realized it, I suddenly thought, *The love you have for your children is like no other feeling. And until you have children, you'll never know.*

I thought how even in the periods when my mother's saying that made me anxious or made me angry, that it was her saying it so persistently that had caused me to pursue a family, even under such complicated and difficult and elaborate circumstances. And it had led me finally to the greatest joys of my life.

 **ANDREW SOLOMON** is a clinical psychology professor at Columbia University Medical Center and writes and lectures on politics, psychology, and the arts. He is the author of *Far and Away: How Travel Can Change the World*, *New York Times* bestseller *Far from the Tree: Parents, Children, and the Search for Identity* (winner of the National Book Critics Circle Award), and *The Noonday Demon: An Atlas of Depression* (a Pulitzer Prize finalist and winner of the 2001 National Book Award). He lives in New York and London with his husband and son, but also has a larger postnuclear family.

Journey Jamison

Theory of Change

When I was ten years old, my best friend died from an asthma attack.

We had spent the day at an amusement park. It was one of the most humid days of that year, July 3rd, 2011, and she'd been struggling to breathe.

After we drove her home, she had the asthma attack, and her dad couldn't get her help in time. The next day my mom got a call that she had passed away.

I took it hard. I knew she had asthma, and I had been able to provide her with some assistance in the past, but I wasn't there this time. I always felt like maybe if I *had* been there, I could have done something.

Five years later my mother and I heard about a gunshot-wound first-aid class. I was immediately intrigued.

And you might be thinking, *Gunshot-wound first-aid class?* But it's not strange, because the lack of resources on the South and West Sides of Chicago make having this information a necessity. It's the unfortunate reality.

I was interested because there would be people who looked like me, teaching me skills to empower myself.

Better yet, they included asthma awareness in the workshop as well. The goal was to create widespread urban preparedness for any situation.

I sank my teeth in. I knew the importance of this training, and I paid attention. I was completely engaged with being a UMedics member. So I knew how to do an occlusive dressing with a credit card and apply pressure with a scarf. But I was also still a regular teenager.

The following summer on a Saturday, I'm coming home from my very first date. I was fifteen at the time. It's just a regular day, two or three in the afternoon. I come inside, I turn on the TV. Nothing major.

And then I hear shots fired.

Pop, pop, pop, pop, pop. They are ringing through my apartment. I can't believe it. You hear all the time about gun violence in Chicago, but I'd never come face-to-face with it like that before.

But immediately I step into my role as a UMedics member and say, "What can I do?"

Step one: be aware of your surroundings. The first step to being a first-aid responder is prioritizing my own safety. I peer out my window so I can see what is going on. I see people running from the gas station across the street toward my apartment.

I'm trying to see if I'm in any position to help. I never planned on going outside, because I didn't want to put myself in harm's way.

But it turns out I don't have to.

Because literally seconds later, a young man flies through my back door, holding his neck, bleeding, saying over and over again, "I've been shot. Can you help me? I've been shot. Can you help me?"

I take a step back, and I just say, "Yes."

And from the moment I say yes, it is autopilot.

I lay him down on the floor. I begin talking to him. The first thing I do is ask for consent to call 911, because that's one thing we emphasize in UMedics training – you cannot assume anything. You have to *ask,* because people are their own person.

So I ask him if I can call 911.

He says yes.

I get on the phone and tell them where I'm at.

They're like, "Okay. We're sending an ambulance."

I'm like, "Perfect."

So then I go back to the guy. I'm talking to him. I'm asking him questions about who he is. I want him to feel safe. And he's telling me his name: Peta. He's telling me how old he is: nineteen. Where he's from: another apartment complex that was pretty close to mine. He tells me he wants to go to college. I'm getting to know him, and at the same time I'm applying pressure. I'm trying to keep the blood in his body, to get the blood to clot.

Once I have somewhat of a stable bandage going, I'm taking this all in, and I realize I'm fifteen years old, I'm home alone with a man who's been shot in the neck.

I should probably call my mom.

I pick up the phone, and I guess you can call it mother's intuition, because as I'm about to press *Call*, the phone rings, and it's my mom.

I'm like, "Mom. You won't believe this. There's this man . . . gunshots fired . . . first aid . . ."

She's like, "Are you serious?"

I say, "Mom, why would I lie about this?"

And she's just like, "Okay, okay, I'm on my way."

I resume treating Peta. And now I'm doing a closer examination of what exactly is going on. He has two wounds – an entrance wound and an exit wound. One is in his neck, and then it goes up through his jaw. Pretty bad, but he's here, and so he's fine so far.

I'm talking to Peta. I'm trying to keep him conscious.

He is extremely eager to live, which I admire. That puts the pressure on me, because I need to be *as* eager to help him.

And I am.

A few minutes later, my mom walks in the house and looks around like, *It's going down.*

She's looking at me. I'm applying pressure.

She says, "Is there anything I can do?"

I'm like, "No."

And for a few moments, it's calm. Peta's calming down. His blood is starting to clot, so the bleeding is not so drastic.

But then, a few minutes later, people start to flood into my house – bystanders, I guess, who had seen what was going on. A commotion forms in my apartment, and it's a lot to deal with, but I'm putting my full attention on Peta.

My mom does a really good job controlling the crowd. She's making sure people are not recording Peta, because that's a violation of his privacy. She's keeping the people trying to question him away so that he's not getting more stressed out. And the only reason she is able to do that is because she got the same training I did. So she knows exactly how to help me in the situation. I'm taking care of Peta's body, and she's taking care of Peta's surroundings.

Then the police come. My mom is apprehensive of the police being there, because it's no secret that black and brown people are not trusting of the police. They make us feel anxious, like we have something to prove.

My mom doesn't want to bring that energy into our apartment. She doesn't want that energy to affect Peta, most importantly. She doesn't want that thought process and that anxiousness to overwork him. So she is going back and forth with the police and bickering with them. But eventually she gives up when they threaten to arrest her for not allowing them on her property.

And so eight or nine police officers crowd into our tiny apartment. They are standing over me, watching me apply pressure to Peta, not providing any assistance. (It's Chicago; they could have been doing something way more important.)

And then, luckily, the fire department gets there. Not the ambulance, the fire department, which gives you a glimpse of what health care is like in Chicago – the ambulances don't come to our communities that fast. My own mother got here first!

So the first fireman comes in to check Peta's vitals, and I have my hands over his neck, and he says, "Take your hand off of him. You don't know what you're doing."

And me, being a little black girl, I am just like, "Okay."

I have all these feelings of doubt, and so I reluctantly pull my hand away.

Just as I thought he would, Peta starts bleeding again.

But then the second fireman came in, and he says, "Actually, she needs to put her hand back."

And I think, *I knew that.*

I don't want to be combative. But it is an important moment for me, because it gives me a boost of confidence, like, *I know what I'm doing. I feel good. I'm doing something good.*

So I keep my hand on his neck, and they are taking his vitals, getting ready to transport him. The ambulance arrives, and a few minutes later they take him on the gurney and whisk him away.

They had to take him all the way to Northwestern, because we don't have a trauma center on the South Side of Chicago.

After that there was still a lot of commotion outside our house. People were looking to me for answers, as if I had anything to do with the actual shooting. It was overwhelming. The news station was there. The police were there.

I remember grabbing my phone, grabbing my keys, locking the door, and making the conscious decision not to engage with anybody, because I didn't want my story to be sensationalized.

I got in the car with my mom, and she just drove. I zoned out, and I was replaying in my mind what just happened.

Then the car stopped, and I snapped out of my trance, and we were at the beach.

I was like, "My God, what is going on?"

And my mom looked at me, and she said, "Let's do some yoga." And so we joined a group of women on the grass doing yoga.

That might seem kind of strange, but for me and my mom it wasn't. We did things like yoga and meditation.

So she looked at me from her tree position, and she said, "Self-care."

And I was so grateful to be able to process everything. I took this opportunity to ground myself, because that really happened.

It was real.

After that day I resumed my life as a normal teenager.

But a few weeks later, I got a call from Peta's mom, and she said, "You know Peta thinks you saved his life, right?"

Until that moment I had never thought about it like that. I just thought I was in the right place at the right time. I had the right information, and I did the right thing.

I took that opportunity to say, "Hey, Peta. Do you know why I knew how to do what I did? I'm not a superhero. It was because I got this training. And how cool would it be if *you* had that training? And your *parents* had that training. And you were able to help somebody you loved who was in this situation?"

He said, "Yes."

So three months later we were able to train his entire family. About twenty-five people, ranging from small children to seventy-year-olds. I kid you not – a complete multigenerational experience.

You know how in school you learn the plot of a story? And it's like: expository, the rising action, the climax, the falling action, the resolution.

For me, change has its own plot. And it starts with taking action, and getting information, and then sharing that information with somebody else. And so being able to train his family was the experience coming full circle for me. It empowered me. It gave me a lot of confidence.

You hear all the time that children are the future.

But I refuse to settle for being the future when I can be right now.

As a young Chicagoan, **JOURNEY JAMISON** witnessed disparities throughout the city and lost her best friend to asthma, prompting her to examine community health. In 2016, she became a trainer for Ujimaa Medics, a black grassroots collective. The following summer she attended Seeds of Peace Camp and she recently interned at Sacred Keepers Sustainability Lab. Only sixteen, Journey has shared her voice on WBEZ, www.Mic.com, and at the United State of Women Summit 2018. Her driving principle – holistic health for the hood – governs her journey toward a peaceful and sustainable life for everyone.

Joshua Wolf Shenk

You Can Come Back

My parents split up when I was seven years old, and they got joint custody. My mom stayed in the house on Hill-top Lane. My dad moved to an apartment about five minutes away, and then to a little house and another house. He was always five minutes away – if you put a compass needle at my mom's house and swung it around, it was always the same distance.

I would go back and forth between them, but I never felt like I was really home in either place.

It was as if I lived in that space in between.

I felt like a pinball. At that time my parents were pretty lonely and unhappy, so I'm bouncing back and forth between these two angry bumpers making loud, screeching sounds.

I left Cincinnati and went to college. I had this split in me. No matter where I lived, there was always one specific, other place I thought I should be.

So I lived in Manhattan but I looked with these wide eyes over the river at Brooklyn. And then I moved to Brooklyn and I looked back at Manhattan with the exact same expression.

I had enough therapy to know what was going on. Brooklyn was like my mom – warm and inviting – and Manhattan was like my dad – elusive and bipolar.

But I couldn't shake it.

I went for a run one day – I had moved to the country, was pining for the city – and I got all emotional. I came back to this country house and called my mom.

We had gotten to be good friends.

I said, "Mom, I had this breakthrough. I see why I can't settle down and get a home of my own. There's a part of me that still feels like the little boy living on Hilltop Lane. And I think that little boy in me thinks that if he gets a home of his own, that means Dad is really not coming back."

My dad was definitely not coming back. After I went to college, he came into some money, and he started traveling the world. He was a photographer – a terrific photographer – and he would pack up his equipment and go.

I often literally did not know where in the world he was.

I would beg him to tell me his itinerary so I could track him in my mind. But that stopped mattering, because even flying commercial became too restricting for him, and he studied for his pilot's license and bought a little plane and began flying himself.

He did *try* to show up. He came to my brother Jon's wedding. He was there for the rehearsal dinner and the ceremony.

But on Sunday morning, when I woke up, I said, "Where's Dad?"

Someone said, "He flew out at dawn."

He was a charismatic and passionate and awkward guy. But the dark heart of his energy in those years was his fury at my mom. Decades after they divorced, he couldn't be in the same room with her. He didn't even want to be in the same city.

And so he just got farther and farther away and higher and higher up in the sky.

Until one day, suddenly, he came down.

In April 2008 my dad was flying from Colorado, where he was living, to Virginia. He was going to stop in Louisville for the night. As he approached the airport in Louisville, something happened with the plane, and it came down quickly through the trees and into this suburban neighborhood and smashed on the ground. It went careening through a yard, across a road, smacked into a retaining wall, and burst into flames.

A little girl saw it from her front window and called 911.

They said, "What's the emergency?"

And she said, "There's a plane on fire in my front yard."

It took at least five minutes for the fire crew to get there. My dad was trapped in the cockpit, burning. And it took a few more minutes for them to get the fire out and extract him from this tangled and twisted plane.

When I saw him late that night in the burn unit at the University of Louisville Hospital, his head had swollen to the size of a basketball, and it was all wrapped in gauze. He had second- and third-degree burns over seventy percent of his body. His back was broken.

If he survived, he would surely be paralyzed.

I ordinarily hate euphemisms, but the doctors used a very good one. They said we should "prepare for the worst."

And the worst thing, for me, was that if my dad died in that moment, he would die with us as strangers.

For as long as I can remember, I'd had this whiteboard in my mind on which were written three phrases that described my relationship with my dad:

- We couldn't connect.
- I wasn't useful to him.
- I didn't know if he was proud of me.

Now, he was in a coma, and I was walking around in a daze, splitting my time between wherever I had to be for work and the hospital. I would come see him for about a week at a time and sit by his side for long hours, with the whirring and clicking of all these machines keeping him alive.

Then he was well enough for them to bring him out of this coma. And one day I was sitting with him. He was unable to speak, but he was awake.

I thought, *Maybe this is going to be like one of those movies where the worst possible thing has this underpinning of light coming up from beneath.*

My mom had come from Cincinnati to Louisville to be with me, and she was in the waiting room. She would never have dared to actually come into the hospital room.

But I said, "Dad, Mom is out there. Would you like to see her?"

He nodded his head.

During this period he was so vulnerable to anyone who had any kind of tenderness for him. He needed to have them in his life.

About a month later, he was high on morphine and my mom was on the phone with one of us.

He asked for the phone, and he said, "Joanne, I know things got a little helter-skelter between us. But if things don't work out with Sidney" – that was her husband of twenty-four years – "I still want to make it work."

Then this really strange thing happened.

I want to remind you of the geography. My dad was living in Colorado, and he was flying to Virginia, and he crashed in Louisville. So after a couple of months in critical care at the University of Louisville, it made sense to transfer him to Cincinnati, about ninety miles away, because he had so many friends and family there.

So we made that move for him, and he was in critical care at the University of Cincinnati for many more months. Then it made sense to move him to a rehab hospital.

The rehab hospital in Cincinnati was five minutes from my mom's house – the exact same distance away as all those apartments and houses where he lived in those first years after their divorce. So in the summer of 2008, my week came up where I could leave work and go be with my dad. I flew to Cincinnati, and I went to my mom's house on Hilltop Lane. I dropped my bags, and I went to see my dad.

That week it was like, one by one, the circumstances and my relationship with my dad took an eraser to those phrases on that whiteboard.

I never felt I could connect with him. It used to be that it was like a miracle to get my dad on the line for two minutes at a time. But now we were talking all day, and we talked about real things. He told me about studying with Ansel Adams, and we talked about Judaism. He was the wise old man with stories, but I was right there with him, asking him questions and arguing with him when I disagreed.

I never felt useful to my dad, but I was so obviously useful. I was *critical*. I was interfacing with the nurses and the doctors about his care, which was constant.

When he was able to have something down his throat for the first time, I went and got him ice chips every hour from the machine. Then he was hot, and I went and got a fan and put it together for him. I shaved him.

When I was shaving him, I said, "Dad, do you remember when I was little, you used to ask me to cut your ear hairs?"

He had these funny little scissors, and he would have

me cut his ear hairs. And I did that again for him in his hospital room.

I never knew if my dad was proud of me, but it just so happened that that week, after months of negotiation with a Harvard psychiatrist who I wanted to write about, we finally agreed on terms for me to get access to this very unusual study. I got the assignment to write a cover story for *The Atlantic*.

I took the call in the room next to my dad's, and I came back and told him. He wanted to know how much I was going to get paid. I told him the number, and he was a little impressed.

Later that day my brother Jon was on the phone, on speakerphone, and he said, "What do you think of our boy Josh?"

And my dad said, "He's not a boy. He's all man."

We'd have these long days together, and then at the end of the day he was tired, he was ready to sleep. And it was just so natural to say good-bye and "I'll see you tomorrow," and I would drive up the hill to Hilltop Lane and go home to my mom's house.

My mom would have dinner waiting for me, and we would talk about the day. She wanted to know how my dad was, and she wanted to know how it felt for me. I would go sleep in my childhood bed and wake up and go do it again.

For once in my life, I felt like maybe I was still a pinball, but I was nestled in this flipper. Everything was okay – both my parents were holding me, and I was holding them. I felt like I could finally shoot out into the world.

The last day was nothing like the rest of the week. I'd had these long, languorous days with my dad and plenty of time, but now we were rushed because I had a plane to catch.

And somehow, even though he was profoundly vulnerable in his body, I wasn't thinking about his body that week, because he was so present in his mind. At one point in the week, somebody came into the room for a little bit to visit, and it was a guy my dad didn't like.

When he left, my dad said, "Somebody crack a window in here."

But this last day the nurses were cleaning him and changing his bedding, and they had him tipped him over on his side. His flesh was hanging off him, and it was so pink and raw – it was like a cut of meat you would see at the butcher.

I was standing at the door. I had to go.

But I was so full of longing for my dad.

I had been so good all week, but I just broke down, and I became a little boy again, and I started to cry.

With some effort my dad turned his head around to face me, and he said, "Josh, why are you crying?"

I said, "I don't want to go."

He said, "You can come back."

And I think I know what he meant. I think he meant I could book another flight, and I could come back to see him. But in the years since – the hard years, while he was still alive and especially since he died, three years later – that phrase has come to mean so much more to me.

It's come to mean you can go back to the places you're hurt and get a little better.

And you can come back to the people in your memory and spend a little bit more time with them.

And, as I think about that week with my dad, I can't help it.

I would give anything to go back.

JOSHUA WOLF SHENK is the author of *Lincoln's Melancholy* and *Powers of Two* – whose essays have appeared in *Harper's*, *GQ*, the *Atlantic*, *Riverteeth*, and the *New York Times*. He is editor-in-chief of *The Believer*, the executive and artistic director of The Beverly Rogers, Carol C. Harter Black Mountain Institute, and a founding adviser to The Moth.

Mary Theresa Archbold

Our Normal

When I auditioned for the university dance department, I quickly realized *one of these things is not like the other.*

All the girls there were tall and lean in their black tights, black leotards, and perfect little buns (with no fly-ways). And there I was, short, muscular, tan tights, bright leotard, and hair just in a ponytail with curly flyways *everywhere.*

As the audition proceeded, all the girls did their pieces, which were important, meaningful pieces of modern dance.

And then I got up there and did my audition piece, which was a jazz dance to Huey Lewis and the News' "Hip to Be Square."

At the end of it, the head of the department looked at me and said, "Wow. We've never had one like you before."

And I thought to myself, *Wow. He's not referring to my music choice. He's talking about my arm.*

You see, I have a prosthetic arm. I've always had a prosthetic arm – I was born with part of my left arm missing, and I got my first prosthetic arm when I was three months old. So I've always worn it.

And I was under this delusion that it was normal, because I went to school in a cocoon, essentially. I was with the same kids from kindergarten through twelfth grade, so everybody knew me. No one ever really thought about Mary's having a prosthetic arm.

So when I was at this audition and this man said this to me, I realized, *Oh, my gosh. This is how the rest of the world sees me.*

At the time of the audition I actually couldn't even wear my prosthetic arm, because I had been injured about a year before, dancing in high school with my rap group, B-PIE (Bourgeois Posse in Effect).

I was not wearing a prosthesis, which seems like it would have been a big deal. But because I was in this cocoon, I was embraced, and it *wasn't* a big deal. To have this man say this to me, it really rocked me back. And I realized I didn't want people to judge me on that. I wanted them to get to know me. So I decided that summer, before I started the University of Michigan, that I was going to go back to wearing a prosthetic arm.

My parents went through the process with me, and I got a lovely arm from a French doctor that was hand-painted by French artists. They even put in little freckles just to make sure that the arm was Irish to go with the girl. And all that for the bargain basement price of twenty thousand dollars.

But when I got to school, I looked normal. Nobody would see me and right away notice anything different. This was great. It was greatly aided by the fact that I wore long sleeves *all* the time.

The only trick of it was not letting my roommates know. It's a little difficult to not have people find out when you live with them, because when you have a prosthesis, you cannot wear it twenty-four hours a day. You must take it off and let your skin breathe, otherwise your skin will break down and bleed and all sorts of bad things happen.

So the way that I got around my roommates' finding out is that every night I would climb into my bed, pull my covers up tight to my neck, and slip my prosthetic arm off underneath the covers. And then when the sun came up and my eyes opened, the arm went right back on, and I would come out of bed. I did this the whole time, four years. I got through college, and very few people found out. It was great.

Then I moved to Chicago, and I was dancing and living my young professional life. I met a fella, and we decided to get hitched. Like any good bride-to-be, I focused on the most important thing: the dress.

I went dress shopping with my mother, and I quickly discovered which dress was *the* dress, because when I walked out of the fitting room, my mother started to cry. The only problem with the dress was that it was strapless. This was a little concerning to me, and I didn't think I could actually wear it.

But my mother said, "You know what? I'm going to get really long gloves made."

And that's what she did. She had super-long gloves made that matched the trim of my dress. On the morning of my wedding, they were laid out there in my mother's bedroom as I was getting all ready to be the bride.

I looked at those gloves.

And I decided not to wear them.

I thought, *I am about to spend the day with my family, my friends, with a hundred fifty people who love me. Why should I care?*

But then I got to the church. I stood right at the back, and as I looked down, I quickly grabbed my veil from behind me and covered my arm. Even on my wedding day, I had to fight to look normal.

But life continued. My husband and I moved to New York, and I was acting and performing and doing great and getting jobs, and for the most part nobody knew.

Sometimes they would find out after the fact, and I'd

be like, *Well, you already hired me. Too bad, so sad. You don't want to be* that *guy who fires me.*

In one particular instance, I was working with a company that is called an integrated company, which means they have able-bodied and disabled actors working together. I was the lead in this play. We were doing a lovely new Off-Broadway play, and the *New York Times* came to review it. Fantastic! The *Times* comes, and they love the play. Their only criticism was that it was unfortunate that the lead was played by . . . an able-bodied actress.

This was my coup de grâce. I had *arrived*. The *New York Times* just called me able-bodied! Who was gonna refute them? Not me.

I felt like the king of the world in this moment.

I thought, *Now I have proof that everyone sees me as normal.*

But then I became a mom. Boy, oh, boy, did this open up a whole new can of worms. Because, as I was expecting my child, I had all the crazy thoughts that you have during your pregnancy, through the long ten months (it's not nine, that's a lie – it's ten months).

You think, *Will the baby have my eyes? Will the baby have my mother's great legs?* All these things that you really hope your baby will possess.

But then I got to add in things like, *Will my baby be embarrassed by me? Will my baby not know what to tell his friends? Will he wish he had another mother?*

So I decided, before I had my son, that I was going to appear normal to him, too. And I brought the baby home and was taking care of this little five-pound, ten-ounce guy and trying to do all these things with my prosthesis on.

And it was challenging.

Changing a little baby in a diaper is hard enough, but to have a six-inch piece of metal hanging at the end of your arm that doesn't rotate or do anything to assist you in changing this squirming baby . . . Now, I was muddling through, doing everything that I could to look like what moms look like. *Two hands, kid, don't worry about it. It's all covered!*

The thing that I was scared of the most was actually bathing my son, because – little-known fact – you cannot get prosthetics wet. Metal, water, not good. So I'd avoided it.

But after about ten days, my mother very lovingly looked at me and said, "You must bathe this child. He's filthy."

So I decided, *Okay, I can do this. I can do this.*

I prepped the sink area. I had a towel on the floor for any splashes. I had a towel off to the side to wrap the baby in. I had the washcloths, the soap, the shampoo, all right there – hypoallergenic, of course. And then I had the little slant that you put into the sink so that he can lie there comfortably while he's getting bathed. All I had to do was get the baby in there and bathe him without getting my arm wet.

So I took the baby in my arms, and I placed him in the sink and took off his diaper. And as the water was getting ready, I could see my son starting to get a little anxious. He'd never been through this before, he didn't know what was happening to him. I slowly moved the faucet over so the water hit him, and he started to get scared, because this was a totally new sensation for him. And I was panicking, because I was trying to hold the baby in place with my hand and at the same time trying to grab the washcloth and soap.

He starts freaking out and crying, and he's looking to me to help him. The one person that he could trust, the heartbeat he listened to for those ten months, he needed me to say, "It's okay. You're okay."

And he looked at me, and all I was doing was crying. I was freaking out that I couldn't do this. I couldn't take care of him because I was so afraid of getting my arm wet and doing it wrong.

And as I looked at my son in that moment, something clicked.

I took off my arm, I threw it on the ground, and I just took care of my son. And we were together, me and my son, discovering our normal. This is how it was going to be for *us*. Nobody else.

As time went on, I really never wore my arm when I was taking care of him, because everything went a lot better without it. Like, I didn't have to rest his head on the metal or wood of my arm while I was feeding him.

I wore my arm so little that, when he was two years old, we were standing in my kitchen, and I put my arm on, and he turned and looked at me and said, "We going out?"

I know that there will still be more questions. He's only four now. And there will be times that he might be embarrassed. He might be ashamed. He might not know what to say.

I also know he'll look at other moms who can do things that I can't do. You know, like give a high ten. (You will always get a high five from me, kid, a high *five*.) Or play patty-cake. Or he'll see other moms hold their kid by their fingers and pick them up with both hands.

I can't do that.

But maybe one day my son will look at those other moms and go, "Wow. I've never seen one like that before."

MARY THERESA ARCHBOLD lives by the motto: "Yes leads to adventure!" – adventures such as taking a Moth Community Workshop. She's told stories with *This American Life*, *Risk!*, and on her podcast, *Funny Parents*. Other adventures include TV (*Law & Order: SVU, Bull*), film, and Off-Broadway. Her show, *Jazz Hand: Tales of a One-Armed Woman*, began at Fringe NYC (Outstanding Actor Award) and went on to run at the Kennedy Center. Her short film, "Jazz Hand," was a finalist in the NBC Shortcuts Festival (Best Actor Award). Her favorite adventure is as mom to two wonderful boys. www.maryarchbold.com.

Sudhesh Dahad

In the Shadow of Fear

A few weeks ago, I was sitting at my desk at work when I overheard a couple of colleagues behind me discussing some breaking news about an incident outside Westminster. I turned to ask them what happened, and they told me that there'd been a suspected terrorist incident there.

As soon as I heard this, my stomach sank, I found it difficult to breathe, and I felt tears welling up.

A sense of dread took over me, like there was something more about to happen. It didn't feel safe to be in the city. Even though I was over a mile away from Westminster, I still felt like I was in danger, so I packed up my bags, left the office, and hurried home.

Fear has become an everyday part of my life now, and it doesn't feel like it's something inside me, but more like something external that follows me in the shadows.

It's not that I'm afraid of death. I'm more afraid of the consequences of my death for the people who depend on me. As a single father, I worry especially what would happen to my daughter if something happened to me.

Back in 2005, one morning, I was on my way to work as usual, and my train arrived at the overground station in King's Cross a few minutes later than usual, so I hurried down toward the Underground.

When I arrived on the Piccadilly line platform, it was a little bit busier than usual, but, as I was late, I was reluctant to change routes, and so I just waited.

A couple of trains passed, and I couldn't board because they were already packed. When the third train came along, I was just bundled on, carried forward into the carriage in the surge of the crowd getting onto the train.

Once on the train, sardines in tin cans came to mind – it was so busy. The driver tried to close the door a few times, but there were still people clamoring onto the train, blocking the doors.

Eventually, the driver did manage to close the doors, and the train left the station.

After a few seconds, I sensed a flash, and then the lights went out.

I heard a loud bang, and a popping sound, and then another popping sound, and then the train jolted to a halt.

I found myself on the floor without really realizing how I got there. And, oddly, suddenly there was lots of space around me.

For a moment, I thought it was a nightmare and some-body would wake me from it. But as I realized that it was probably a terrorist attack, the blood drained away from my face.

The next thing I thought was that I was probably dead, and the scene around me was something like some artis-tic illustrations I'd seen of purgatory in Dante's *Inferno*.

Under the dim lights of mobile phones, I could see some people on the floor, some people standing, and some people in between. I could hear some screaming and crying, but it seemed to be in the distance – I didn't know where it was coming from. The smell was like the day after Guy Fawkes Night: quite unpleasant.

I felt my head and my limbs, and I realized I was actually still alive. In that moment, the only thought in my head was that I needed to get home to my daughter as quickly as possible.

After a few seconds, there was something smoke-like drifting through the carriage, and I felt horror. I thought it was probably a chemical attack, some kind of toxic gas or something, and I got down on the floor, hoping that whatever it was would be lighter than air and rise to the ceiling. Luckily, it was just some sort of soot.

After a few minutes, the driver managed to start passing a message down the carriage, saying that we could evacuate through his cabin and walk down to the next station.

As I got down from the train onto the narrow and uneven gap between the tracks, I still felt a sense of dread, because I thought, *This can't be the end of it. Something else is going to happen, or I'm going to fall over and electrocute myself on the rails*, because none of us knew whether the rails were live or whether they'd been switched off.

It took us about ten minutes to walk down the tunnel and reach Russell Square station. When we got there, the station staff helped us off the tracks and onto the platform, and then they showed us up the stairs.

The 171 steps up to the top seemed endless, but as I ascended I felt an increasing sense of relief as we got closer to daylight.

Up at ground level the station was empty, because everybody was being kept out for obvious reasons. I didn't know what to do, because I had cuts and bruises, and some blood on me. I didn't really know whether I was injured and needed medical attention or not, so I waited.

But then after a while, I saw other people who were much more seriously injured emerging from the staircase, some being helped up or carried on stretchers. So, I thought I should probably just move away and let them get attention first.

After a while, the station staff ushered us into the hotel next door and said we'd be more comfortable waiting there. But soon somebody ran in panicking and saying there'd been another explosion, and we should all get out.

It made no sense at all, because nobody knew where it was safe and where it wasn't safe at that time, so even though it seemed irrational, we all complied with the instructions and ran out, scattering in different directions.

I started running towards King's Cross and, after about fifty yards, I stopped and noticed a couple of other people who looked like they'd been on the same train. So we got to talking, and then we all headed towards King's Cross together.

One of my fellow survivors had a gash on his head, and another one had a gash in her arm. We were all covered in soot and looked disheveled. All our clothes were bloodstained. But amazingly, nobody seemed to notice us as we were walking through the busy streets – nobody even gave us a glance.

That was until we got just outside Camden Town Hall, and then a council worker asked us if we needed some first aid, and she said the city was on lockdown, so we wouldn't be able to go much farther anyway. All of Bloomsbury was inside a police cordon.

So we went inside, and the staff gave us some fresh clothes and tea and sandwiches, and we waited in the lounge. While we were watching TV, we heard of the other incidents, and the true horror of what had happened on that day started emerging.

After a few hours, we were able to get outside the police cordon, so I made my way to Euston, where my brother was waiting in a car. I got in, and we set off up the A1 towards our hometown.

Once we got beyond Mill Hill and into the green belt just outside London, the sounds of sirens and helicopters stopped, and it was beautifully peaceful.

That evening, on the first night, the nightmares began.

Every time I closed my eyes, the whole scene from the morning replayed in my head – the train pulling out of the station, then a loud bang, then the pop, and another pop from the shockwaves.

And then I'd find myself waking up with my head and chest bathed in a cold sweat.

Sometimes I'd see the scene even while I was awake.

I felt scared to close my eyes or go to sleep.

I went to my GP a few days later, not knowing how to deal with this, and asked for advice, but he said that it was too soon to get any help, because it takes about two months for the adrenaline levels to return to normal in your body after a physical shock like that.

I wasn't prepared to wait for two months, so after about a week I heard that an emergency response center had been set up near Victoria station, so I went to get some more information and see what help was available.

Some Red Cross ladies invited me to sit down and have a cup of tea, and tell my story. So I did, and as I got towards the end of the story they told me that, while I had thought I was at the opposite end of the train from where the explosion was, that the explosion was actually in my carriage. As soon as they said that, I felt a chill go down my spine.

I went home, and I tried to get back to normal as soon as I could. I tried to work from home for a while, but I couldn't really focus on anything or concentrate. I couldn't even laugh or smile for weeks.

So I spoke to my HR department, and they said, "Well, we recommend you take a couple of weeks off on special leave."

So I booked a holiday to the Lake District, and took my family up there for a week.

On the way up to Lake District in the car – it's about a five-hour car journey – I kept dreading that anything that *could* go wrong *would* go wrong. Like maybe somebody crashing into us, or something falling out of the sky, or even concrete blocks being dropped from bridges like vandals used to do in the decade before.

But we got there unharmed, and had lots of long walks and good food, and I came back with the nightmares receding a little bit.

For years after that, I avoided the Underground, and preferred to walk or cycle through London whenever I could. But sometimes the weather didn't permit, so I'd have to go down and take the Tube.

Whenever I did so, I'd feel my heart pounding as I approached the Tube, and my palms sweating. And then sometimes I'd let the trains go, and it would be two or three trains before I had the courage to board one.

For a long time, I thought these fears were just my own, and I'd never spoken to any of my family members about it. I didn't really want them to know or hear too much about my experience.

But a couple of years ago, I noticed that my daughter was having the same fears as I was – she was afraid every time I went away. Every time I went on a flight or the Eurostar, she was worried about what would happen to me.

I didn't want her to grow up with these thoughts. We had to take back control of our lives and stop hiding away from these fears, and start living life to the fullest.

I knew something had to change, but I didn't know how, because how do you allay your child's fears when you have the same fears yourself?

Then a year ago, my daughter was diagnosed with a long-term, stress-related illness, and I knew that I had to do something, as it was having an impact on her physical health.

So the only way was to begin moving past my own fears little by little, to take small steps towards doing the things I used to enjoy so that she would feel more emboldened to take those steps herself. The more she saw me being at peace, the more likely she would move past her own fears.

People often tell me how lucky I am to be here today, lucky to be given a second chance, and lucky to be relatively physically unharmed.

But not all injuries are visible to the eye.

The truth is, I don't think I'll ever escape from the fear, and it's always going to be there overshadowing us in the background. I know that I don't want it to dominate, and I know I don't want my daughter to be affected by that either, but also I accept that it is there.

So sometimes, especially when events like those in Westminster take place, I know it's okay to have these irrational thoughts, and just pack up my bags, and go home.

SUDHESH DAHAD is a risk specialist in the City of London. He is also a trained sound therapist, using his experience to help trauma victims. Sudhesh moved to the UK from India before the start of his earliest memories. Growing up in northwest England left him with a funny accent and a fondness for pies. His accent was further scarred after moving to Hertfordshire in his teenage years. A healthy dose of Radio 4 and a return to Manchester for higher education aided the healing. Sudhesh sometimes surprises his daughter's friends with his unexpected knowledge of hip-hop and RnB artists.

Jeni De La O

Can I Get a Witness?

It was my thirty-third birthday. I don't celebrate my birthday, because I'm one of Jehovah's Witnesses, but I know it's my birthday.

Hitting your thirties as a single woman can be tough, but hitting your thirties as a single woman who's a Jehovah's Witness is brutal.

A couple of weeks earlier, I'd heard a statistic that confirmed something every single Witness girl already knows:

The ratio of single women to single men in our organization is *nine to one*.

Yeah. So that's tough.

When you factor in the rule that we cannot date or marry outside our faith, it gets even tougher. So this was weighing on me as I was sitting with my gorgeous, funny, smart, single girlfriends.

I had dreams. I had things I wanted to do. I wanted to be a writer. I wanted to put myself out there. I wanted to find love.

But the idea of finding a mate had become such an unattainable goal, such a pipe dream, that by extension *all* my dreams seemed unattainable. I felt, at thirty-three years old, as though my entire life had already passed me by and I'd missed it.

I'd lost my joy, and joy is a fundamental requirement of being a Jehovah's Witness. Only joy can get you out of your bed on a freezing-cold Michigan Saturday morning to go knock on people's doors and try to talk about God. You have to have joy, and I'd lost mine.

I talked to the brothers in my congregation about it. They told me to read the Scriptures, to meditate on them, and I did. I prayed. I read the Bible. Wasn't really working.

During this time there was one Scripture that I meditated on specifically, and that was Philippians 4:8: "Whatever things are chaste, whatever things are lovable, whatsoever things are pure, think on these things."

And I did. I kept myself busy, so that I wouldn't think about what I felt was missing in my life.

But I thought about other things, too. Like what it would feel like to have a life partner and what it would feel like to wake up in the arms of a man who loved me.

So on my thirty-third birthday, surrounded by all my gorgeous, funny, smart, sexy, single girlfriends, I made a decision:

I decided I needed more than Scripture.

I needed more than prayer.

I needed Tinder.

Tinder, for the uninitiated, is neither chaste nor lovable nor pure. It's also a visually based dating app, and that presented a problem for me because I couldn't have my face out there.

Can you imagine going to someone's door, knocking, saying, "Hi, I want to talk to you about God's—"

"Aren't you that girl I saw on Tinder?"

"No, no, no, no, no."

It's a sure way to get caught.

Remember, Witnesses can only date other Witnesses, and that's not a suggestion, that's a rule. And if you break that rule, there are consequences.

So I'm a planner. I launched a plan.

I put on my best wrap dress, I took a really flattering picture, and then I cropped my head out and prayed for the best.

There were some creepy responses to a headless torso on Tinder – there were. But there were some, the gentlemen of Tinder, who were nice, and one of these nice gentlemen was a guy named Josh.

Josh and I hit it off immediately. We're both obsessed with Parliament-Funkadelic. He had great taste in music, he was funny, he was smart, he was witty, he was not a creep. Best of all he was a grad student – he was doing his capstone – so he was perpetually busy and four hours away. That was perfect for me, because we became texting buddies.

Most guys on Tinder, they want to text one day, maybe two, before you meet and get the show on the road. Josh was always busy and far away, so we texted, and the texting was delicious. All that flirting. I was sizzling, I was vivacious. Here was a man who saw me as a woman, not as a spiritual sister. It was awesome. I had a pep in my step, and it spilled into the other parts of my life. I found the joy in my ministry, I was friendlier at work, I wasn't the wet blanket at parties anymore.

People noticed, but I kept the reason to myself. I had to keep it a secret, because Josh wasn't a Witness.

So one day I get a message from Josh, and he writes, I'M IN YOUR NECK OF THE WOODS, WHAT ARE YOU DOING?

I happened to be home by myself that day, and I had this rush of boldness.

I texted back, I'M HOME ALONE. DO YOU WANT TO COME OVER AND MAKE OUT FOR 15 MINUTES?

To which he said, YEAH.

And I immediately started to question every life choice I'd ever made, because *I am not this girl, this is not me.*

This is the start of every Lifetime movie ever made. My roommate's going to come home and find my dead body splayed on the living-room floor, and what are my parents going to think?

I'm spiraling. But before I can cancel, Josh is at the door. I open the door.

Wow. Tall, dark, and handsome.

I let him in, we sit down on the couch, I set my timer. He makes small talk because he's a polite Midwestern boy. And then he leans in for the kiss.

That kiss was magic, it was electric. I felt it in my toes. I'm telling you this story years later, and I feel it in my toes *right now*. My whole body was buzzing.

And then the *timer* was buzzing, our time was up.

I thought, *Oh, no, I want more.*

But I stood up dutifully and said, "Okay, thank you."

He said, "Really? Okay."

And then he said, "Can I see you again?"

I told him I'd have to think about it, and I did. I had to think about it, because the texting, the flirting, that was good and fine, but we'd crossed a line. I knew where this could go, and I knew what the consequences could be.

But I also knew I wanted more. It felt good. So I started carving out time to be with Josh.

Jehovah's Witnesses, we have a big culture of accountability. If you miss your meetings, people will text you or call you and ask where you were.

If you have a roommate and you're out late, that roommate might call you and say, "Where are you, what are you doing?"

So I had to start lying. I started "going to the gym" a lot, I started "working late" a lot, to carve out time for me and Josh. We'd meet and we'd go to a movie or we'd cook a meal together.

I remember one time we ordered takeout and watched *Sherlock* at his apartment, and I was so deliriously happy. I wanted to call my parents and my friends and tell them how happy I was. But I couldn't do that because, not only was Josh not a Witness, he was a lapsed Catholic altar boy who questioned the existence of God. And if you Googled Josh (like I did), the first thing you would see is an article he wrote while he was attending MIT about leaving religion behind altogether.

Yeah, this is not a guy I could take home to my family.

I realized I was falling in love with Josh when my youngest brother got engaged and my first thought was, *I can't wait to dance with Josh at the wedding,* and my second thought was, *Have you lost your mind? You can't take Josh to this wedding!*

So I launched a four-part plan.

Phase one, introduce Josh into conversation: "There's this really nice Midwestern guy. He keeps asking me out. I'm dutifully rebuffing him because of my faith."

Phase two, and this one was tricky: convince my family to convince me to take Josh to the wedding as my date.

And I did it. Here's how: I called up a couple of escort services and priced how much it would cost to rent a date, then called my family and said, "Listen, guys, it's about three hundred fifty dollars an hour – can you pitch in?"

When my mother picked her heart up off the floor, she said, "Why don't you just ask that nice Midwestern boy to come with you?" Mission accomplished.

Phase three was simple: take Josh to the wedding, keep it platonic, have him charm the pants off everybody.

That's easy, he's a really lovable, affable guy.

My grandmother fell in love with Josh. She's not a Witness – she's a little old Cuban lady – but the Grandma Seal of Approval? Super important.

Phase four, I will admit, maybe I didn't plan it out as carefully as I should have, but here was the general idea:

We would get back, I would wait two weeks, and then I would announce that I had decided to start dating Josh. He wasn't the big bad wolf anymore – people knew him, they liked him. I knew I'd take my lumps and maybe lose some friends, but I didn't think it would be the end of the world.

You know what they say about best-laid plans.

By week one of phase four, a Witness friend had put two and two together.

She says to me, "Have you been secretly dating Josh?"

I was exposed. The lying, the dating, the intimacy, all of it.

I couldn't ask her to hold that secret. I knew what the next steps were.

So I called the elders in my congregation, and I told them everything. The decision was made to disfellowship me.

So for those of you who don't know what disfellowshipping is, it's a disciplinary action that Jehovah's Witnesses take when someone is an unrepentant wrongdoer, a fornicator such as myself.

What it means in practical terms is your family can no longer talk to you, your friends can no longer talk to you. You walk into a room full of people who've been your only social network your entire life, and they can't even say hello.

Some of them won't even look at me. It's not to be mean, it's because they're hurt.

So now, for the first time, everything is on the table. On the one hand, there's my family, my friends, my community, my God, my faith.

On the other hand, there's this man who loves me, and his parents, who have my picture on their mantel, and his friends who have welcomed me, and the wedding we talked about, and the life that we wanted to build together, and that feeling of joy that he gives me. It's time to strip everything down to zero and come clean to myself about who I am and figure out what I want.

I break up with Josh.

In the absence of that culture of accountability, where no one is checking on me and no one is calling to see where I am, I surprisingly find myself still going to my meetings. The doctrine feels insurmountable, but I keep going, and I realize that I believe, I *really, truly do believe,* what they're teaching here. And, to my shock, I want to be a part of this organization. I want to find my way back.

There is a path back. You go to all your meetings, you pray, you study, you stop doing what you're not supposed to do, and then you meet with your committee.

And it was interesting, because I didn't just *go* to my meetings. I went to my meetings, and I *marched all the way up to the very front row, and I sat there.* I made sure everyone could see me.

I wanted them to know, *I'm human, I fell short, but I'm still here. I'm not giving up.*

But I missed Josh. I missed him so much it hurt to breathe, and I'm not one of those girls, I never have been.

So, four months into this ordeal, I called him up and I said, "This is how I feel. How do you feel?"

And he said, "Whatever it is, we can figure it out together. This is not insurmountable."

I had to believe that the God who loves me wants me to have love, too.

So we decided, "Why not?"

Josh and I got engaged in June.

I'm still disfellowshipped. I'm still going to my meetings. We're figuring it out together.

It's messy, it's work, but it works for us because we love each other.

There have been times through this journey where things get dark, and I feel like giving up because it's hard.

And in those moments Josh has never once said to me, "Why don't you walk away from this faith?"

He's never asked me to give up my religion.

So I have to have faith that, if this man can make room in his life for my faith, with time my community will make room for him in my life.

So Saturday, two days from now, Josh and I are getting married. I'm still disfellowshipped, so it's going to be a small ceremony. My family will not be there, and I'm not going to lie, I'm sad about that. It's a small sadness, though; it's a tender spot that I know will heal with time.

I'm excited about the prospect of being reinstated with time. I'm excited to be part of the congregation again. I can't wait to go knocking on people's doors again.

But what I am most excited about is that Sunday morning I'll finally get to wake up in the arms of a man who loves me.

Born and raised in South Florida, **JENI DE LA O** moved to Michigan eight years ago. She is the founder and director of Relato:Detroit, the nation's first bilingual community storytelling series. When she's not telling stories or writing poetry, she's trying to convince her Cuban family that she's is not now, and has never been, a commie-pinko.

Aleeza Kazmi

Pastels and Crayons

I was six years old in the first grade, and I was sitting at a table with my three best friends. We were all really similar. All of our moms bought us clothes from the Children's Place, we all liked to play house during recess, and all our names started with the letter *A*. It was Ashaya, Alicia, and Aleeza.

We were working on a first-grade icebreaker project, which our teacher, Miss Pennington, had assigned to us. It was gonna be self-portraits that we could hang up on the wall and get to know each other's faces and names. I was really excited for this project. I knew it was really special because there were three drafts. And we were working on the final draft, which was going to be colored in.

I was super stoked for this. Over the summer my mom had bought me this coloring book that taught me all these great techniques for how to draw properly, and I finally mastered coloring inside the lines. I was so excited to show my friends my new skills. I was basically young Picasso.

I also knew this was a special project because we were using oil pastels. I loved oil pastels – they're really soft, so I would pinch off a little bit and melt it between my fingers. They were expensive for my public school in New York City, and so each table got one box. And each box had one of each color, so you had to be patient and wait for your color.

At this point I had colored in my shirt blue and the background green, and there was a little tree. I had drawn in all the features of my face, which the book had taught me to do first. I had drawn in my lips and my nose, and I was ready to color in my face.

All my friends had used the peach oil pastel to color in their faces, and since we were basically all the same girl, I would use peach, too. So finally, when it was available, I picked it up, and I started drawing so slowly, going around my lips and my eyes and coloring in all one direction. I was watching as the oil pastel melted into the paper and my face came alive, and I colored inside the lines.

When I looked down, it was like I was looking into a mirror. This girl I had just drawn was exactly how I saw myself. I felt my teacher, Miss Pennington, over my shoulder.

Miss Pennington loved it when people drew well, and so I was getting ready for her to praise me, to say, *Aleeza, that is the most beautiful self-portrait I have ever seen. I'm gonna hang it above my desk so everyone who comes in can see it.*

Instead Miss Pennington says, "Aleeza, that's not your color."

I'm confused by this, because I don't understand how colors can belong to people.

But before I can find a way to ask her, she's gone to the oil-pastel box and started looking for it. She doesn't find the color that she's looking for, and so she goes to the crayon bin.

Now, every school had this infamous crayon bin that had bits and pieces of gross crayons that had been rolling around in that bin forever, and I *never* went to the crayon bin. Nonetheless, Miss Pennington is rummaging through it, and she reaches in, and she pulls out this little nub of a brown crayon that's unwrapped and gross.

And she hands it to me.

I'm still really confused by all this, but I notice my friends are staring at me, and my heart is beating really fast, and I want this to be over. So I just grab the crayon, and I start coloring in my face, and I'm going in all different directions. But wax crayon and oil pastel don't mix together. They don't belong on the same paper. So it doesn't matter how hard I'm pushing, because I can't get the crayon to stick, and I'm coloring outside the lines.

When I look down at the paper, I am this grotesque monster that can't decide if she wants to be peach or brown.

And I want to beg Miss Pennington, *Please don't hang this up. I'll do it all over again. I'll use the colors that you want me to.*

But before I can find the right words, she's taken my self-portrait and put it into a pile with all my even-toned peach friends, and it gets hung up.

That night I go home and I ask my mom why I wasn't allowed to use peach. And she explained it as best you can to a six-year-old who's just gone through an identity crisis.

She says, "You know, I'm not peach, and your dad isn't peach. And since you're our daughter, you're not peach either."

But this confused me even more, because my parents are just like my peach friends' parents. They sound the same. They make the same small talk at school pickup. But they're apparently not the same. And everyone seems to understand this concept of color. I'm not getting it, and

I don't want my mom to think that I'm stupid. So I don't ask her anything further, and I try to not think about it.

But it wasn't that easy. A couple months later, we had a day called International Day. We had it once a year at my elementary school, where everyone would dress up in the traditional clothing of the country that they're from or that their parents are from and then march around the school. It was meant to celebrate diversity and heritage.

I hated International Day.

First off, my mom is from Afghanistan and my dad is from Pakistan, so each year I'd have to alternate who I marched with.

But no matter who I was marching with, they always seemed to understand the traditions better than I did, or they spoke Urdu or Farsi, which I did not. And so, even though we were the same color, I didn't belong with them completely, just like I apparently didn't belong with my peach friends.

I didn't know where I fit, and I was stuck in this color limbo.

But I finally graduated elementary school and moved on to sixth grade and thought I had left this whole concept of colors behind me.

So, on the first day of sixth grade, I was really excited. It was a brand-new start, and we were all trying to get to know each other by asking questions, like "Where'd you go to elementary school?" and "What's your favorite book?"

And this one kid comes up to me and says, "What race are you?"

I had never been blatantly asked this question before, and so I didn't have a prepared answer.

I thought back to Miss Pennington and that brown crayon, and I told him, "I'm brown."

He gets this confused look on his face, and he says, "What do you mean you're brown? Brown isn't a race."

And I couldn't believe it. I couldn't believe that I had finally said "I'm brown" and it still wasn't enough. And then this little six-year-old girl deep inside of me gets angry. And then I get *really* angry. And then I'm screaming at him.

I said, "You know what? If I say I'm brown, then that's it! I'm BROWN!"

And he never spoke to me again.

Which was fine, because I had finally found the words to stand up for myself, and I had finally come to terms with who I was.

I want to say that was the end of it, that because I was, you know, okay with who I was, that I never had to stand up for myself or defend my race again. But that just wasn't true. I was growing up in post-9/11 New York City, where being brown put me in this category of "other," and I have been questioned about who I was many times after that.

I had to reaffirm over and over that "I'm brown, I'm brown, I'm brown," because nothing anyone says to me will ever make me question that again. I've worked so hard to love the skin I'm in, and nothing anyone says can take that away from me.

Today if you ask me to draw a self-portrait, I'd draw a confident young woman who's proud of her Afghan and Pakistani heritage, who is a proud American. And I would find the most beautiful, soft brown oil pastel to color in my face. No one would have to tell me to pick it up. It would be my first choice.

ALEEZA KAZMI is a senior journalism major at Stony Brook University. She first got involved with The Moth during the Education Program in high school and has since told her story for The Moth on stage at Lincoln Center and on *The Moth Radio* Hour. She is not quite sure what she will be doing after graduation, but as long as she is telling stories in some way, she will be happy.

The Wattage of Our Inner Light

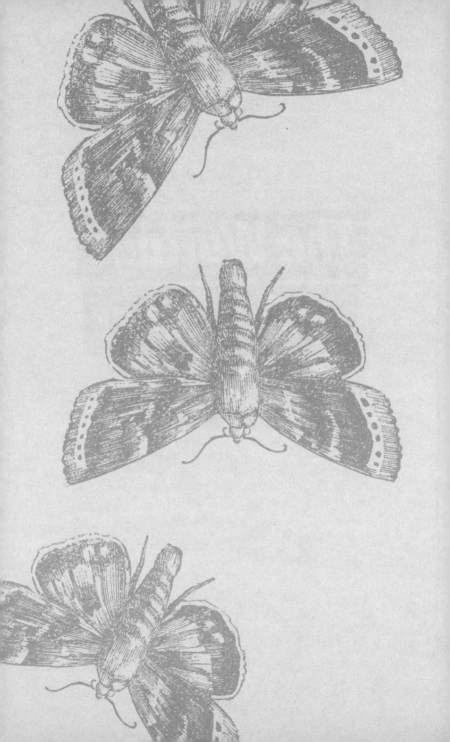

Sheila Calloway

True Justice

There I was, standing at the podium with my client. I was a public defender, and I was representing him on a burglary charge. They claimed he had broken into a store and taken some money out of the register.

Now, the video they had wasn't really clear. And they had his fingerprints, but he used to work at that store, so there was a good reason why his fingerprints were on the scene.

I thought I had a winnable case – I could probably come out good on this one.

But I was practicing in front of Judge Lacy Johns at the time. And Judge Lacy Johns had this long list of rules you had to follow in her courtroom. If you missed one single rule, that could be the difference between freedom and jail.

So I had sat with my client, Mr. Coleman, and we had gone over these rules. I mean, I *literally gave him a copy* of the rules. And I read them out to him:

1. You must use the title of anybody you're referring to – no first names.
2. You must wear professional clothes.
3. You must have a job each time you come to court.
4. You must always answer questions "Yes, ma'am" or "Yes, Your Honor."

These were the rules you had to follow.

So when I first saw Mr. Coleman come into court that day and he had on a polo shirt and khaki pants, I got a little nervous, but I thought, *We're going be all right. Not what I told him, but not too shabby.*

But then when the judge asked him where he was working and he said, "Well, I don't have a job," I felt the ground open up just a little.

Then she went on to ask him, "Well, why don't you have a job?"

And he said, "Well, *Sheila*" – referring to me by my first name – "told me I should get a job, but I thought I should just wait until the case was done."

That was it – the ground completely opened up, and sure enough he was carted off to jail. He was revoked on his bond because he didn't follow those arbitrary rules, and he ended up spending about six months in jail, pleading guilty to get out for two years on probation. I started feeling bad about our justice system.

Was this really justice?

But then one day my boss came to me and said, "We're going to switch you to Judge Thomas Shriver's courtroom."

I had heard about Judge Shriver. He seemed pretty fair. And when I went into his courtroom, it felt different. There wasn't a long list of rules you had to follow. There was no dress code.

People seemed fairly relaxed. It seemed like a place of peace in the midst of a broken justice system.

I started to think, *There might be some justice in* this *courtroom.*

I had a client, Mr. Blacksmith. He was an older gentleman. He had never been to court, and it was a minor charge. But when we got to court, I could tell he was real nervous. He smelled like a distillery. I mean, I thought he had *bathed* in a bathtub full of beer. He smelled so bad, *everyone* could smell him a mile away.

It was just *terrible*. I didn't know what to do.

I was hiding him.

I felt dread. I didn't know how to handle it.

I was giving him every mint I could find, I was spraying him with perfume I had in my briefcase, I was trying whatever I could do to keep him from going to jail.

Finally they called him into the courtroom.

And immediately the prosecutor stood up and said, "Your Honor, I want his bond revoked. He's been drinking."

Judge Shriver looked at us. And he must've sensed that fear, that dread.

He said to my client, "Mr. Blacksmith, have you been drinking?"

My client was very honest with him, he said, "Well, yeah, I had a beer."

And Judge Shriver said, "Well, when did you have this beer?"

And my client said, "Well, I drunk it last night."

"How much beer did you have?"

"Well, I only had *one* beer, but it was a *forty-ounce*."

The floor started opening up. We were done. I just knew it.

But then I heard Judge Shriver snickering.

He was *laughing*.

The judge was *laughing*?

He said, "Now, Mr. Blacksmith, next time you come, don't drink before you get here. You can go."

Judge Shriver wasn't being lenient on him. He was being fair. He recognized that this gentleman was nervous and he had made a mistake. And he recognized that he deserved a second chance.

Now, Mr. Blacksmith's case was eventually resolved, and he was given a second chance. He was able to get back on the right track and never returned.

And what it showed me was that Judge Shriver understood that you can make mistakes, but that doesn't mean that your life is over. You can have another chance. He showed compassion and empathy to all the clients who came in there.

Over the next three years, I learned so much from Judge Shriver. He became a mentor to me, a father figure.

He was someone who always treated everybody with respect and with fairness, while holding them accountable for their actions.

True justice.

One Saturday morning my supervisor called me and said, "Are you sitting down?"

I said, "Well, I can sit down. What's going on?"

She told me that, the night before, Judge Shriver had died in his office.

At first I was numb. I didn't know what she was saying. It didn't make sense to me. And then it hit me. I became overwhelmed with emotion, and I burst into tears.

It broke my heart. Losing this man who had become my mentor, my family, was devastating. Judge Shriver's death was like losing a piece of me. It was one of the hardest things I'd ever had to deal with.

His courtroom was closed for several weeks. When they opened it back up, they had to get an interim judge until they could find someone to take his place permanently. And, wouldn't you know it, that interim judge just happened to be the retired Judge Lacy Johns. I thought, *Oh, no, not again. We're going back to that system of arbitrary rules and unfairness.*

As I practiced in Judge Johns's court again, the struggle grew, and I got more and more frustrated with the system.

And then one day I had a young kid, about nineteen years old at the time. He had made a really serious mistake. He was at the ATM machine, he found a card. He took it with him and started using it.

He went and bought some gas, he bought some pizza, he got a DVD player.

And then all of a sudden, it clicked – *This is not right. I shouldn't be doing this.*

And so he actually backtracked. He went back to the stores where he'd been buying stuff and returned everything he could. It was everything except for, of course, the pizza and the gas. But he recognized the wrong that he did, and he was trying to make it right.

So I was asking the district attorney in the courtroom if he would consider giving him what we call expungeable probation. It's like if you do everything you're supposed to do – you know you're wrong and admit you're guilty, you comply with the conditions that are set and do what you're supposed to do – then, at the end, the felony charge gets erased from your record.

In this case it was so important for this felony charge to be erased from this kid's record, because if he had a felony, he couldn't get a good job, he couldn't go to college, he couldn't get good housing.

He admitted it. He knew that he'd made a mistake. All he wanted was a second chance.

If a DA doesn't agree to expungeable probation, every once in a while you get an opportunity to ask the judge if they would consider overruling the DA's decision. And, if Judge Shriver had been here in this case, there was absolutely no doubt he would have overruled it.

He would have said, *Oh, yeah, this is a kid who has made a mistake, and he's ready to make it right. He can have expungeable probation.*

But Judge Shriver was dead.

And I knew in my heart of hearts that this judge would never give this kid expungeable probation. The frustration grew in me, and the more I talked to the DA about it, the smugger he seemed to be.

The DA would say, "Well, he did the crime, he's gotta do the time."

He kept saying that to me *over* and *over* and *over*.

And it just built inside of me. The anger was so deep that all of a sudden I snapped.

I put down my files, and I pointed my finger in his face, and I said, "You don't know what justice is, you are blah, blah, blah, blah, blah, *bleep, bleep, bleep,* blah, blah, blah, blah, blah, BLEEP, BLEEP, BLEEP, BLEEP, BLEEP, BLEEP, *BLAH, BLAH.*"

Now, mind you, this was a courtroom full of people – there were attorneys, my supervisor, my poor client, all watching this.

But at that moment I didn't care who was watching. This was *not right,* this was *not fair.*

My supervisor came over quickly to try to calm me down.

She got in front of me so that I couldn't see what was going on behind me, and she said, "You've got to calm down, you've got to calm down. You can't act like this in court. You've gotta calm down."

But in my ultimate upsetness, having my out-of-body experience, I looked around her, and I saw the DAs talking about what I had just said. And I saw that they were being smug about it. It looked like they were making fun of what I had just done.

And so I said to my supervisor, "I'm sorry, I need to go handle some more business."

I proceeded to go around her and go up to the other DA and say, "Now, if you've got any questions about what I just told *him*, I'll tell *you* the same thing, which is bleep, bleep, bleep, bleep, *bleep, bleep, bleep, bleep,* BLEEP, BLEEP, BLEEP, BLEEP."

And boy, did I feel good.

But my client didn't get the expungeable probation.

And at that moment I knew that it was time for me to do something different. I could not practice law in a place that I didn't feel was fair or just, that was controlled by someone's random, arbitrary rules.

I struggled in that court for a little while longer, about two months. But then one of the public defenders who worked in the juvenile division was leaving, and they needed someone to take his place. I quickly volunteered.

The first day I went to juvenile court, it felt like Judge Shriver's home all over again. It felt like people were really working with our youth and trying to make a difference in their lives. These were people who knew that our youth were going to make mistakes and they would sometimes need second chances.

And so, almost twenty years later, I stand before you as the juvenile court judge. And every day, as that judge, I think about the lessons I learned from Judge Shriver.

People make mistakes.

People are unique.

But it's up to us to build them up and to give them a second chance.

Not long ago one of the attorneys who used to practice in front of Judge Shriver had a case in front of me.

After she finished, she came up to me and said, "Practicing in front of you made me feel like practicing in front of Judge Shriver all over again."

It was the biggest compliment I've ever had. And something that I always try to live up to.

SHEILA CALLOWAY, a Louisville native, moved to Nashville to attend Vanderbilt University. After receiving her JD at Vanderbilt, she began working at the Metropolitan Public Defender's Office in both the adult and juvenile systems. In 2004, she was appointed juvenile court magistrate and served in that position for nearly ten years, until she was elected juvenile court judge in 2014. Judge Calloway is an adjunct professor at Vanderbilt Law School, Belmont College of Law, and American Baptist College. She combines humor, passion, and judicial wisdom to change the way we look at justice.

Ana Del Castillo

Jump from a Plane

Twenty years ago I was living out my dream of being an actress and a singer in New York. At the time I was a swing on the national tour of *Les Misérables*. If you don't know what a swing is, it means I understudied all the women, which was awesome.

So I was living out my dream when I got a call from my brother, Danny, letting me know that our father and our brother, Alberto, were both dead. They had been brutally murdered in our hometown of Miami. My father owned an import-and-export electronic-goods business, and Alberto worked with him.

I didn't know this at the time, but business wasn't going well. One of them made some sort of shady deal, and that deal went south – so south that one day some men came to the office, took my father and my brother into the warehouse, and then tied my father's hands behind his back and taped his mouth shut. They made him watch as they tortured and murdered his favorite son. (Alberto was everybody's favorite. If you had met him, he would have been your favorite, too.) When they were done with that business, they shot and they stabbed my father to death.

There was a million dollars' worth of merchandise in the warehouse, and they took nothing, except of course the lives of my father and my brother and the possibility of my family ever living a normal life again.

I was in a fight with my dad when he died. I wasn't speaking to him. And the day that they died, this overwhelming sense came over me – there was a voice in the back of my head that kept telling me, *Call him. Call them both. Tell them that you love them. Tell them.*

And I was just like, *No.*

I had my reasons, and I thought they were good ones at the time. But when I got that call, I fell to my knees, and I screamed out loud that I hadn't told my father that I loved him.

After they died, my life got really small.

I had always been the life of the party, the kind of person who was the first one on the dance floor, the first one to laugh, the first one to be out there, just *first, first, first.* I used to sing all the time – singing was a prayer for me.

I got off the road, stopped singing, and could barely leave my house. I was almost agoraphobic.

I developed, unbeknownst to myself at the time, a panic disorder, which, if you've never had a panic disorder, means you panic because you think you *might* panic. It's very odd.

So I'm going to say something that sounds a little crazy, given what I just said: I'm really lucky. I have amazing friends, and they dealt with me during this time like, *Okay, this is a rough patch you're going through right now.* But they listened to me when I needed to talk, they got me out of the house, and they never lost sight of who I was, even when I had lost sight of myself.

One day one of these friends, Sandy, says to me, "Oh, you know what we should do? Whenever one of us hears the other one say, 'Oh, I've always wanted to do *x*' or 'I've always wanted to do *y*,' it then becomes the other person's responsibility to make sure we do that."

I thought, *Okay. I'm barely leaving the house. That might be a good idea.*

So fast-forward a few months later.

Out of the blue, she says, "Oh, I've always wanted to skydive."

So first I thought, *Fuck . . .*

But then I thought, okay, if it was just her and me going skydiving, I was not going to skydive. I'd chicken out. And I wanted to make sure that we did – integrity was a big deal to me. I do what I say I'm going to do.

So I went around for a while introducing myself, like, "Hi, my name's Ana. Would you like to skydive?" "Hi, I'm Ana. Would you like to go skydiving?"

I figured that if I got as many people as possible to go along, I would do it.

I ended up getting nine people to come along with us. The day comes, and we pile into two cars. One is a neon-green Geo Metro, and the other was this boat of a Monte Carlo.

We drive two and a half hours to the middle of New Jersey somewhere.

We get there, and the woman who's driving the Monte Carlo only has an American Express, and the place doesn't take American Express, so she says, "I'll be right back."

She never comes back.

This is way before Uber, so we are like, "What are we going to do? Oh, my God!"

We're conferring like crazy people, when all of a sudden, out of the corner of my eye, I see this beautiful man come toward us. He looks like he's eight feet tall and eight hundred pounds of pure muscle. He's this Paul Bunyan man, lumberjack-huge. He's Australian, and I think to myself, *You eat Vegemite and vagina for break-fast every day.*

He's our jumpmaster, and he gives us this ridiculous thirty-second demo of how to jump from a plane, which is just, "You put your foot here, and you jump out of the plane, and then we'll put a shrimp on the barbie. I'll see you up there!"

So we put on these one-size-fits-all onesie outfits and goggles, and then we go to an outdoor waiting room. We watch people fly up and then come down to the ground.

I start to freak out a little bit. But what has me *not* run after the woman with the Monte Carlo are two things:

First of all, everybody's flying up there and jumping, and nobody's dying.

And second, once people land, they have this look on their face like the wattage of their inner light has been turned up to maximum.

I knew I didn't have that. And I wanted it.

Finally my name gets called, and I walk over, only I can't feel my body. I'm just like a floating head walking over to the plane. We get in, and it is this ridiculously small plane – it's literally small enough that my back is up against the pilot's seat and my feet are touching the back of the plane. Claustrophobia.

We start to go up, and my adrenaline's pumping. You ever get that feeling where you can't hear anything because the blood is like *boom, boom, BOOM!* in your head?

And then I have this really weird response to the adrenaline.

Songs start bubbling up, and I began to sing maniacally. I belted out *Les Miz* songs.

I sang this one section in particular:

But the tigers come at night,
With their voices soft as thunder,
As they tear your hope apart,

As they turn their dream to shaaaaa . . . aaa . . .
 aaa . . . aaa. . . AME.

Yeah, it's all fun and games for you now, but I sang that *over* and *over* and *over again* while I was on the plane, like a crazy person. My Aussie jumpmaster just smiles at me as though this is something he sees all the time.

We finally get up to the right altitude, which is three miles above the earth. We get into jump position, which is like doggie-style crouching right before the plane door.

Because it's a tandem jump, he straps himself onto me (and that might have been fun at another time, but I'm about to jump from a plane).

He opens up the flap, and it's shocking, because freezing air rushes in. It's August; it's ninety degrees below, but it's like February up there.

I take a peek down at the earth, and I suddenly think, *I'm not jumping from this fucking plane.*

What the hell was I thinking, jumping? I'm not doing this.

And I am starting to panic. I'm hyperventilating and trying to catch my breath, and I'm thinking, *I can't, I CAN'T.*

He's in my ear saying, "Ready?"

And I'm like, "No! I'm NOT jumping! No! No!"

He's wrestling with me a little bit. He's got a hundred pounds on me – the man is huge, you know? He could have just grabbed me and thrown me out of the plane.

But instead he does this amazing thing. He wraps his arms around me, and he whispers in my ear like a lover.

He says, "I promise you I will get you down in one piece, and I swear that you are safe with me."

What he says just like opens me up, and I start to cry. I'm letting go. And I realize in that moment that the day my father and my brother both died, I died with them. And that I had a choice in this moment.

I could continue leading the pathetic life I had led since my father and my brother died, or I could jump from this plane with this beautiful Aussie man strapped to my back, and I could live.

So I chose to live.

We get into jump position, which is insane – it's one foot on the wing, a knee inside the plane, straddling the open air.

"You ready?"

"I'm ready."

"Okay. Let's do it."

So we jump.

And we're falling away from the plane.

The earth comes at you pretty quickly.

Then we go into full flying position, and it's so loud. Your skin is stretched back, like your lips are wrapped around your face.

We fall away into my grief and my despair and my hopelessness and my rage. My missing my father and the fact that I didn't call him.

And, finally there was nothing there.

Just me.

He taps me on the shoulder and tells me to pull the ripcord. And it was so loud before, but then all of a sudden the parachute opens, and it's just *silence*.

The kind of silence that's thick, that does not exist here on earth.

So we float down to earth.

He tells me to "Bring it in, baby," and we bring it in.

Friends all come over to me – we're all these little beams of light, you know? I can feel my own light up to maximum. And we pile into that stupid neon-green Geo Metro like Keystone Cops.

We don't even drive back to New York, we *float* back to New York, back to figuring out how I could live my life again, one day at a time.

I realized that part of it was I had all this love to give to my father and my brother that I didn't give. And when you don't give love, it rots inside you. So my life rotted for a little while. But when I jumped from that plane, it stopped.

I started figuring out how to tell people "I love you" (even when I was angry).

It's been twenty years now. And I'm still here because I've chosen to live every day.

ANA DEL CASTILLO is a certified desire and life coach and course and seminar leader. She is also a professional actress and singer and has been in shows such as *Nunsense, Les Misérables*, and her own one-person show, which she wrote and produced. She is writing her second show, of which this Moth story is a part. Ana thanks her mother, Reina, for her unique style and always providing her with material; her dearest friends, Christen Bavero and Carla Vilches, for their unfaltering love and support; and the incomparably talented Seth Barrish, who believed in her and this story.

Aaron Naparstek

Honku

It was December 2001, and I was living in a one-bedroom apartment on the third floor of an old brownstone on Clinton Street in Cobble Hill, Brooklyn. It was a nice place, very affordable. It had three big windows facing the street and got lots of great light.

There was just one problem with this spot, and it was the honking.

Endless, nonstop car horns directly beneath my three big windows.

At the time I was working as a web producer. I was what back then was called a community producer. That was the person who set up and ran chat rooms and message boards and did a lot of the stuff that today you would just call social media.

I was living and working by myself most of the time in this apartment, and I really got to know the honkers.

I could tell from just the sound of a honk, without even seeing it, what kind of vehicle it was.

So the bright major chord with a bit of a dual note – that was the Ford Crown Victoria, the yellow cab. Real blood-pressure spiker.

The deeper, more bone-jarring, discordant honk – that's the Lincoln Town Car. One of the worst sounds in the world. It got to the point where I felt like I could understand the honks, like I could translate this awful monosyllabic language into actual thoughts and feelings and meaning.

So the quick *honk-honk* over there by my living-room window? That's somebody saying, *Hey, buddy, light turned green.*

The deeper *hooonk* over there by my bedroom window? That's somebody who's eight cars back and can't really see anything and is telling the guy in front, *Yeah, you should run over the pedestrians because I've got places to go.*

I thought I'd heard pretty much all the honks that you could hear on Clinton Street – had cataloged them, knew them. Then one day I was sitting down to work on a mindfulness and meditation website that I happened to be producing at the time. And I heard this honk that I'd never heard before.

It was essentially just a *HOOOOOOOOOOOOOOOONK*.

You get the idea.

Whereas most honks have clear start and end points, this honk was essentially *infinite*. It didn't stop.

So eventually, as the honk passes the three-minute mark, I come up to the window to see what's going on. I look outside, and I can tell it's coming from this blue sedan directly beneath my window.

I notice that this honker is actually honking at a *red light*.

This just seems unacceptable.

I decide in that moment that I'm going to my refrigerator.

I'm getting a carton of eggs.

I'm returning to my window.

And if this honk is still going by the time I get back to the window, the driver is getting an egg on his windshield.

When I return to my window the honk is still going. So I start pelting. My first egg misses, but I was a pitcher in high school, I feel like I've got this. My second egg *explodes* across the roof of the blue sedan in this very satisfying thud.

It stops the honk.

And I probably could've left it there. That could've been it.

But I kept throwing. *I kept throwing the eggs.*

Now the honker is out of his car, and by the time the egg is actually splattering across his windshield, he is standing in the middle of Clinton Street staring up at my third-floor window going completely ballistic.

He's a middle-aged guy, balding, fortyish, indeterminate ethnicity, and his general message to me, which I will have to paraphrase, is, "I know where you live, I am coming back tonight, and I am going to kill you."

So . . . clearly a flaw in my plan that I had not thought about ahead of time.

The guy drives off, but I'm shaken. I'm agitated, and for the rest of the day I can't focus. For the next couple of days, I find myself milling about my apartment looking for household items that would make for good self-defense weapons.

I actually go to sleep with a large plumbing wrench next to my pillow.

I realize I need a different way of handling the honking.

So the next time it really starts to bother me, I decide to take some advice from the meditation and mindfulness website that I'm working on. I decide to sit down, take a deep breath, and just *observe* the honking on Clinton Street. And then I take those observations and I start boiling them down into pithy haiku. Haiku is a traditional form of Japanese poetry, three lines of five, seven, and five syllables. Its goal is to observe quietly and leave the reader with a kind moment of Zen.

I call my poems *Honku.*

And it feels good to do this. It feels good to write them.

My first Honku is simply this:

You from New Jersey,
Honking in front of my house
In your SUV.

Just a snapshot. The essence of Clinton Street.

This poem really pleases me, so I print up fifty copies, and I go out very late at night (because I'm sort of embarrassed about this), and I tape the Honku up and down Clinton Street on the lampposts.

This becomes my regular honking therapy regimen. Whenever the honking really starts to bother me, I sit myself down, I write some Honku. Toward the end of the week, I pick my favorite one from the latest batch, I print fifty copies, I go out very late at night, I tape 'em up.

It feels like I'm honking *back* now in my own quiet way, and I have some power over the honkers.

One night I'm out there taping up my Honku. I've been doing this for about a month, and I'm still kind of surreptitious and a little embarrassed about it. I turn around, and I see that a woman is standing near me. She's been out late walking her dog, and she sees me standing there, caught red-handed with my heavy-duty tape dispenser.

I brace myself, and she comes up to me and says, "Excuse me, but are you the Bard of Clinton Street?"

I'm like, "Yeah, okay, I guess so."

And she gets very excited.

She says, "Well, we just love your work. It's fantastic! We're so sick of the honking, and my daughters, they're now writing Honku, too. Would you sign one? Could I get your autograph? My husband would love that."

As I make my way down Clinton Street that night, I notice that a few other Honku written by strangers have popped up on the lampposts.

I'm like, *Okay, this is interesting.*

Over the next few days and weekends, many Honku blossom on the lampposts of Clinton Street, and I realize suddenly, *I'm not alone here. There are other people who feel the same way.*

The next time I go out posting Honku, I decide to put a website address on my poem: www.honku.org.

At www.honku.org I do my online-community producer thing, and I create a message board. I call it the Lamppost. And within days of my putting this thing online, there are dozens of neighborhood people hanging out on the online Lamppost. They're chatting with each other about problems in the neighborhood, trading Honku, talking about solutions.

I say, "Guys, let's get together in person. Why not? Saturday, eleven a.m. on my front stoop, come on out."

About a dozen people actually show up. And it turns out to be this diverse, funny, smart group of people who'd all been living next to each other – in some cases for years – but had never actually met. We're having a good time, and someone notices that on the lamppost on my own corner there is a sign very high up that says NO HONKING, $125 PENALTY.

I had seen this street sign before, and I'd never really thought much about it. But everybody gets excited about it, like, "Hey, the law is on our side. Let's make this city live up to its no-honking ideals!"

So that afternoon I go home and I type up some letterhead for something called the Honku Organization. I fire off letters to my local elected representatives and community organizations, and I decide to attend a community meeting.

I show up at the monthly community meeting of the Seventy-Sixth Precinct, the police station. It's probably the least dot-com place you can imagine. It's got the puke-green subway tile on the walls, the fluorescent lighting, the burly mustachioed cops. I'm easily the youngest person in the room by a good twenty years. The other attendees seem like regulars.

I'm really nervous, like, *What the hell am I doing here?*

But the first guy stands up, and he says, "Look, this new bar that moved next door to me, it's making too much noise. You've got to do something about it."

A woman stands up, and she's complaining about the speeding and the double parking on Court Street. The next guy's angry about his neighbor's dogs barking all the time.

And it slowly starts to dawn on me: *These are my people. I have found the place that is possibly where I most belong.*

I'm starting to get up the nerve to raise my hand and speak when, very late into the meeting, in walks this six-foot-five-inch-tall, smiling bearded guy, and the commanding officer of the precinct says, "Hey, everybody, welcome our brand-new City Council member – he's just been on the job for a few weeks now – Bill de Blasio. Come on in, Bill."

If you recognize the name, he is now the mayor of the City of New York.

Bill sits right next to me, and I notice at the very top of the stack of papers on his lap is a piece of letterhead from the Honku Organization.

I think, *Okay, I'm going to wait and see what de Blasio does.*

He takes the floor immediately, and it's almost like Bill is my downstairs neighbor on Clinton Street.

He goes into the most perfect description of the honking crisis. It's not just a minor quality-of-life issue. This is a serious public-health and safety issue. He firmly but politely asks the police to get out there and enforce that no-honking sign.

The police say, "How's a three-week no-honking blitz on Clinton Street sound to you?"

And I'm like, "That sounds incredible."

The next Monday morning, for the first time in as long as I can remember, I oversleep.

Clinton Street was quiet.

There were no horns!

When I do finally wake up, I jump over to my window to see what's going on. I see that guys from the Seventy-Sixth Precinct are standing there and talking to every single driver coming up Clinton Street.

You know, the Honku Organization, I'll just be honest with you, we did not accomplish our ultimate mission of ending horn-honking in New York City. That battle is still there to be fought for someone else.

But we did start making a bunch of changes and fixes on Clinton Street and the streets around it, and this actually became my work and my career – doing advocacy and community organizing and media to make cities better for pedestrians and cyclists and transit riders.

The real success of Honku, though – the thing that I think was most significant – was that now, when my neighbors and I are walking down Clinton Street, instead of being in our little bubbles of honk anger, we talk to each other.

Clinton Street wasn't just a street anymore – it was a neighborhood. And we were really producing community.

AARON NAPARSTEK is a journalist, activist, teacher, and the founder of www.streetsblog.org. Since its launch in 2006, Streetsblog has informed, inspired, and helped to build a Livable Streets movement that is bringing a more human-centered, less automobile-oriented urban design and transportation policy approach to cities across North America and around the world. Aaron was a 2012 Loeb Fellow at Harvard University's Graduate School of Design and is the author of *Honku: The Zen Antidote for Road Rage.*

Jason Trieu

Operation Babylift

It was an early spring day in 1975, and my two younger brothers and I were waiting in a cargo airplane to go to America. We were with about fifty other orphans, mostly babies and young children.

This was in Saigon, South Vietnam, and near the end of the war. I was fourteen at the time, old enough to understand the grim situation that South Vietnam was facing: South Vietnam was collapsing rapidly under the advancing North Vietnamese army. I could sense the panic in the air and the urgency in the people, and the airport was buzzing with military vehicles, airplanes, personnel.

But for my brothers and me, the only thing that was on our minds at that time was that we were going to America. It was a lifelong dream that was coming true for us. It was something I had waited for most of my life.

Nine years earlier, our dad died fighting in the war. A year later, our mom passed away in a traffic accident. So the neighbors brought the three of us to an orphanage.

It was after living in the orphanage for a while that I came to understand the situation my brothers and I were facing: that we were not normal, that we didn't have parents to provide for us, to support us as we were growing up. We didn't have parents to prepare us for life, to give us a future – we were on our own.

And as the oldest child, I took over the parental responsibilities, following the Vietnamese tradition. I had to be parents to my brothers, to take care of them. So as a seven-year-old *parent,* I worried a lot. I worried constantly.

I always worried about how I was going to take care of my brothers, how we were going to survive in a country where ordinary people were having a tough time, struggling with life because of the war.

So now I was sitting in this airplane, waiting with my brothers, just moments before taking off for America. We were ecstatic.

About a year before, we had met Cherie Clark, an American lady who was head of a charity organization called Friends of Children of Vietnam that was helping orphans. Now she was helping us leave Vietnam as part of their Babylift operation that was trying to bring orphans out of Vietnam before South Vietnam fell completely.

I was so lost in my own thoughts and excitement that I didn't see a South Vietnamese police officer approaching me until he was just right in front of me.

The officer looked me over, asked me a couple of questions, and said, "You cannot go. You're too old. The country may need you."

I can only imagine that he wanted me to stay back and fight when South Vietnam amassed all its resources in a last ditch to defend the capital against the North.

I was stunned. The thought of not being able to leave for America with my brothers never crossed my mind. The police officer proceeded to take me and another boy about the same age off the airplane. I felt like I was being dragged into a deep, dark tunnel. I was devastated.

I looked over to my brothers, and they were shocked and confused. I could see the fear in their eyes of now not having their parent. *What were they going to do?* I didn't know what to do. I wanted to tell them to take care of themselves and take care of each other in the new land, but I couldn't say anything. So I just left, silently.

The pilot was the president of World Airways at the time and was spearheading Operation Babylift – I learned later that he tried to bribe the police officer with a hundred-dollar bill to let me and the other boy go. But the police officer refused and ripped the hundred-dollar bill in half.

Shortly after the plane took off, I went back to the shelter.

That was a long night for me. I tried to come to terms with what had just happened – my lifelong dream that was so close had just slipped away, maybe forever. I was filled with hopelessness, disappointment, and despair.

At the same time, I felt a sense of relief knowing that my brothers were now in a good place, that I didn't have to worry for them anymore.

So I convinced myself that now, not having to worry about taking care of my brothers, just me, I could survive anything. I could find a way to handle anything that may come my way.

But a few days later, Cherie came by and showed me a newspaper. Since my brothers had left on one of the earlier flights of the Babylift operation, they'd made big news when they landed.

The newspaper had a photo of my two brothers playing in the snow and, as soon as I saw this photo, it hit me like a freight train: I had now lost all my family. We'd lost our parents, and after that my brothers were my only family. Now I had lost them, too.

All of a sudden, I was overwhelmed with emotion and the desire to be with my brothers again – and this notion of trying to find ways to survive alone, facing what may come to me in Vietnam, dissipated.

I begged Cherie, I asked her, "Anything you can do, help me. I want to get out."

I was facing the distinct possibility of North Vietnamese communists overrunning the South, which would mean that all communications and ties would be cut off.

This did not sit well with me. The idea of being left behind, of perhaps never seeing or hearing from my brothers again, was too much for me to bear.

Shortly thereafter Cherie came to me and said, "Get in the van to go to the airport, there may be a plane that you will be able to get on."

I jumped into the van with pretty much the clothes I had on at the time. But this trip was much different from the first trip. I was filled with fears and anxiety.

I knew that I was defying the government order. I felt like I was on an escape mission. At the airport they rushed me onto a military airplane. I took my seat next to an American who was also trying to get out. I tried to lie low, to be invisible, hoping for a quick departure.

I looked up, and I saw another police officer coming on board.

My heart stopped. I was frozen.

The officer made his way toward me and asked me a couple of questions, and then, again, he told me I could not go.

My world crashed down on me, and I knew my fate was sealed.

But instead of taking me off the airplane right away like the first officer did, he told me to wait for him there. He proceeded to talk to the pilot and then went inside the building. I waited there, expecting him to come back anytime with maybe more police officers or soldiers to haul me away.

Time passed very slowly.

Minutes seemed like days.

After what seemed to me like an eternity, I started hearing the engine roaring and the doors closing. I pinched myself. I thought maybe I was imagining it, maybe my mind was overworking, but no, sure enough the plane started moving.

I was thinking, *Is the pilot gunning for it? Is he going to defy the order? Is he going to leave without authorization?*

I could only hope.

And then the plane started moving a little faster. My heart was racing, pumping. I could feel my heart in my chest, expecting that at any time the government, seeing the plane moving, would send troops, guns, and vehicles to stop us in our tracks because we weren't supposed to leave.

But the plane kept moving.

I found myself holding my breath, watching the plane rolling down the runway, ever in slow motion. Finally the plane went off into the air, and I found myself breathing again, a sigh of relief. But even after the plane took off I was still full of fear that they would send military jets to intercept us and force us down.

It wasn't until after we landed in the Philippines hours later that I completely realized I had now escaped and was out. I flew to the US the next day, two weeks before South Vietnam fell completely to the North.

I will never know what prompted the pilot to take off, defying the order, but I'm forever grateful. I often think about how my life would have turned out had it not been for a series of kind acts from strangers like this pilot.

Cherie helped me reunite with my brothers. She also gave me the half of the ripped hundred-dollar bill that the first pilot had given to her and told me to keep it as a memento of the battle for my life.

When I first saw my brothers again, I looked at them before our big embrace, and they looked at me. It reminded me of the look we had when we were on that last plane and I was taken off – a look of complete disbelief.

But this time the emotion was reversed – it was pure joy, tremendous happiness.

It was a huge relief knowing that I was with my brothers again, with my family again, and knowing that from now on I no longer had to worry about how my brothers and I were going to survive.

JASON TRIEU was born in central Vietnam, and came to the US as a child in 1975. After graduating from high school in the US, Jason worked for a few years, then went on to earn his BS degrees in Speech Communication and Computer Science and has worked in IT/ Software engineering ever since. Jason currently lives in Washington with his wife, Jaclyn, and two daughters, Tionni and Lena, and works as a Software Engineer Principal for XPO Logistics. In his spare time, Jason enjoys art, traveling with his family, skiing, playing tennis and ping pong, and being in the outdoors.

Krista Tippett

Gaggy's Blessing

So there's a story about my childhood that my children loved to hear when they were little, and wanted to hear over and over again. We called it "The Gaggy and the Snake Story." Gaggy was my grandfather, the Reverend Calvin Titus Perkins. Everyone called him CT.

He was a roving evangelist. He was a preacher. But he never had a big church for any period of time. He pastored tiny little country churches, and he would kind of bring them back to life and then move on.

And this story was a memory I had of a day, I believe it was a Saturday, when I followed my grandfather to the little country church of the moment. He was mowing the lawn, and I was poking around in a shed out in the yard. I looked down beside me, and there was this enormous snake coiled up and just looking up at me.

So I race out of the shed. My grandfather hears me. He comes to rescue me. In my memory the snake follows me out of the shed and rears up – it's taller than my grandfather. He has a hoe, which he swings, and in one fell swoop he kills the snake.

He has vanquished evil. He's vanquished the serpent.

And that is a perfect story to capture my grandfather. Faith for him was a battleground. The world was a treacherous place. It was full of dangers. It was full of temptations to sin.

He was an expert on sin. And the result of that was a list of don'ts, of rules to avoid sinning. I didn't have to follow all his rules as my mother had as a child, but it was very clear to us that he'd prefer it if I would.

You weren't supposed to drink or smoke or play cards or dance or go to movies or even go swimming, because if you went swimming, you might have to wear a revealing bathing suit, and you might tempt someone to think about sex. The older I grew, the more I was sure that all these rules really came back to trying to avoid having us think about sex.

I went far, far away to college, and that whole religious world of my childhood just ceased to make sense. I grew very "smart" and learned things that I hadn't known before. I learned in history class why Southern Baptists were Southern Baptists. It wasn't anything I'd ever wondered about. It wasn't a question I'd ever asked. And the reason was that Southern Baptists were the ones who wanted to keep their slaves.

And yet, growing up, I had learned that Southern Baptists were the only ones going to heaven. Methodists didn't even have a fighting chance.

So I went home for Christmas that year. I didn't confront my grandfather – that's not how I would approach him.

I asked him, "Gaggy, why the 'Southern' in Southern Baptist?"

He hesitated. I don't think he knew the answer.

Then he finally said, "Well, Jesus was born in the south of Galilee."

I was furious. I was disgusted. Whether he was being deceptive, whether it was willful ignorance, or whether he wasn't brave enough to say "I don't know," I was done with his religion.

I became a very political person. In my twenties I ended up in divided Berlin. I ended up on this great geopolitical canvas where good and evil were being acted out again. It was very easy to believe that in a grand way in that Cold War world of the 1980s.

But in that place, too, those clear, crisp distinctions left me wanting. I knew people on the eastern side of the Berlin Wall who had nothing and who created lives of dignity and beauty and poetry and intimacy and meaning. And I knew people on the western side of that wall who had everything by definition and whose inner lives were impoverished. And none of that was dependent on politics.

So I found myself asking questions which I very reluctantly realized were spiritual and religious questions. Questions like why are we here? What makes for a worthy life? What are we to each other? I resolved that I couldn't possibly take religion in myself or in the world seriously if it couldn't be very different from that world of my childhood, of my grandfather. I had to be able to apply my mind. I had to know that it could be relevant and reconciled with all the complexity that I had experienced in the world.

I ended up taking myself to the British Isles. There I discovered the world of the great mystic writings, like Julian of Norwich's *Showings* and Brother Lawrence's *The Cloud of Unknowing*. I listened to the BBC. I discovered this quantum physicist, John Polkinghorne, who had also become a theologian later in life and who talked about how he could take what he was learning about the cosmos as a quantum physicist in chaos theory and find echoes and explanations of reality that could infuse his sense of the nature of God and what happened when he prayed and what happens when we die.

I gained this ever-growing sense that both reality and mystery are much larger than we can possibly imagine. And that mystery is absolutely rooted in physicality and in both the mess and the beauty of human life.

And I found this described most exquisitely in the Bible itself. It has no fairy-tale heroes, only flawed, flamboyant human beings as prone to confusion as to righteousness. Like us, millennia later, they have trouble reconciling the political and the private, the sexual and the societal. Moses quarrels with God. King David is at once a great leader and also an adulterer, a military hero who sends the husband of his mistress to the front lines to die. Jacob is a quintessential late bloomer, a conniver, and an egotist. The Bible calls him "clay-footed." He becomes Israel after many foibles and false starts and through wrestling through the night with an angel who just might be God.

I was also very drawn to the Celtic idea of thin places – "thin places," "thin times" – the idea that there are places we can experience where the veil between heaven and earth is worn thin, where the temporal and the transcendent seem to touch.

I had experienced a place like that. I remember standing on the west coast of Scotland, which is one of these places that is physically both bleak and gorgeous at the same time, and feeling like, *Here I can breathe, God.*

And so I followed that feeling. I went to divinity school. I studied theology. And the funny thing is, all that took me straight back to my grandfather. If I was thinking about my sense of who God is or what it means to be religious, it was all infused with him. But it wasn't infused with his rules. It was infused with Gaggy's physicality, with the fullness of him, which I now realized was full of contradictions.

He was strict, but he was also one of the funniest people I knew. He was playful. He once broke his ankle chasing me around the house. After he retired from preaching, he bought a farm and planted vegetables, and he had pecan trees, and he built birdhouses. In fact, he was one of the earthiest people I knew as well.

I had experienced enough of the world to be smarter than I was as a sophomore in college, and I realized that even his rules made some sense. They had intelligence behind them. Only a couple of generations ago, things like drinking and gambling, addictions, alcoholism – before AA, before the Twelve Steps, these were death sentences. They were things that devastated lives and families. And so, in another time, did getting pregnant under the wrong circumstances.

I also remembered and cherished the fact that my grandfather actually had a very interesting mind. He had a second-grade education, but you could throw a mathematical problem at him and he would be able to calculate this thing in his head in an instant. You could pull out a calculator and check it. It was very strange. He didn't know what to make of it. We didn't know what to make of it. It was kind of a party trick.

But I think that Gaggy held the strength of his mind in tension with his faith – and not a creative tension. He held it off to one side of the passions and beliefs that were so important to who he was in the world. I don't believe he ever felt that his mind – and its questions – were invited into his faith.

I came through all this and ended up creating a radio show where I take up the animating questions behind religion and spirituality, this question of what it means to be human, and look at how that runs through modern lives and all the disciplines we're engaged with, in the twenty-first century. And I came to feel early on that I was studying theology and leading this life of conversation, asking these questions *for* my grandfather, *with* my grandfather.

Fifteen years after I heard John Polkinghorne on the radio in England, I had him on my show. I was talking about quantum physics and theology, somehow with Gaggy in mind, asking questions he couldn't have asked.

But my show was also in and of this twenty-first-century world, not just talking to Baptists and the occasional Methodist, but to Buddhists and Jews and Muslims, Atheists. I really could not imagine that would ever be something that Gaggy would be comfortable with, that he would give his blessing to. And that was a real source of sadness to me.

When I wrote my first book, which was a kind of spiritual memoir, I ended up writing a lot about my grandfather. And I wrote this whimsical passage, which was edited out of a very early draft, where I fantasized that somehow, wherever my grandfather was, beyond space and time, he was cheering me on. I imagined my grandfather, who was a teetotaler all of his ninety years, raising a glass of champagne in my honor. As I say, I edited that out early on because it wasn't serious enough, and I thought it might erode my credibility.

But later in the process of writing, I took myself again back to those magical British Isles, this time to the west coast of Ireland. I was there with a bunch of writers, and a lot of these other writers were taking a pilgrimage to the local lady who "read stones." This is the last kind of thing that I would ever take seriously or consider doing. But when everyone else came back, they would tell these stories at breakfast every morning about how she had seen inside their souls. She had told them about things that she couldn't possibly have known. She talked about their past and their present, their future, people who were living and who were dead.

So I finally thought, *Okay, fine. I'll try it. I'll do it.*

I find myself then, about a day later, sitting with this absolutely beautiful view over the Bay of Mishkish, with this woman named Mary Maddison, who has the most beautiful, ageless, wizard-like face. My feet are bare, in a bowl full of stones from the Irish coast.

And she is in fact telling me things she can't possibly know. She knew nothing about me. She doesn't even ask your name or what you do. She told me about my work. She told me about myself. She described my children exquisitely. And then she started describing this gentleman she was seeing, and clearly it was my grandfather.

And here's what she said:

She said, "He's proud of you."

"He's not as serious as he looks."

She said, "I think he was pretty stern in his lifetime. He must've had a lot of rules. He realizes now that he was even too strict with himself, that he denied himself some things."

"He realizes now that we can become closed-minded when we could be investigating."

I don't know what happened in Mary Maddison's house that day. I don't know what she taps into. It's in that realm of mystery for me, which I honor. I do know that since that day I have felt that I have my grandfather's blessing.

And I forgot the best part. When she finished describing him to me, she said, "He's raising a glass to you. He's toasting you."

Maybe he's toasting all of us right now.

But I knew on that day that I had his blessing. And he has mine.

KRISTA TIPPETT created and leads the On Being Project, hosts the *On Being* radio show and podcast, and curates the Civil Conversations Project. She received the National Humanities Medal at the White House in 2014. Krista speaks widely and is also the author of three books: the *New York Times* bestselling *Becoming Wise: An Inquiry into the Mystery and Art of Living*, *Einstein's God*, and *Speaking of Faith* (in which Gaggy features prominently).

Ophira Eisenberg

Inside Joke

I never wanted to have kids, and when I was in my thirties all my friends were sweating about having a family.

They would say things to me like, "When you see a baby, don't you just want to gnaw on its pudgy little thighs, and inhale its forehead, and then grab it and run away?"

And I was like, "No! What are you talking about?!?"

I did not understand their weird Hansel and Gretel fantasies. I just didn't get it.

When I was in my thirties, I had goals. They were to feed and clothe myself while living in New York. I wanted to have a bedroom with a bed that I could walk around all three sides of. And then there was one big item that I thought, *If I owned that, I've made it!* And that item was: a wine fridge.

That was my dream.

And with wine in it that lasted more than one weekend.

So I'm the youngest of six kids and, growing up, my mother always said to me, "Never get married and never have kids. They'll ruin your life!"

It's not exactly what you want to hear from your mother, but what she meant was that she wanted me to be able to have a career, follow my dreams, not feel pressured to settle down. Do whatever I wanted. It was very much what she *wasn't* able to do, and I took it to heart.

Now, in my forties things started to gel. I had a bit of a career, I was married to a guy I loved, I traveled. It felt pretty good. So I ordered a wine fridge.

And then the next second, a sledgehammer went through the whole thing.

After a routine mammogram, I was diagnosed with breast cancer (early-stage breast cancer but, as you know, there's no such thing as lucky cancer).

I fell apart. Thus started a year of hell.

And I did not respond to it by having a Tig Notaro moment and spinning the whole thing into comedy gold. I was destroyed. I fell apart. I dragged myself to one surgery and then another surgery, appointments and tests, and then thirty days of radiation.

I completely lost any sense of myself. I didn't relate to who I was in the past. I didn't even know if I could think of who I would be in the future.

There's this little bit of wisdom people say all the time, that you should *live in the moment.* Let me tell you something: there is nothing worse than being forced to live in the moment. Thinking about the future, just musing on what could happen next, that is for the happy and the carefree.

So at the end of that year, I went back to the doctor, and of course they don't really use the word "remission" anymore, but she said, "You responded well to all the treatments, and things look really good. So we'll see you in a year and test you again."

I tried to ease myself back into my old life, or figure out what my new life was. But before I could really even get it together, I got pregnant – by accident. It was unbelievable, mostly because I honestly didn't think my body was capable of ever doing anything beautiful again.

I didn't think that I was ever going to be able to do anything normal. It was like looking out onto a cracked, barren, soil field and seeing a tiny green shoot. I have to admit, I didn't think so much about gnawing on pudgy thighs. I was just elated that maybe this meant I was supposed to survive.

Could I get excited? Should I be concerned?

Before I could even pick one, I miscarried.

I hate saying that word. I know you hate hearing it. It's so common, though. It makes me think we should talk about it more.

But I got a call from my ob-gyn, saying that the miscarriage was something called a "partial molar pregnancy." It's a genetic mistake. It's not based on age or prior health history – bad luck, as she said. What was growing in me wasn't so much a fetus but an irregular group of cells. And what is an irregular group of cells considered? Cancer.

My own pregnancy had given me another cancer scare.

To make sure that it didn't develop into cancer, I needed to get tested by giving blood every week for six months. I couldn't believe it. I felt like I was never going to be able to move forward. I was depressed.

That is an understatement.

I wasn't suicidal. That wasn't enough.

I didn't want to destroy myself. I wanted to destroy *everything*.

I wanted to rip up the sky, and light everything on fire, and watch it all burn to the ground.

Now, at the end of that, six months later, I'm back in my ob-gyn's office. My husband, Jonathan, is with me, and she delivers the great news. "Guess what? It's great. You're cleared. You're good to go."

And then she says, "So you guys can try again."

And we are just sitting in silence, shocked silence, so much so that she goes, "Well, don't you want to try to have kids again?"

So interesting. First of all, we never tried to begin with. Second of all, we were just trying to get to a place where I felt normal and in control of my body again.

And, man, I have been asked if I want to have kids thousands of times in my life, and I usually just responded with a bit of a joke, to be honest.

I would say, "Sure I do, but who's going to raise them?"

Or, "Yes, of course, but I live in New York. Where am I going to put 'em?"

But this time I looked her right in her eyes, and I said, "It's too late. I'm too old."

She reminded me that she had many patients of an advanced maternal age, and she suggested that I go get an egg-count test, a blood test.

She ended the appointment saying, "Why don't we just see what happens?"

Now, if anything seemed routine and normal to me, it was giving blood. So I went into Quest Diagnostics, one of the most casual medication facilities on the planet. I mean, it's hard to believe that that exists.

You walk in, and there's a woman faxing forms, and you say, "Hey, I'm here to give some blood," and she puts down the toner and snaps on gloves. She fishes out a syringe from a pencil case, and there are no diplomas on the walls – there are just lock-up instructions.

But she took my blood, and then a few days later I got an email from my ob-gyn with a weird number and a one-line note, and it just said, *"An encouraging number for someone your age."* And I cried, because it was the nicest thing anyone in the medical community had said to me for years. I looked at the calendar, and I thought, *Maybe I'll see if Jonathan wants to try.*

I told him about the results of the test over breakfast. I said, "Oh, the omelet you made me reminded me that . . ." and I was like, "Encouraging number . . . My age . . . Encouraging eggs."

Jonathan nodded, and he looked very pensive, and he said, "While I can imagine us having a life with kids, I can also imagine us *not* having a life with kids, and we'd be okay. We'd be okay together, you know. We'd travel, and we'd do nice things. We'd have a nice life, just the two of us."

I knew he was being honest, but I also felt he was trying to protect me. He didn't want me going through anything more. He didn't want me to be put in another medical situation or have something – another physical thing – happen to me.

And I got it. I was equally terrified. I wanted nothing more than to feel like nothing could ever get to me again.

But later that day, weirdly, I found myself writing him an email, my own husband.

I wrote, *"I think we should try, because we can't guarantee that we're going to have a kid. We can just try and see what happens. But if we don't try just because we're scared, then the fear has won, and I can't live in that world."*

And he responded, *"Great. Let's do it."*

So I will admit, though, that after month one, when I got my period, I wasn't all like, "We can't guarantee it. We'll just try and see what happens."

I swore at my period. I swore at my body.

I was like, "What's going on, encouraging eggs?"

I was so mad, and I felt this primal urge in me. I was like, *I have to have a baby, and it has to happen now.*

And then the second month when I didn't get my period, I was just silently terrified.

Now, through all of this, people kept telling me, "You need to think positively."

And I would just go, "What are you talking about? How can I look at myself in the mirror and lie to myself?"

Because I know what it's like when things don't work out the way you want them to.

But now I understand what that's about, because it really doesn't matter if you think positive or negative. It has zero influence on the outcome, but it certainly changes how you experience the moment.

I'm lucky. I have a one-year-old baby boy at home right now. His name is Lucas. His crib is taking over the room that was supposed to be my dream office. He's learning how to walk, and he's always tripping over the wine fridge. And he's sweet. He smiles all the time for no reason.

And I'm still full of fear. Oh, my God, so many question marks loom in the future, but I try to challenge myself.

I try asking myself, *Okay, if everything fell apart, if everything went to hell the worst way possible, would I think to myself, I am so glad I did not let myself experience joy or enthusiasm in the good moments because it really protected me from the future?*

No. Life doesn't work like that. Nothing protects you.

So I practice enjoying.

And now my goal is sort of like my mom's joke about kids ruining my life. My goal is that me, Jonathan, and Lucas, we all get to ruin our lives together.

OPHIRA EISENBERG is a comedian, a writer, and the host of NPR's *Ask Me Another*. She has appeared on HBO's *Girls*, Comedy Central, *Live from the Comedy Cellar*, *Gotham Live*, *The Late Late Show*, and more. She recently appeared at the New Yorker Festival and the *New York Times* called her a skilled comedian and storyteller with "bleakly stylish" humor. Her debut memoir, *Screw Everyone: Sleeping My Way to Monogamy*, was optioned for a feature film with Zucker Productions. Her comedy special, also called *Inside Joke*, is available on iTunes and Amazon.

Ali Al Abdullatif

The Patriots' Game

It's February 2015, and I'm in Boston on the T, heading home after Sunday brunch. The T is what we in Boston call the subway.

So I'm on the T, doing what I assume everybody else does, which is daydream and contemplate my own existence, when a screw pops off the panel right in front of me and falls down on the seat. Being the Good Samaritan that I am, I pick it up and put it back in place with my fingers.

I go back to contemplating my own existence when my contemplation is broken a second time, this time by a man yelling from behind me.

Now, it takes me a while to realize he's yelling at me, but then I get up and I look at him.

He puts his finger in my face and says, "I saw what you just did there."

I'm not sure what he's talking about, and I don't know how to respond.

And then he goes, "I saw you plant a bomb on the T."

My heart sinks. I don't know what to say, because I've never heard what he's just said, directed at me. Before I can formulate a response, the T comes to a halt, two stops away from my apartment.

A lot of people hear the word "bomb" and the yelling and decide to leave, but I'm frozen in place. The man runs

THE MOTH | ALI AL ABDULLATIF

to the front of the train and quickly comes back with the conductor.

He points me out and says, "I saw that man plant a bomb on the T."

A couple of guys stood up, and they said that I didn't do anything. The conductor considered the situation. It was literally impossible for me to plant a bomb the way he said I did. I would have had to put it right on the seat, which clearly I hadn't.

So the conductor decides everyone can sit down. I can come to the front of the train, sit right behind him, and, when we get to my stop, I can leave.

I was a little bit relieved, and I thought, *This was dealt with properly.*

So I went to the front of the train with the conductor, but the man who accused me didn't feel the same way. He was still upset, so he dialed 911.

Now, apparently dialing 911 activates some sort of transport-authority protocol. I'm not allowed to sit anymore. I have to stand next to the conductor as he puts one arm on me and steers the train with the other hand.

We go another stop, one stop away from my apartment. And that's when the train is taken out of service. Everyone is asked to leave the train; the train is sent back to the station. Another train comes, and everyone's allowed back on – with the exception of me, the man who accused me, and a female officer who was waiting at the stop.

This was one of the outdoor stops Boston has, and we were standing outside in February, during one of the coldest winters Boston had seen in over a decade. We were told to wait for the police.

My mind began to race. I'm here on a visa. I don't know what this means. I don't know if I'll get searched, if I'll get hauled to the station, if they'll check my apartment, if my visa could be terminated and I could be sent back home. I don't know what comes next.

I panic, and I unzip my jacket, and I throw it on the ground. I run up to the female officer, and I ask her to frisk me. I tell her to check my pockets – I have nothing on me. She tells me to calm down, put my jacket back on, and keep waiting.

So I do. We wait outside in the cold for thirty minutes.

I look at the man, and he starts to hesitate.

I think maybe we have a connection now, and he says, "I'm sorry."

For the first time, I get a human moment from him.

Then he brushes it off, and says, "No, but I saw what I saw, and you did it."

Now I am angry, and I want to yell. I want to tell him that he is ignorant and wrong. But I don't. I calm myself down. I tell him I understand why he did what he did, but he just got the wrong guy.

He doesn't like that answer. He gets close to me, and immediately the officer separates us. She puts him on the next train, tells him that they'll call him later to come in and make a statement, and then she and I continue waiting for the police.

We wait for another half an hour outside in the cold. Then she gets a phone call. The police say that they've shown up to the wrong Harvard Avenue station and it would be hours before they got to this one.

So she decides if I leave my address and number with her, I can go home. Later that night they'd call me and I'd go into the station to give my full statement. I tell her that's okay. I give her my information. She asks me if I want to get back on the T, but we're one stop away from my apartment and I'm not quite ready yet, so I tell her I'll walk. And I do.

My mind begins to race on my walk home. I'm from Saudi Arabia. It's a conservative country, but I was a liberal-minded kid, so I didn't always feel like I belonged. Everyone wanted to talk about traditional family values, and I wanted to know who would win in a fight, Batman or Superman.

So when it came time to pick colleges, I knew immediately that I wanted to come to the States, and I picked Boston. I was looking for my people, and it took me a second, but then I found them in the comic-book lovers, the Dungeons and Dragons players, and the video gamers.

It turns out that my people are what you guys call nerds.

The nerds and I got along great, and it was awesome until close to the end of our senior year. We were all about to graduate, and everyone would go back home after that. I'd have to go back home, too, unless I was able to find a job, and it didn't look like anyone was hiring.

I had been anxious and afraid, and now I was dealing with a much bigger issue, race. I mean, I'm not a stranger to racial slurs, racial comments – being detained at the airport. I've been "randomly selected" more times than random would allow.

But this was different. This was an *accusation*. It was immediate, and I didn't know what it meant.

I get to my apartment that night, and I am angry and frustrated and afraid. If I don't belong back home, and I don't belong here, then what comes next?

I pick up my phone, and I call my friend Jackie. She was one of the few people who was thinking about staying in Boston, so I clung to her like a life raft. She immediately reaffirmed my situation. She told me how messed up everything was.

I got a little calmer.

She then reminded me that that day, February 1, 2015, was the day of the Super Bowl. Our New England Patriots were set to play the Seattle Seahawks, and I was invited to a party at her place.

I told her that I didn't care about football and I didn't want to go to a party. But it was really me being afraid of the phone call I knew was going to come.

Jackie doesn't take no for an answer, so I cave like I always do, and I tell her I'll go.

Before I walk out, I take my phone and I put my ringer on the loudest setting so I can hear the call when it comes.

I headed outside. I could have taken the T fifteen minutes to her place, but I didn't know if I was allowed, so I walked forty minutes in the cold until I got there.

As soon as I walked into the hallway, I could hear the loud sports-party sounds and excitement. I calmed myself, and I opened the door.

Immediately everyone went silent. I saw a couple of friends, but it was mostly friends of friends and loose acquaintances. Apparently Jackie had told everyone what just happened to me.

I got hugs from my friends, and a couple of people told me they were sorry that this had to happen and that they were there for me. I appreciated it, but a party is a party, and pretty quickly everyone went back to the game.

Every once in a while, though, someone would sit next to me and tell me how messed up it was that that happened. I knew they were being genuine, but I couldn't connect just yet. I was so intensely focused on this phone call that I wasn't there. I would constantly pull out my phone and check if it had rung.

And then it did.

I look across the room at Jackie, and she signals for me to take the phone call outside because it was quieter, so I did. I pick up the phone, and the man on the other end of the line introduces himself as Jim. Just Jim.

And Jim had dialed the wrong number.

I kindly let Jim know, and I hung up. I picked myself up from my breakdown again, and I allowed myself to go back into the room.

This time, though, everyone was up and putting jackets on. I was confused.

I asked them what was going on, and they told me, "Oh, we're coming with you."

Apparently in their minds I was going to walk into the police station with an army of nerds in Patriots jerseys who would one by one proclaim my innocence.

I told them that it wasn't necessary, but I appreciated it, and I was really thankful.

We ended up winning the game that night, and everyone stormed outside into the same cold from earlier, but this time celebrating and partying and yelling. It was amazing.

I didn't end up getting that phone call, though. Not that night, not the next – or ever.

Every once in a while, I wonder if the phone call could still come. When I'm at airports, I get a little bit nervous that they'll bring it up. I don't know if it's on record somewhere or if it will ever lead to anything.

But out there in the cold, I realized something. It took one man to alienate me and make me feel like I completely didn't belong.

But then seventeen amazing nerds let me know that I *did*.

And I knew right there that these were my people, Boston was my city, and I wasn't leaving the US anytime soon.

ALI AL ABDULLATIF was born and raised in Saudi Arabia. He received his B.A. in Psychology and Neuroscience in 2015 at Boston University. Most recently, he was a researcher at the Laboratory of Neurodegenerative Disorders at Boston University working on ALS, Alzheimer's and Parkinson's disease. He is currently living in Baltimore working on a master's degree in Biomedical Engineering. Ali also writes comedic short films and hosts a podcast titled *We Have the Facts* on iTunes. He hosts a taco night every Tuesday, too.

We'll Come
with Lions

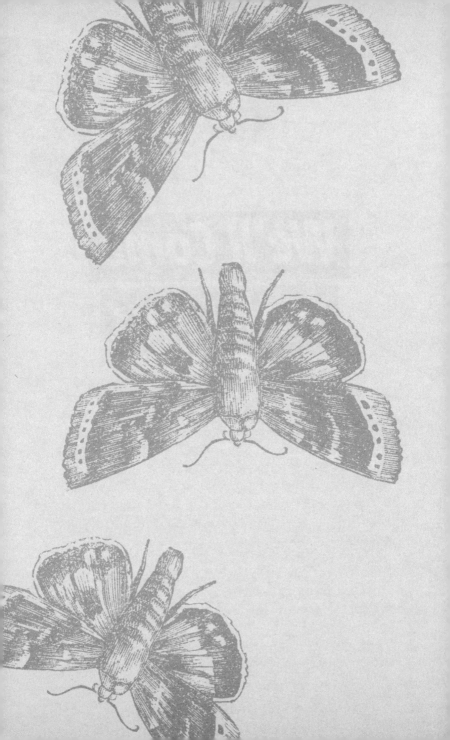

Neil Gaiman

Liverpool Street

I was just sixteen. It was Easter 1977 and it was seven o'clock in the morning. My train had pulled in to Liverpool Street station in the East End of London.

I got off on my own looking for my parents who were going to pick me up and take me home.

They weren't there. And I wasn't really surprised by this because I had the kind of parents who were always late.

I don't know how you went to school, but I went to school by getting up and going, "Oh my God, is that the time?" and leaping in the car.

My father would say, "We'll go the quick way."

The school was about eleven miles away, and we would go "the quick way," which involved driving down tiny country lanes where only one car could go, around hairpin turns, at seventy miles an hour, which would get me to school only three or four minutes late.

So it's seven o'clock in the morning, and my parents are late. And I am at Liverpool Street Station, which is a fairly long way away from Sussex where I lived in the south. But I'm not worried and I go and I wait.

Every now and then I look up and see if my parents are there.

(They're not.)

We were early for school once. It was a couple of years before, and we drove to the house of Robert Leeson, who lived in the same town. Some weeks I'd take him to school and some weeks he'd take me to school, and so we drove to his house, and he was always waiting impatiently out at the end of the drive.

But he wasn't there, so we got out and we rang the doorbell and after a while somebody leaned out from an upstairs window and told us that it was four o'clock in the morning and please would we go away. It was April 1st, and it turned out that as an April Fool's joke my sister had put all the clocks in the house four hours early.

That was the only time that we were ever actually early.

So I waited on the platform with my suitcase and I read my book.

I had been in Hamburg, in Germany. I had to go as part of a German exchange and I should have come back with lots and lots of friends a week earlier. But I'd been in a Greek play, *Antigone*, which the headmaster had decided had to be performed once in Greek and once in English. I was a messenger in the English version, and so I'd stayed a week after everybody else and I'd had a really interesting time.

I had a passport, which was kind of exciting. It had a photograph of me looking really nervous in my school tie, but it was my passport.

And I had my first girlfriend – I'd met a girl in Hamburg. She was English; a girls' school had also gone out there. And I'd been informed by my friend Baggie Wilson that he'd already called dibs on her (his real name was Simon, but his nickname was Baggie, and then very rapidly after that it became Simon-Don't-Call-Me-Baggie Wilson, which is actually a worse nickname to have than Baggie). But he hadn't mentioned this to her and she called dibs on me.

I felt so incredibly grown up.

And now I was sitting at Liverpool Street station and time was ticking away. By then it was lunchtime and I was getting hungry and my parents still weren't there. And I didn't have any money because, glorying in my newfound adulthood, I had bought cigarettes – an entire carton of cigarettes – on the ferry home from Hamburg using up the last of my money.

So I sat on a bench and smoked cigarettes. I hadn't quite got the hang of it, but I did.

I thought about phoning home and did.

No answer.

Phoned my dad's office.

No answer.

Started nervously making collect calls to every phone number I could remember.

No answer.

I was starting to get worried.

I decided it was probably my own fault because of the problem with the five-pence pieces. We'd all of us kids gone to some little town on the border with East Germany, where they hadn't seen any English people since 1945. We'd discovered that our English five-pence pieces were the same size as a German Mark (but worth four times less) and had used our five-pence coins to buy cigarettes and chocolate from the German vending machines. Two days later we found ourselves in the English Consulate in Hamburg, where they pointed out that, seeing that they hadn't seen any English people except the liberating English army and us in the last thirty years, the fact that all of their cigarette machines and chocolate machines were now filled with English five-pence pieces meant that they were pretty damn sure it was us. This also meant that I had no English change to use in the chocolate machines at the station.

Now I'm really starting to get nervous, because this is Liverpool Street station. It's over forty years ago, it was a fairly rough, nasty station back then, and fairly rough, possibly nasty people kept looking at me.

Only a week ago I had been an adult with my own passport and girlfriend and cigarettes and now I was Paddington Bear.

So I'd watch as people would circle me and eye me and move away. A little old man came and sat down next to me, pulled out a packet of Capstan full-strength cigarettes (possibly the scariest cigarettes ever created in the history of the human race), and offered me one.

"You want a cigarette, boy?"

"No, thank you."

He said, "You want come back to my flat with me?"

I said, "No."

He said, "I've got apples!"

It's now four o'clock in the afternoon; my parents are the latest they've ever been.

It's still not entirely beyond the bounds of possibility that they're just late. I once had measles, and they took me back to school the day that I recovered and dropped me off and I got out, and the school was locked. Eventually I found a nice groundsman who told me this was half-term. But that time they phoned my parents, who took me away.

I am desperately phoning every number I know and finally one gets answered and it's my cousin Leigh down in Sussex and I say, "Leigh! I'm at Liverpool Street station!"

She says, "Why are you there?"

I said, "Well I just came back from Germany! I have no money, I don't know what to do! Where are my mom and dad?"

She said, "Oh, they've gone on holiday."

I said, "What?"

She said, "Well, it was Easter; they took your sister on a skiing holiday in Austria. It was a sort of spur-of-the-moment thing."

I said, "What about me?"

She said, "What *about* you? Why don't you come home?"

I said, "I have no money."

She said, "Why not?"

I said, "I bought cigarettes."

She said, "It's your own bloody fault."

I said, "I have to get home."

She said, "Stay there."

I said, "I'm not going anywhere."

Everywhere I went I had to haul my suitcase with me. I sat down at the station. I had smoked as many cigarettes by now on that one day as I had smoked previously in my entire life.

At five o'clock, there was an announcement over the terminal: "Will Neil Gaiman please come to the station-master's office?"

I went up to the stationmaster's office, and my Aunt Rhoda, Leigh's mother, was on the phone. She had come home from work; Leigh had explained my predicament.

She said, "It's your own stupid fault."

I said, "What do I do?"

She said, "Hang on. Put the stationmaster back on."

I gave him the phone back. They talked for a while.

She said, "Alright, I've paid your ticket from Victoria station, in the south of London, down to Sussex."

I said, "Okay."

She said, "There's only one problem."

I said, "What's that?"

And then I realize what that was.

I said, "I have to get to Victoria, don't I?"

Victoria station is in the south of central London. I'm on the east of London, at least half an hour away by tube.

She said, "Yes."

These days you can buy tickets that will take you from your trains all through the London Underground , but not then. Then the Tube system didn't talk to the railway services.

I said, "What do I do?"

She said, "Show them your passport."

I said, "What?"

She said, "Well, what can they say?"

I said, "I don't know."

But I had to find out. I got my suitcase, and I marched down to the Underground and I showed the ticket collector my passport. They weren't used to schoolboys showing them passports instead of tickets.

They didn't know what to do – they let me on the Tube.

Eventually, I got to Victoria, without a ticket. I showed the ticket collector my passport. They wrote down my name and address, and let me leave the Underground. I got on the train in Victoria and, an hour later, I got off and there was my aunt, waiting rather nervously for me.

And I'd been an adult, and then I'd been a kid, and now I wasn't sure what I was. But adult or child, I'd made it home, with only my passport.

NEIL GAIMAN is a *New York Times* bestselling author of books for children and adults. His award-winning titles include *Norse Mythology*, *American Gods*, *The Graveyard Book*, *Good Omens*, *The View from the Cheap Seats*, and the *Sandman* graphic novels. Several of his titles have been adapted for TV and film, including the critically acclaimed, Emmy-nominated television adaptation of *American Gods* and the forthcoming miniseries adapted from *Good Omens*, the novel he co-wrote with the late Sir Terry Pratchett. Originally from England, he now lives in the United States.

Mike DeStefano

The Junkie and the Monk

When I was a kid, I had a spark in me. I was a happy kid. I always had a little bit of a flame going, and nothing could really knock it out. I went to Catholic school, but even the nuns couldn't extinguish the flame that dwelled inside me. (They tried.)

At the time of this story, I was twenty-eight years old, and I was living in West Palm Beach, Florida. I was in the Winn-Dixie supermarket shopping when this weird feeling came over me, and then I fainted, I blacked out. That had happened to me before, but it was on purpose, with drugs. This time it was a little scary.

I was in and out of consciousness. I knew something was wrong. I was put into an ambulance, and I ended up in the Palm Beach Gardens Medical Center. I had a tube in my nose, and I was in this incredible pain and couldn't really move much.

It turned out I had pneumonia. I had double-lobal pneumonia in all five of the lobes.

So I was lying there, and for a minute I was really concerned about myself. This was weird. I hadn't worried about *myself* for a few years, because at home my wife was dying of AIDS, and she was really sick, obviously. At the time they didn't have diagnoses for women when they had AIDS – they just called it "wasting syndrome."

All I could think about is, *I've gotta get out of this hospital. I've gotta get home and take care of her.* Because all I did was take care of my wife; that was my life, my job. And it wasn't a problem, I loved it.

People would say, "How do you deal with it?"

How do you ask a question like that? Like, have *you* ever loved somebody? It was weird to me that they'd ask that.

So I was lying there, and the phone rang. It was my friend Jimmy, and he said, "Mike, Frannie was in a car accident."

I said, "No. She can't even fuckin' walk. She's on so much morphine, there's no way."

He goes, "Yeah, she got in the car."

And I believed it, because I knew her. We were reformed drug addicts, recovering people. With drugs it's like if you cut my leg off, I would be upset, but if you gave me heroin right afterwards, I'd be like, I can handle it, I'll be all right, you know? So even though she was suffering with AIDS and going through all this horrible stuff, the morphine helped her feel better, like she would be okay, and she probably just thought, *Hey, I can drive.*

She tried to, and he told me the car flipped over several times. I knew she was dead, so I laid back, and I was just like, *Wow.*

And I had these Buddhist rosary beads on the side table. I was sort of between religions at the time, if anybody knows what I'm talking about. I needed something, you know? Because, quite honestly, my life – the drugs and the tragedy and people dying that I loved, and most of all, my wife being so sick after being off drugs for so long and us really trying to get our lives together – it just seemed really unfair.

And all I knew about God was the one that I was told about as a kid, you know, *God's watching. He knows.* So I figured that the god who's doing this to me and my wife, I'm not gonna fuckin' pray to *him,* you know?

What am I gonna say? *Can you help me?*

No. I'm gonna say, *What the fuck are you doing? Get off the fence. Make a move. Kill us or help us. Do something.*

That wasn't really working for me, so I went to this Buddhist place, because I saw an ad in the paper.

I thought, *I'm gonna go see.*

When I got there, it was just a monk sitting there. They just sit there, these people, and there's no nails or blood or anything.

I was like, *I can do that. I probably can do that sitting stuff there.* So I walk into this place, and they told me to take my shoes off.

I was like, "I'm from the Bronx. I'm not taking my shoes off!"

Then I saw everyone else had their shoes off, so I took my shoes off, because that was all they really asked. They were just nice people, you know? They were very sweet and kind, and they had a lot of compassion. (Here we friggin' call that "codependency" and charge you money to get rid of it.)

Then this woman, a really sweet, kind, darling, she said, "Would you like to see the lama?"

I'm thinking it's an animal they've got somewhere, like a sheep type of thing or whatever, so I said, "What's a llama?"

She said, "No, it's a Tibetan priest."

I said, "All right," though when she said the word "priest," I immediately thought of, you know, a scary Catholic priest . . .

I went to the room, and I don't know about anyone else, but as a kid if I was in church kneeling and my knees didn't hurt, I was in trouble. Your knees had to hurt in order to be really praying right. There was none of this "comfort" shit, you know what I mean?

So I walk in there to meet this guy. He's a little man, and he's just sitting there, bent over, and he's mumbling a chant, and I'm like, *What's he doing?*

She says, "He just prays and meditates. He's been doing that since he escaped Tibet with his family. He does this for twenty-some-odd hours a day, and then he eats and goes to sleep for an hour."

Who the fuck's paying for this? I wanna know. *Is this guy getting federal assistance? Are my tax dollars paying for this guy?* This is what went through my head.

The woman says, "Well, come sit near him."

So I actually got on my knees, like a good Catholic, and she goes, "No, relax, relax," and he looks at me.

He couldn't speak any English, but he said, "Oh, West Palm Beach. Thank you. Thank you."

I said, "What is he saying?"

"Well, he's just letting you know that you're in West Palm Beach, and he's saying thank you for being here. It's a simple thing."

I'm like, *I'm not going to hell or nothing if I don't sit right?*

And then he puts his hands out.

She said, "Oh, put your hands out!"

She was excited that he put his hands out to me.

I put my hands out, and he took my hands. And when he touched me, I felt so relaxed. I was just there in the moment. I wasn't scared. All the pain went away.

And then he put his forehead out, and she said, "Put your forehead out."

So I did, and he put his forehead against mine, and he said some Tibetan stuff, I don't know what. All I know is I just felt really good and happy. It gave me a great feeling. I went there every day for a few weeks, meditating and praying.

But now I'm in the hospital, waiting for my friend to call me back with more news about my wife's accident. But I've got these Tibetan beads, and I'm thinking of this man, and I'm okay. He blessed these beads for me, by the way, so every time I touched those beads, I thought of him. Whenever I saw orange or yellow, I thought of him, too, because that's the colors of the robe he had on. To this day when I see orange, I think, *Wow, I love that color,* because of him, you know?

And then the phone rings again. But it's not my friend, it's my mother, and she says, "Daddy has a brain tumor."

Yeah, this was a bad day.

And I sat back, and I had the beads, and I was so overwhelmed that I wasn't feeling anything per se. This news just froze me. There was no feeling.

I took the beads, and I threw them.

I was like, *Fuck this.*

You know what? I've been a Christian, Catholic, angry person for twenty-seven years and eleven and a half months, and now I'm a Buddhist for like three weeks? Fuck Buddhism. I don't want that little bit of peace, man. It just makes the rest of life seem so much shittier. So screw this. I don't want nothing to do with this.

The phone rings again, so now I'm like, *Okay, they are going to tell me my wife's dead.*

And it *was* Jimmy, but he said, "Mike, I'm outside. I'm coming up. Frannie's okay. Relax."

I said, "Oh, my God. That's amazing."

I got up out of the bed, because she had actually been

taken to the same hospital I was in, so I had to go visit her down in the emergency room. And I had this robe on and my morphine pole and another machine that's giving me oxygen, and I took my robe off and turned it on backwards so that my balls were hanging out.

I think it was just me saying, *Fuck you, everyone.* You know what I mean? *Will you give me a break here? My dad has a brain tumor, and I'm going to visit my dying wife down in the ER. She didn't die from flipping over the car, but she's gonna die soon anyway. I'm gonna go visit her now, and I've got pneumonia. Who knows what the hell's going on here?*

I go down, and she's sleeping sitting up in the hospital bed. She's got a little cut on her lip from the accident – a tiny cut. Car flipped five times on I-95.

I woke her up, and I said, "Honey, honey."

She goes, "Hey . . . what are you doing?"

She was wasted on morphine.

She said, "I wanted to surprise you."

I said, "Well, you did!"

A couple of weeks went by, and she ended up in hospice. She was in hospice two or three times.

Young people don't like to die, you know? Not that old people do, but some old people can say, *I had a good life.* She didn't feel that way. She was *pissed.* She didn't wanna die.

She was thrown out of hospice for not dying.

They put her in, but she didn't die, and they said, "Look, you can't stay here. You've been here for four months. Hospice is supposed to be for a week, two weeks. You've gotta go home." But then she got worse, and she came back again.

This happened three times.

But finally, this time, she died. They told me she was gone. I was at home. I *never* stayed home, I stayed with her every night. But her mother was in town, so I took a night and stayed home, and she died that night.

When they called me, the emptiness was there again. There was no feeling about it, you know? I froze. I held in all that death that I had because I knew my father was now going to die, too, and I loved my father. We were so close.

So I was like, *You've gotta save this angst up, man. You've gotta hold on. You can't fall apart.*

Nine months after my wife died, I was out at a movie. I came home, and there was a voice mail from my brother, "Mike, pick up the phone. Mike, pick up the phone."

Every time I heard him say "Pick up the phone," I felt a little more fear of what he was going to say.

Finally he said, "Mike, I'm sorry to tell you this on the phone, but Daddy's gone."

I'll never forget where I was. I was standing in front of my laundry machines, listening. And I felt my heart get ripped outta me. Like I actually reached for my heart. It was the weirdest feeling.

And that was it. The flame that I had as a kid – all of it – was gone, because now everyone had died.

I made arrangements to fly home the next day, and when I got on the plane, I decided that I was going to end my life. I was done. I wasn't telling anyone. It wasn't a threat, it was a decision that I'd had enough of this. There was nothing else to live for.

I got on the plane. I was so excited because, *I'm really gonna fuckin' die. This is so great.* I was at peace. I couldn't wait until the funeral was over, because that was when I was going to do it.

I wasn't going to jump off a building or jump in front of a car.

People haven't heard of overdosing on drugs?

So I'm on the plane, and I've made this decision to end my life, and I'm at peace and I am happy.

But all my life God or the universe, or whoever the fuck's running this thing, would always go, *Yeah, it's really awful now. You're almost out of hope. But here's a little something nice to keep you going.*

I got up.

I went to the back of the plane to go to the bathroom.

And the lama, the monk that I had met, is sitting in the back row.

He sees me, and he says, "West Palm Beach!!"

And I said, "You little motherfucker."

He put his hands out like he did before, and he put his head out.

What he was doing is called *tonglen*. You have to have amazing karma, they say, to have a lama actually want to do *tonglen* with you, which is giving and taking. When they put their head to yours, what they are doing is saying, *Give me all your pain, and I'm gonna give you all my joy.*

The reason he sat for thirty years in meditation was to open his heart so much that it gets as big as the ocean, so that if you pour some of your pain into it, it absorbs it. That's what his whole life was about.

And it worked for me, that particular *tonglen*.

I got home and I quit my job. I said, *I want to be a standup comedian.*

So that's what I did.

MIKE DESTEFANO was a comic who overcame torment to become a regular at top clubs in New York. He was on Sirius Satellite Radio and numerous television networks, including Comedy Central, Showtime, and NBC. He was featured at HBO's U.S. Comedy Arts Festival in Aspen and the Just for Laughs Comedy Festival in Montreal. His one-man show, *A Cherry Tree in the Bronx*, garnered critical acclaim. Mike died of a heart attack at age forty-four. A documentary is in progress – about how he rose from addiction and showed those who are suffering that they can recover and do great things. www.mikedestefanodoc.com.

Abeny Mathayo Kucha

Are We There Yet?

When I first arrived in Portland, Maine, I walked off the plane with my twelve-year-old brother, my eight-year-old daughter, and my two little boys, age four and two. The woman from social services who met us took us directly to this room with a conveyor belt.

I had never seen anything like it before.

We stood there in silence, watching the bags, and she asked me, "Do you see your bags?"

I told her I didn't have bags, only the plastic bag I was carrying.

That's all we had.

She said, "Right. Okay. Well, then – let's go home."

And that word "home" – I hadn't had a home since my village. I was born in a small village called Bor in South Sudan. We knew Africa had its troubles, but we had food, and we had each other, until one day, the spring after I graduated from high school. I was in the market getting meat for my family. Baskets were raised, and people were shouting. The meat wouldn't go far, and we all wanted some.

Over the noise and chaos, the unmistakable sound of gunfire filled the air. Some people dropped to the ground, and some people ran.

I chose to run.

My stepmother and I grabbed what we could and ran into the jungle and on to another village.

It would be eleven years before I stopped running from that war. I never knew peace in Africa again.

Later I met my husband. All my children were born in refugee camps.

Then things changed from bad to worse. My husband was killed in the war, and I lost my second daughter. She died of starvation and disease as we were wandering from place to place.

So when this woman said, "Let's go home," there was nothing else I wanted.

She brought us to an apartment. We had never been in an apartment before. We had lived with thousands of other refugees, wandering from under the tree to under the tree, so this apartment was different.

She showed us around the apartment. She showed us the bathroom and the shower. I remember she opened the refrigerator, and it was full of food, but there was nothing familiar to us. We saw a big bottle of orange soda, and we thought it was juice, so we tasted it. (It tasted very bad. So we left it.)

Before she left, she said, "This is a fire alarm. When you hear it, just go. Go outside and wait there until it's all clear."

Then she left. And all five of us were standing in this strange place, very scary.

I told the kids, "Let's sit down. We are home now."

I kept remembering the word "home."

There were two couches in the living room. My children had never seen a couch before, or a carpet.

So I went to the kitchen to warm up some milk. But before we drank our warm milk, we heard a noise.

I told the kids, "Let's run! That's the fire alarm the woman was talking about."

Back at the refugee camps, we had a plan, because one time the village was attacked and I had to run with the children, and it was very difficult for me to collect all of them. So we made a plan that when something happened, my brother would grab the baby, I would grab my four-year-old, and my daughter would hold my skirt, and we'd run.

So here we were in Portland, Maine, in this apartment, hearing this noise, so we went into our plan, and my brother grabbed the baby, I grabbed my four-year-old, my daughter held my dress, and we ran out of the apartment and across the street.

We stood there.

And I asked them, "Do you see the fire? Do you smell the smoke?"

They said no.

We stood there for a while, and then we said, "We should probably go back inside the building."

So we walked inside, slowly. But we didn't know which one was our apartment! We looked, but all the doors looked alike. We tried a few of them, but they were locked.

Finally I saw one door a little bit open, so we thought, *This might be our apartment.*

I went in first, slowly. And it *was* our apartment.

There was a woman standing by the door. She told us she accidentally rang our doorbell. So we learned it wasn't a fire alarm at all – it was a doorbell!

The woman from social services would come to visit us from time to time. And when she came, she would always find me sleeping.

One day she asked me, "Why do you sleep so much?"

I told her, "For the last eight years, I walked from Sudan to Ethiopia.

"And I walked again from Ethiopia to Sudan.

"And again from Sudan to Kenya.

"And from Kenya to the border of Somalia.

"I walked from under the tree to under the tree, from hunger to hunger.

"From gunfire to gunfire.

"From death to death.

"I walked the *entire eastern continent* of Africa with these children.

"I am sleeping because I haven't slept for *eight years.*"

Portland was different from my village. My village was a small village, maybe around five thousand people. It lies on the eastern bank of the White Nile. My father had four wives, as is custom in my village. I lived among many brothers and sisters. I went to school and learned English, my third language. I was happy.

But in Maine we felt so alone. A woman helped me find some friends, people from my tribe who had made it to Minnesota. So with the help of social services, we were able to move to Minnesota.

In Minnesota my children had their first opportunity to go to school. I managed to get them enrolled. I bought them school clothes and the supplies they needed.

The woman who helped me told me that the kids would need to wake up early in the morning and go to the school-bus stop. She told me that we would need an alarm clock. So I went to Kmart and I asked the ladies there if they had an alarm clock that sounded like a rooster. They helped me find one!

We set the alarm clock in the morning. The kids woke up. I walked my now twelve-year-old brother and my eight-year-old daughter to the bus stop, which was just behind our apartment.

I watched them climb onto the bus with tears in my eyes. The bus took off. The other parents left. I was still standing there with tears in my eyes, wondering if they would come back.

Hoping they would come back to me.

I went back to the apartment to my little boys. They were still sleeping. My tears were still falling. I thought about everything my children had gone through. Everything they had seen.

When my baby Jok was born, the village was attacked. Nine hours after his birth, I was forced to leave with him. And now we had made it, with God's help we had made it.

My children would never walk two hundred miles again. They would never starve again. And they would always be happy, even when I'm not around.

I thought about all of this the day my daughter graduated from law school – I was so proud of all my children.

Today I think about that first day in the Portland, Maine, airport when the woman said, "Let's go home."

And home means hope to me.

Home means I would never have to run again.

ABENY MATHAYO KUCHA is a single mother who survived the civil war and genocide in her homeland of South Sudan and immigrated to the United States. She became a certified nursing assistant and worked at the Mayo Clinic for almost ten years as a surgical processing tech. She has two daughters, three sons, and one grandson. Atong, her oldest daughter, graduated from law school in 2012. Abeny is especially proud, because few refugees' children graduate high school, let alone attend college. Abeny lives in Lincoln, Nebraska, and is the author of *Tears of a Mother: A Sudanese Survivor's Story*. www.Tearsofamother.com.

Jim Obergefell

Love Wins

I fell in love with my husband, John, the third time we met. I knew right from that moment that he was the person I wanted to spend my life with.

I told him, "I want to be a couple. I want to date."

He tried to talk me out of it.

He said, "I'm not good at relationships. I've dated a lot of men" – and he had – "and it didn't go well."

But I wouldn't be talked out of it, and so we became a couple, and we built a life together. Over the years we talked many times about marriage, but we decided, instead of having a symbolic ceremony, we would only marry if it actually carried legal weight.

One day John was walking around our condo, and I noticed that his walk sounded different. His left foot seemed to be slapping the floor harder than his right foot. When you've been with someone for eighteen years, you pick up on those small things.

I asked him, "Did you sprain your ankle? Did you pull a muscle?"

He said, "No."

But that slapping sound didn't go away. So I convinced him to see our doctor, and that started a series of doctor visits and tests that lasted several months.

One day I was sitting at the kitchen island when he came home from a neurologist appointment. When he walked in the door, I jumped up, hugged and kissed him, and asked how it went.

The tears started to fall, and his voice faltered as he said our worst fears were confirmed: ALS, Lou Gehrig's disease.

ALS is a death sentence. There's no cure and no effective treatment, and most patients die within two to five years of diagnosis.

Now, John had always been the dreamer, the flighty one. He always saw possibilities and not necessarily reality. That was my job as the practical one – I kept us grounded. Friends liked to describe me as the anchor to John's kite.

With his diagnosis, we changed roles. *He* became the practical one. He was the one who talked about what we needed to change, what we needed to do, what we needed to plan for, specifically worrying about me after he was gone.

When I needed it most, John became *my* anchor.

ALS progressed quickly. Barely two years after I asked about that slapping sound, the love of my life was bedridden, incapable of doing anything for himself, and in at-home hospice care.

I was his caregiver full-time. Every routine we had built over twenty years together was supplanted with a new routine of caring for John, making sure he was safe and comfortable. After all, that's what you do when you love someone – you take care of them, during the good and the bad.

A few months later, I was standing next to his bed, holding his hand as we watched the news. We were expecting a decision from the Supreme Court on the Windsor case. The news came out, and the Supreme Court struck down part of the Defense of Marriage Act.

In a spontaneous, joyful moment, I leaned over, hugged and kissed John, and said, "Let's get married," and luckily he said yes.

For us this was so important, because we only wanted to marry when our government would say we exist, would acknowledge our relationship, and that's what the Windsor decision did. It didn't bring marriage to any new states, but what it said was that the federal government had to recognize lawful, same-sex marriages for tax returns, federal benefits, social security, things like that.

Now I had to figure out how do I get this bedridden, dying man to another state, just so we could do something that millions of people take for granted?

So I started to do my research, and we settled on Maryland as the place to get married, mainly because Maryland was the only place that did not require both people to appear in person to apply for a marriage license. My whole goal was to make this as pain-free on John as it could be, so that helped.

Okay, so now we know where we're going. How do we get there?

We live in Ohio, and I wasn't willing to put him in an ambulance for that long of a trip. It would have been just too physically painful on him.

He couldn't fly commercially.

That left one option for us, a chartered medical jet. And let me tell you, if you've never priced one of those, they're not cheap.

I went to Facebook, and I thought, *Maybe one of our friends will know somebody – a pilot, someone who works for a chartered medical-jet company, something – just to make this a little easier.*

And the most amazing thing happened.

Our family and friends immediately started replying, "Sorry, Jim, we don't know anyone. We can't help in that way, but you and John deserve to get married, and we want to help make it happen."

Our family and friends banded together, and through their generosity they covered the entire thirteen-thousand-dollar cost of that jet.

So, on a beautiful July morning in 2013, I dressed John in a pair of khakis and a plaid shirt with Velcro closures in place of buttons. I put on a crazy plaid pink jacket, and we rode in the back of an ambulance to the airport. We boarded this tiny jet along with John's Aunt Paulette, who would marry us. And we flew to Baltimore.

We landed at BWI Airport and parked on the tarmac.

I raised the head of John's gurney so that he was sitting up, and I took his hand.

And in that cramped medical jet, Aunt Paulette married us, and we got to say those magical words that we never expected to say: "I do."

It was the happiest moment of our lives.

We were on the ground for maybe thirty minutes before we were back in the air flying home to Cincinnati as husband and husband. And we said that word an awful lot. In the days that followed, I don't think two sentences left our mouths without the word "husband."

"Good morning, *husband*. Would you like something to drink, *husband*? I love you, *husband*."

And that was all we wanted, to live out John's remaining days as husband and husband.

A few days after we married, friends were at a party and ran into a friend of theirs, a local civil-rights attorney named Al Gerhardstein. Our story came up in conversation. Our friends got in touch and asked if we might be willing to meet with Al.

John and I discussed it and said, "Well, why not?"

Al came to visit, and in walked this brilliant, kind, gentle man. He sat down and talked with us. He pulled out a piece of paper – a blank Ohio death certificate.

He said, "Now, guys, I'm sure you haven't thought about this" – because who thinks about a death certificate when you've just gotten married? – "but do you understand that, when John dies, his last official record as a person will be wrong? Ohio will say he's unmarried. And, Jim, your name won't be there as his surviving spouse."

We were speechless.

Al was right. We hadn't thought about it, and goddamn it, we'd just jumped through all these hoops to get married, and the state of Ohio is going to pretend that we don't exist. They're going to erase our marriage from John's last official record?

It hurt. It was painful, and it was personal.

So John and I, we were never political. We weren't activists, other than signing checks. But we decided to fight for our marriage and for people like us across Ohio.

We filed suit. We sued the state of Ohio to say the state had to fill out John's death certificate accurately when he dies and recognize our marriage.

Eleven days after we married, I left home to John's words, "Go kick some ass, Jim."

I went to federal court, and I took the stand, and I had the chance to read a statement to Federal Judge Timothy Black. I got to explain to him what John meant to me, what our marriage meant to us. And how harmful and hurtful it was to know that the state of Ohio wanted nothing more than to erase the most important relationship of our lives from his last record as a person.

The state of Ohio kept saying, "But the people of Ohio

voted for this, and that carries more weight than your constitutional rights."

I will always remember how Al, our attorney, replied to that.

He said, "The surest way to abridge the rights of a minority is to allow the majority to vote on it."

At five o'clock that day, Judge Black released his ruling, starting with the sentence "This is not a complicated case." He ruled in our favor and said, "When John dies, the state of Ohio must recognize their marriage on his death certificate."

John and I had three months more together as husband and husband, and in October of 2013 I read out loud to him from one of his favorite books, *Weaveworld*, by Clive Barker.

I still remember the last sentence I read: "Lions. He'd come with lions."

And then he died.

I'm grateful the last voice John heard was mine.

A few months later, the state of Ohio couldn't let this lie, so they appealed to the Sixth Circuit Court of Appeals. And our case, along with several others, was heard by that court.

About a year after John died, I got a phone call. "Jim, the court of appeals just ruled against you. They have given Ohio the ability to erase your marriage from John's death certificate."

I worried every day when I went to the mailbox. I thought, *Is this the day I'm going to pull out John's updated death certificate with the most important relationship of my life erased?*

But I wasn't going to give up. I was going to fight, and I was going to take this all the way to the Supreme Court if I had to.

And that's what happened. In April I walked into the Supreme Court of the United States of America. I took in this grand room – the marble walls, the marble columns, the red, white and blue ceiling, and these dark red drapes with gold fringe that honestly put me in mind of a French whorehouse.

I wondered, *Will the court live up to those four words inscribed in the pediment of their very own building, "Equal justice under law"?*

I thought about John. I thought about our marriage. I thought about my co-plaintiffs – another widow, parents, couples, children. And I wondered, *Are we going to walk out of here knowing that our marriage licenses, our death certificates, our birth certificates matter? Are they accurate, do they hold value?*

Now we had to wait for the court to deliberate and write an opinion.

A short two months later, I was back in that courtroom waiting to hear their decision. The chief justice announced that Justice Kennedy would read the first decision, and they read our case number. I startled in my seat, and I grabbed the hands of the friends sitting on either side of me. I listened as Justice Kennedy read his decision.

I struggled to understand the legal language, and I thought, *Well, we won . . .* but then I wasn't so certain. And once it finally hit me that we *did* indeed win, that the Supreme Court had made marriage equality the law of the land, I burst into tears.

And I wasn't the only one breaking the usually staid decorum. The typical silence of that courtroom was broken by gasps and tears and sobs.

It was such a beautiful feeling realizing I could walk out and no longer worry about getting that updated death certificate.

Al and I led our group of plaintiffs and attorneys arm in arm through this amazing crowd to the plaza of the courthouse. The air was electric with a palpable sense of joy. As we wound our way through the crowd, it split before us, and we were showered with cheers and tears and smiles and this amazing, utterly happy feeling of celebration.

In that moment, for the first time in my life as an out gay man, I felt like an equal American. And I did it all because I loved my husband.

Now, a bit over a year later, I chuckle when I think about *Obergefell v. Hodges*. I have to pinch myself that the "Obergefell" is me. And I laugh when I think about all those law students, for the rest of time, having to learn how to pronounce and spell Obergefell.

But mostly I think about John. I think about the love we shared, and I think about the fight that we were willing to fight, along with so many other plaintiffs.

We fought for pieces of paper: marriage licenses, death certificates, birth certificates. When I realize that it was all about a piece of paper, it takes me back to how I ended my vows the day we got married:

"I'm overjoyed that we finally have a piece of paper that confirms what we've always felt in our hearts – that we're an old married couple who still love each other. I give you my heart, my soul, and everything I am. I am honored to call you husband."

JIM OBERGEFELL is an LGBTQ activist, speaker, and author. He co-founded Equality Vines, the first cause-based wine label. Jim is a speaker with Keppler Speakers and co-authored *Love Wins* with Debbie Cenziper. Jim is on the board of directors for SAGE, devoted to advocacy for elder LGBTQ Americans. He is a member of the national advisory boards for the GLBT Historical Society and the Mattachine Society of Washington, DC. Jim was inducted into the Ohio Civil Rights Hall of Fame in 2018. He was named on *Foreign Policy Magazine*'s 2015 Global Thinkers list and *Out Magazine*'s 2015 Out 100 list.

Dylan Park

Roadside

After graduating high school, I was looking for a way out of my quiet hometown in Northern California. A military recruiter on campus told me that if I enlisted, they'd pay my tuition to any college I could get into.

I'd be able to travel the world. And if I got lucky, I might be able to blow some shit up.

He sweetened the pot by saying that he would give me a ten-thousand-dollar bonus by extending a three-year enlistment to a short six-year enlistment. And ten thousand dollars was a lot of money for a nineteen-year-old, so I was sold.

Six months after basic training, I found myself in Kirkuk, Iraq, which is one of the largest oil fields on the planet. Because it's one of the largest oil fields, it's also one of the most dangerous places on the planet – it's a hotbed for terrorism.

Now, my job was mainly to patrol the city around the base's perimeter, but sometimes I would be posted at the front gates or at checkpoints – patting down potential suicide bombers, hoping to live another day.

Working those "suicide gates," as we called them, was like this sick lottery that you didn't want to win.

I knew a few guys who weren't so lucky.

But for every suicide bomber, for every enemy insurgent, there were a thousand friendly faces in Kirkuk. And one of those friendly faces belonged to a teenager named Brahim.

Brahim was one of a group of kids of all ages that would follow us around while we were on patrol. They would ask us for candy, soda, magazines. They wanted to talk American pop culture.

And I'd always entertain Brahim. I loved having him around. But some of the guys in my squad, not so much, because, after all, we were in a war zone where enemy combatants didn't wear a uniform.

But in my heart I knew that these kids weren't terrorists – they were just trying to make the best out of a bad situation, kind of like I was.

This kid Brahim, he reminded me of my younger brother, Rory, back home. They were both very mature for their age. That was to be expected. I mean, Brahim was raised in a war zone, so he'd probably seen things that none of us ever had.

Over the course of that deployment, we had some very deep and intellectual conversations about life and death and religion and politics – conversations you shouldn't be having with a sixteen- or seventeen-year-old.

When he was a kid, my brother Rory would follow me and my friends around. He'd tag along everywhere. So by the time he was a teenager, he had this very adult sense of humor.

Rory was five years younger than me, but he was my best friend. We did everything together.

And I think in a way Brahim filled that void for me. He was like a little brother.

Brahim worked on our base as a janitor. I thought that was kind of odd, because my brother, who was the same age, was back home going to prom and applying for college.

So I asked Brahim, "Why aren't you going to school?"

He said, "I don't have a school to go to. It was bombed out."

He told me that he was biding his time to become an interpreter for the U.S. Army, because that's where the real money was. You could make *two hundred fifty dollars* a week.

See, the U.S. government had this agreement with Iraqis that if you worked a certain amount of years as a translator, once your contract was up, you'd get a visa to come to the United States. The opportunities were there because there was high turnover – not because Iraqis were quitting but because they were all getting *killed*.

These terror groups, they would execute anyone they suspected of working with the Americans. And sometimes they would kill your family or your friends, just to prove a point.

Brahim said that he understood the risks, but he was willing to do anything it took to feed his family and help end the war in Iraq.

Now, as the deployment went on, I learned a lot of things about this kid. We became really close. He told me about all the friends and family members he'd lost in the conflict. He told me about how he was the sole provider for his household, a house that only had electricity every other week because of the rolling blackouts. The house had piss-poor plumbing, so something as simple as personal hygiene became a struggle.

And I felt partially responsible for that, because after all I was a cog in this war machine that had destroyed this kid's home country.

So when I got a chance, I went down to the base's PX, which is like a mini grocery store, and I bought him twenty dollars', maybe thirty dollars', worth of soap, shampoo, deodorant, toothpaste – just, like, the bare necessities. The next time I saw him, I presented him with this box of toiletries, and he looked at me with tears in his eyes, like I had just handed him the keys to a brand-new house. And it was an incredibly humbling experience.

I wanted to see how Brahim was living up close. So one day I snuck off base.

He gave me a tour of the city. We hailed taxis, hitched rides, walked for miles. Along the way he pointed out historical landmarks. He pointed toward an ancient citadel that was built two thousand years before Jesus was born. He showed me the tomb of the prophet Daniel from the Bible; he said people of all faiths went to pray there – Jews, Muslims, Christians. He told me how Kirkuk was one of the oldest regions in the history of human civilization.

I could tell how proud of his culture he was. It was pretty impressive stuff.

I told him that Campbell, California, the town I'm from, is famous for inventing the fruit cup.

He didn't know what a fruit cup was.

We went to a marketplace, and we stopped for kabobs and fresh-baked bread. And I don't know if I'm romanticizing this meal in my head, but to this day I say that that was the best meal I've ever eaten.

I asked Brahim, "How is this bread so good?"

He looked at me and rolled his eyes, and he said, "Because we *invented* bread."

A few months later, toward the end of my deployment, Brahim finally got the chance to become an interpreter. And for me that was bittersweet. I knew that he was finally able to provide for his family. But on the other hand, he had just volunteered for his own death.

I knew that I was leaving him to die.

That was a sickening feeling, but what could I do? I wished him the best, and I got on a plane and flew home.

When I got home, things were different. *I* was different. There was this ultra-vigilant muscle memory that I had.

I remember walking in downtown San Jose with my friends, and I would look at rooftops and windows, searching for snipers. Or I would be at a gathering somewhere, or at a restaurant, and I would be looking at the torso of every single person that walked in the building just to make sure they didn't have a suicide vest on – it was just second nature at that point. Living like that can be hard – it can make a person angry – and my behavior was straining all my relationships.

I decided I needed a change of scenery, a fresh start, so I moved to Phoenix, Arizona.

I enrolled in college, went to ASU. But things didn't get better. Actually, for the next five years I struggled with my mental health. I started abusing drugs and alcohol. It was hard to keep a job, because I was in and out of the court system.

There was even a period of homelessness.

But, despite weekends spent in the county jail and different homeless shelters, I was a pretty decent student and was able to muscle my way through college.

Then, one Saturday morning, I woke up to a dozen missed phone calls and text messages. I called my mother back first, because her name was the first and the last on the list.

When she picked up the phone, there was this fear in her voice that I'd never heard before. Then there was silence. She couldn't get out what she was trying to say.

But when she did finally speak, she told me that the night before, my brother had been murdered in a carjacking.

I didn't believe it, because things like that didn't happen where I was from. I had just purchased plane tickets to fly home to spend the holidays with my family. Only now I was flying home to bury him.

I remember spending that Thanksgiving in a morgue. And then, a few days later, I spent my birthday staring at his freshly engraved tombstone.

That Friday, when Rory was killed, he was walking out of a grocery store with his best friend. They were celebrating – he had just gotten a new car, a new apartment, a new job. He was about to turn twenty-two. He was starting his adult life.

As he was sitting in his car, two men wearing ski masks, brandishing firearms, ran up on him. They told him to get out, but for whatever reason they didn't even give him a chance to comply. One of the men shot Rory three times in the chest and face as his best friend watched in horror from the passenger seat.

I know these details because I watched it.

I watched the high-definition security-camera footage during his killer's trial.

I watched my brother take his last breath, and it's something I can still see every time I close my eyes.

I had been through a lot in Iraq. I'd survived suicide bombings and mortar attacks and sniper attacks. But Rory's death caught me more off guard than any roadside bomb in Iraq ever could.

I was destroyed.

I decided I should move home to be closer to my family, but before I did that, I would have to go back to Arizona to pack up my apartment.

When I landed in Arizona, I got off the plane and exited the terminal. I remember thinking it was odd that the sky was gray and it was pouring rain.

I went straight down to the taxi stand and got into the first taxi I saw.

We were driving down the 202, and I wasn't feeling very conversational, but the taxi driver didn't know that. He started up that standard small talk: *Where you from? What do you do? Why are you here?* That sort of thing.

And obviously I didn't want to talk about my brother's murder, so I half lied and said, "Oh, I just got out of the military a few years ago, and I got this new job in California."

When I said military, he asked if I'd been anywhere special.

I said, "Sure, I've been all over the world. I just recently did a year in Iraq."

He said, "Iraq?"

And when I said Iraq, his tone changed a little bit, and he said, "I'm from Iraq."

He said, "Where in Iraq were you stationed?"

I said "In the northeast, in this city called Kirkuk."

And he paused, and he said, "I'm from Kirkuk."

And just as soon as the conversation started, it was over.

I knew something was wrong, and I was thinking, *What just happened? Did I harm one of his loved ones intentionally or unintentionally?* Or maybe he was really antiwar, and, if he was, could I blame him?

We sat there in silence, for miles, and I could feel him staring at me in his rearview mirror.

I was trying to avoid eye contact by looking out my own window, and it was in that moment that I saw he had passed our exit.

Now I was terrified.

I told him that he'd missed the exit, but he didn't respond. He just took the next exit.

When he got off, we went down a few blocks, and he pulled the car over to the side of the road.

Now the red flags were going off!

I didn't know what he was thinking, but I could see him gripping his steering wheel – working up the guts to do something. What he wanted to do, I didn't know, but I didn't want to be there to find out.

So I grabbed my backpack, and I kicked open the door.

But before I could get all the way out of the taxi, he grabbed my leg – and he turned around and said, "Hey, Dylan, Do you remember me? It's me, Brahim."

And I looked at him, and I just didn't understand what was going on.

But he sat a foot taller. His voice was deeper, his English was better. He didn't have that goofy bowl cut.

Seventy-five hundred miles away from Iraq, there was this kid who had saved my life a lifetime ago.

We got out of the car, and we were hugging and sobbing in the pouring rain, like a scene out of *The Notebook*.

He explained to me that, after I left Iraq, he was an interpreter for four years, and when he finished his contract and got his visa, they asked him where he wanted to resettle. He said he didn't know, but he wanted to go somewhere where the weather was like Iraq.

So they sent him to Phoenix, Arizona.

I'd learned a lot of things about survival in the military. During POW training, one of the things the instructors tell you is that sometimes the pain can be unbearable and the outlook can be pretty grim. But you have to look for these glimmers of hope to keep you going to that next day.

I think that day on the side of the road in Arizona was my glimmer of hope.

I'd lost one brother, and I got another one back.

DYLAN PARK was born and raised in the San Francisco Bay Area. From 2004 to 2010, he served in the US Air Force and was deployed all over the world. Once home, he became a social worker for homeless veterans and a victims advocate. In 2016, Dylan moved to LA and became a writing fellow at AMC Network. He's had scripts optioned for television and film and also works as a director. You can find Dylan with his face buried in a laptop, or hiding in a café or a bookstore in Santa Monica, the city he now calls home.

Adam Gopnik

Charlie Ravioli

My wife and I left New York for several years. We lived abroad, in France. We decided we would come home in the year 2000, for a lot of reasons but essentially because we wanted to see our children grow up in New York City.

We didn't want them to have the experience that kids have growing up in Paris, where every child, at four thirty, when school is finished, looks like a Democrat – they look completely depressed and kind of dog-eared, with enormous circles under their eyes. They've been beaten and abused for the last nine hours, and they have no idea how to respond to the force of unappeasable authority at every moment.

We wanted them to have the kind of light-footed, spring-hearted sense of ownership that New York children seemed to us to have. We came back to be in New York so that they would have a childhood in New York and be able to be *part* of New York.

We had just come back when the greatest tragedy in the city's history happened, and a long shadow spread out over every life and I think particularly over the lives of parents with small children. We wondered if we should stay in New York, if New York was the right place for us to bring up our children.

We were all full of doubt, and my wife, Martha, would put on my pillow, night after night, brochures for real estate in Connecticut and houses in New Jersey and even things clipped from the paper about the farthest reaches of Brooklyn.

And it was just around that time that my daughter, Olivia, who was then three, told us that she had an imaginary friend and that this imaginary friend's name was Charlie Ravioli.

At first Charlie Ravioli seemed like a terrifically attractive, Manhattan kind of character. His apartment was at the corner of Lexington and Madison, which seemed like a great neighborhood. He lived, Olivia explained, on grilled chicken and water, sort of like a fashion model, and it was a great New York diet – we knew a lot of people who lived on exactly that.

But then something a little disturbing began to happen. Olivia would be talking on her cell phone – we gave her one of those toy cell phones that they had then.

We would hear her say, "Hello, Ravioli, Ravioli? Okay, call me when you get in."

She would hang it up, and she would turn to us and say, "I always get his machine."

And we realized that she had invented an imaginary friend who was always too busy to play with her. She had an invisible playmate whose salient characteristic was that he was too busy to play.

She would come to the dinner table every night and everyone would recite the things that had happened throughout the day.

We'd turn to Olivia, and she'd say, "Oh, I bumped into Charlie Ravioli today. We grabbed a cappuccino, but then he had to run."

Or she'd say, "I bumped into Charlie Ravioli today. We got into a taxi, but then he had a meeting, so he had to go."

It turned out Charlie was working in television in those years. That's how Olivia explained it.

What she actually would say was "He's working on a television," and we could never figure out if he was a talk-show host, sort of like Charlie Rose, or if he was a guy in the electronics business with a little repair shop someplace in Queens.

But that was what Ravioli did. And he was always too busy to play with her.

Now, I should explain, of course, that Olivia at that moment had no life where she was bumping into people or grabbing cappuccinos. She was simply expressing and imitating the world that she heard all around her, and particularly that she heard from her mother every night when we would come to the table.

I would say to her mother, "How was your day?"

And her mother would say, "Oh, you know, it was one of those days. I bumped into Meg downtown, and we grabbed a coffee. But then I had a cell-phone message from Emily, but we couldn't connect, so we came back uptown," and on and on and on, a whole history of miscommunication that had enveloped eight hours.

Olivia was taking that in. She had one person in her life who was out there in the world. Her older brother, Luke, is exactly five years older than she is (to the day, which tells you more than you really want to know). Every day, at the end of the day, they would sit down together for cookies and milk when Luke came back from school, after Olivia had spent a day at the Central Park Zoo, taking naps, doing the things that three-year-olds do.

She would say, "Luke, how was your day?"

And he would say, "Okay."

"Luke, did the teacher like your essay?"

"Yeah, I guess."

"Luke, what did you have for lunch?"

"A sandwich, I guess."

"Luke, how was *my day*?"

The basic rhythm of men and women. It gets started about the ages of seven and two and never alters throughout a lifetime.

Well, Charlie Ravioli seemed to us like such a strange character that I decided I would call my sister. I have five sisters. They all have Ph.D.s. They all teach in universities somewhere or other. Growing up, when the moths would come onto our porch, they would dissect them and figure out exactly what genus they belonged to.

One of my sisters is a developmental psychologist out in Berkeley. I called her up because it seemed a little strange to me to have an imaginary friend who was always too busy to play with you. I wondered if this was something that came up a lot in the psychological literature.

I said, "Listen, Olivia has got this imaginary friend, but she's always trying to connect with him and never can. He's always too busy to play with her."

And she said, "Oh, that's completely normal. Children make their imaginary friends out of whatever experience they have at hand. If they're living on mountaintops, they have imaginary friends who are made of clouds. If they live by the seashore, their imaginary friends are waves. So what could be more normal than that her imaginary friend, growing up in Manhattan, would be always too busy, would be a creature of interrupted occasions, of constantly occluded connections? It makes perfect sense. The kids understand that these imaginary friends are fictional. You have absolutely nothing to worry about."

So I told my wife, "We have nothing to worry about. Completely normal. Every child in New York has a busy imaginary friend."

It would seem that this was going to be okay. But then a new character arrived in the story. We would listen to Olivia talking on her little toy cell phone, and we heard her talking to someone called Lori.

She would say, "Hello, Lori. Hello. Is Ravioli there? No? Okay."

And at first we thought that Lori was sort of the Linda Tripp of the whole Ravioli operation. She was the person you spoke to when Ravioli was ignoring you, the big creep that he obviously was, and you confided in Lori, as she was recording your conversations and so on.

But then we listened more carefully, and we realized who Lori really was: Lori was Charlie Ravioli's assistant.

She was the person on the phone who tells you, "Oh, I'm sorry, Mr. Ravioli is in a meeting. He'll try and get back to you as soon as he can."

Martha turned to me and said, "This is wrong. This is really wrong. I'm not a child psychologist, but I know that imaginary friends should not have assistants.

"They should not have agents. They should not have personal trainers.

"Imaginary friends should not have *people*.

"They should *play with the child who imagined them*."

So I called my sister again and said, "Ravioli has an assistant who's answering his phone now. Would you describe this as normal?"

She said, "This never occurs in the psychological literature."

I said, "Oh, so you think we should look into it?"

And she said, "No, I think you should move."

But then something very interesting began to happen. Olivia didn't seem to get any closer to Charlie Ravioli. She didn't come any nearer to actually having the play dates and the good times with him that it seemed to us she deserved. But she would report to us at the end of the day that she had gone out into the world in search of Charlie Ravioli and something amazing had happened to her.

She had gone out looking for Charlie Ravioli and ended up in the zoo, and she had released all the animals from the zoo, and they had had a dance.

She came home and told us about a day (which she of course spent entirely inside, watching *Caillou* on television and taking a nap) when she had gone out in search of Charlie Ravioli on the streets of Manhattan, and the taxi driver had a heart attack, and she'd gotten into the front seat of the taxi, and driven through the city.

She had gone looking for Charlie Ravioli downtown somewhere, and she had ended up telling jokes in a nightclub with a microphone.

And we realized that Charlie Ravioli, for her, was truly the prince of the city. He was the prince of our disorder. He was the representative of the spirit of New York, which is always the spirit of attainment. It's the spirit of the thing that lies before us. It's always the place that we haven't quite got to yet but that we'll get to someday.

Ravioli wasn't, we realized, just an incarnation of the insane busyness and missed connections she saw around us. He was also her hero, her demigod, her fictional version of the endless possibilities in New York, which always lay just around the corner and on the other side of a cappuccino.

And so I knew that we could stay in New York.

Because I understood that all we really wanted from this city was to go on bumping into Charlie Ravioli for as long and as often as we possibly could.

ADAM GOPNIK has been a staff writer at the *New Yorker* since 1987. He has written fiction, humor, memoirs, critical essays, and reported pieces from at home and abroad for the magazine. His books include *The Table Comes First*, *Paris to the Moon*, *Through the Children's Gate*, and *At the Strangers' Gate*. A musical, written in collaboration with David Shire, *The Most Beautiful Room in New York*, opened in 2017 at New Haven's Long Wharf Theatre. His one-man show, *The Gates*, based on material developed with The Moth, played for a sold-out week at New York's Public Theater in 2018.

Wang Ping

The Book War

I was six when the Cultural Revolution began in China, and it crushed my dream for college. Everything was shut down: the factory, the store, the school and library. My father was exiled, and my mother was once arrested and later released for teaching Western music. As the oldest daughter, I took on the duty of feeding my family: my grandma, sisters, and brother.

I raised chickens and grew vegetables in the backyard, which had been plowed for me by bombs. Every day I rose at dawn, walking through minefields, checkpoints, bullets, and grenades, to search for food and fuel. My college dream seemed so far away – dangerous and impossible.

Early one morning I took out the stove to light a fire to make breakfast for my family. When I opened the door. I saw Jiajia, the new girl from Beijing. She was reading Mao's Little Red Book under a streetlight. Her head and shoulders were covered with frost, and she was sobbing.

Who would be weeping like this reading Mao's words these days? I wondered, let alone Jiajia, the very uppity girl who had just moved to our navy compound on an island in the East China Sea? She dressed like us – the ugly gray Mao suit – but she wore it as if it were a ballet outfit, and she walked like a ballet dancer.

I tiptoed closer and peeked over her shoulders.

I gasped.

The book she was reading was not Mao's book. It was Hans Christian Andersen's *The Little Mermaid,* the very story that had fired my imagination and my dream of college. I had begged my mother to let me start school a year early so I could start reading on my own. My mother agreed and even promised that she would buy me Andersen's fairy tales if I got straight A's.

But the Cultural Revolution broke out before I finished the first grade. Students became Chairman Mao's little Red Guards. They rounded up all the books, condemned them as poison, and made the teachers kneel in front of the bonfires, watching their treasures burn.

I had raked through piles of books on the streets before the burning, hoping to find my mermaid, but no luck. Here she was, wrapped in Mao's Little Red Book in Jiajia's hand. Jiajia was so deep in her story she didn't realize I was standing right behind her until she heard me weeping loudly with her.

She jumped, clutching her book to her chest. Her face told me if I dared to report her, she would fight me to the death. We stared at each other for an eternity.

Suddenly she burst out laughing, pointing at my face wet with tears. She knew I was a kindred spirit and her mermaid was safe.

I begged Jiajia to loan me her book just for three hours. I would read in the fields on my way to the food market.

She refused. I knew she didn't trust me.

"Oh, please, please, don't go away. Just give me a minute. I have something to trade with you," I said.

I ran to the chicken coop and pulled down *The Arabian Nights* from the roof.

I had found this in the book pile outside a tuberculosis patient's apartment. He was dying from coughing up blood and pus, so the Red Guards wouldn't touch his books. It had been yellowed by the sun, rained upon, and was missing many pages, but I didn't care. I hid it in the chicken coop and read the stories whenever I could.

Jiajia squealed with delight and snatched the book from my hand. We agreed that we would meet tomorrow to return each other's books. If we couldn't finish reading them by then, we would renegotiate our terms.

It took us more than two weeks to finish the books. My problem was finding a place to read. I shared my bed with my two sisters and my brother. My grandma also had her bed in the same room.

Jiajia had her own bedroom, but her apartment was watched by soldiers day and night. Fortunately, her father liked to take long walks, followed by the soldiers. So, whenever he went out, I would sneak into her room and we would roll around in her big bed, reading and daydreaming about a possible underground book club so we could have more books to read besides *The Arabian Nights* and *The Little Mermaid*.

My daily chore was to feed the chickens. I had ten hens and a rooster. My favorite was Silky. She had long white silky feathers, black feet, and a black face.

Silky was brooding. She would need twenty-one days to hatch the babies. So that day I was going to dig a hole to make a nest for her behind the chicken coop in the woods to keep her safe – away from foxes and weasels and my mother, who all wanted her meat.

I was digging, and my pickax hit a wooden box. I pulled it out, pried it open, and found Shakespeare, *Tom Sawyer*, *Huckleberry Finn*, and my mother's music scores of Beethoven and Schubert! And in the bottom *The Complete Fairy Tales* by Hans Christian Andersen – hardcover, gilded title.

On the first page, my mother's words: *"To my stubborn girl. May you be as beautiful and courageous as the Little Mermaid. Your mother."*

I screamed with joy and ran to Jiajia and brought her to the treasure. We cried in each other's arms. Our dream for a book club would finally come true. We each found a bunch of kids who also had a cache of banned books. We went into the woods, cut our wrists, and mixed our blood together as a pledge to guard our books and each other with our lives.

So while everyone else was busy killing each other, we read poetry, drama, philosophy, medicine, military training manuals. Our days were filled with joy and hope.

Jiajia got ambitious. She wanted to expand the club to a hundred members.

I begged her, "Please wait."

Something bad was coming. I could feel it.

That night I dreamed of a monster yanking me up by my hair and throwing me down into a firepit.

I opened my eyes, and my mother was thumping my head with Andersen's fairy tales.

"Where did you get this book?" she hissed. *"How?"*

I looked at her. She knew where I got this book. I wanted to know how she found it. I had hidden it under my grandma's mattress, the last place she would check.

She slapped my face with the book and took out a bamboo whip.

"You want to kill me and your father? I'm going to kill you first."

She whipped and whipped me until the whip broke. I covered my head with my arms. The pain was unbearable – not from the whipping but from my bleeding heart. I knew this was the last time I would see my *Little Mermaid.* My mother was going to burn it.

"Where are the rest of the books?" she asked.

I remained silent. I understood she must find all the books from the box and destroy them before they destroyed us, but I had sworn I would guard the books with my life.

She threw down the whip and started searching. I listened to her pulling up every floorboard, turning over the mattresses and drawers.

My heart shriveled. I knew she was going to find all the books, because she was my mother. Soon she had a huge pile by the window.

She sat down, ordered me to bring the stove, and tear up everything, page by page, book by book. My face was covered in blood, I listened to my Little Mermaid scream in the fire as she turned into ashes.

When every book was gone, my mother went back to bed.

I walked out to sit by the chicken coop. Everything was so quiet and peaceful, as if nothing had happened. I looked up; no star in the sky. The night had entered its darkest moment. I thought of tomorrow: What was tomorrow without books or hope?

I was choking with tears when Silky came to me, along with her chicks, their soft feathers rubbing against my feet and hands as they begged for food.

I sat with them till the dawn came. I got up and did my chores as usual, but in silence, feeding the chickens, my family, cleaning up.

When night fell again, I went into the woods with Jia-jia, empty-handed this time. Nobody asked what had happened. The cuts and bruises on my face and limbs said it all.

I stood in silence for a long time. Then I started talking, words coming out of my mouth like seas and stars, forming a constellation of the Little Mermaid – her courage to go after her dream at any cost, which had become mine.

Everyone listened as if it were the first time. My Little Mermaid had come alive again through my mouth, more beautiful than ever.

So I started telling stories to the members in the woods, then my siblings and neighbors. When the indoors became too small, we moved to the yard. Night after night under the stars we gathered – children, parents, grandparents – from spring to summer to fall.

When the winter came we brought our own wood to make fires. I told stories of Romeo and Juliet, Tom Sawyer, Huckleberry Finn, Ali Baba, and Jiajia told her stories of Swan Lake, the Red Shoes, Lady Macbeth.

We were hungry and cold. Our future was bleak, without jobs or college. But we had our stories.

One night I was telling the mermaid story again for my best friend, Jiajia. She was leaving the island with her father to go to Mongolia, and I knew I might never see her again. Across the blazing fire, I saw my mother in the crowd. She had tears in her eyes, shining like stars in the night sky.

My voice quivered with joy. I might have lost my book battle with her, but I had won the war. We had won the war.

WANG PING was born in China and came to the US in 1986. She's published fourteen books of prose and poetry, including her latest, *Life of Miracles Along the Yangtze and Mississippi*. She's also a photographer, filmmaker, and installation artist. Wang has received NEA, Bush, McKnight, and Lannan fellowships and numerous book awards. She is Professor of English at Macalester College and founder/director of Kinship of Rivers project (www.kinshipofrivers.org). She dedicates this story to children fleeing war and injustice, and children separated from their parents at the U.S. border. May the story bring light to their dreams. www.wangping.com.

THE MOTH'S DIRECTORS

The storytellers featured in this book developed and shaped their stories for the stage with The Moth's team of directors:

Meg Bowles is a Senior Director and one of the hosts of the Peabody Award-winning *The Moth Radio Hour*. Like many of the Moth staff, Meg started as a volunteer in 1997, helping to curate early Mainstage events and teaching storytelling workshops. In 2002, she was pulled away by Discovery Communications, mainly because she needed the paycheck, but when Moth founder George Dawes Green asked her to return to help curate the Mainstage in 2005, she found it impossible to say no. While directing stories for the Mainstage, Meg has had the privilege of working with a NASA astronaut who commanded the first shuttle mission after the loss of *Challenger,* a doctor who saved Mother Teresa's life, a member of Churchill's Secret Army who trained spies during the Second World War, an innocent man who spent eighteen years on death row, a Nobel Laureate, a lobster fisherman, neuroscientists, veterans, musicians, chefs, fugitives, mothers, fathers, and countless people who have found themselves in sometimes ordinary but often unique situations and have generously shared their experiences and emotions, exposing their imperfections – the very thing that makes us human and ultimately connects us to one another.

Catherine Burns is The Moth's longtime Artistic Director and one of the hosts of *The Moth Radio Hour*. As a lead director on the Mainstage since 2003, she has helped hundreds of people craft their stories, including a retired New York City detective, a jaguar tracker, and an exonerated prisoner. She is the editor of the two bestselling books, *The Moth: 50 True Stories* and *All These Wonders*. She is the director of the solo shows *The Gates,* written by and starring Adam Gopnik, and *Helen & Edgar,* written by and starring Edgar Oliver, which was called "utterly absorbing and unexpectedly moving" by Ben Brantley of the *New York Times*. Prior to coming to The Moth, she directed and produced television and independent films, interviewing such diverse talent as Ozzy Osbourne, Martha Stewart, and Howard Stern. She attended her first Moth back in 2000, fell in love with the show, and was in turn a GrandSLAM contestant and a volunteer in The Moth Community Program before joining the staff full-time. Born and raised in Alabama, she now lives in Brooklyn with her husband and young son.

Maggie Cino is an award-winning director and playwright living in Brooklyn. Her plays were published by Indie Theater Now, and excerpts appear in the Smith & Krause Best Men's and Best Women's Monologue series. The *Villager* called her "A writer of extraordinary versatility and imagination" and *Time Out New York* says, "Cino has a gift." A former Senior Producer for The Moth, she directed storytelling shows nationally and internationally at venues including BAM, Lincoln Center, and the main stage of the Sydney Opera House.

Jenifer Hixson is a Senior Director and one of the hosts of *The Moth Radio Hour*. Each year she asks hundreds of people to identify significant turning points in their lives – fumbles and triumphs, leaps of faith, darkest hours – and then helps them shape those experiences into story form for the stage. She falls a little bit in love with each storyteller and hopes you will, too. In 2000, she launched The Moth StorySLAM, which now has a full-time presence in twenty-nine cities in the United States, the UK, and Australia and provides more than six thousand individual storytelling opportunities for storytelling daredevils and loquacious wallflowers alike. Jenifer's story "Where There's Smoke" has been featured on *The Moth Radio Hour* and *This American Life* and was a part of The Moth's first book, *The Moth: 50 True Stories*.

Sarah Austin Jenness joined the staff at The Moth in 2005, and as Executive Producer she has worked with hundreds of people to craft and hone their personal stories. She is one of the hosts of the Peabody Award–winning *The Moth Radio Hour* and launched The Moth's Global Community Program – coaching storytelling workshops in the US and Africa to highlight world issues, including family homelessness and public health. Moth stories she has directed in the past decade have been told before the UN General Assembly and as far afield as the Kenya National Theatre. She believes that stories have power and can change the world by creating connection.

Catherine McCarthy is the manager of The Moth's Education Program, where she helps students and educators to build community and challenge dominant narratives through personal storytelling. She is a story director for the Mainstage and is the co-editor of the Penguin Random House Teachers' Guide for *The Moth: All These Wonders*. She has facilitated storytelling workshops for the U.S. State Department, the Albert Einstein College of Medicine, the DreamYard Project, and at dozens of high schools around New York City. She also directed the award-winning solo show *The Secret Life of Your Third-Grade Teacher* at the 2016 NYC Fringe Festival. She is currently pursuing a master's degree in social work at Fordham University.

Larry Rosen is a master instructor with The Moth. He has been performing, teaching, directing, and producing storytelling, theater, improvisation, and sketch comedy for twenty-five years through institutions including Second City, the People's Improv Theater, and the New York International Fringe Festival. A proud member of The Moth's Global Community team, Larry has had the privilege of working with storytellers representing diverse communities throughout the United States and in Kenya, Tanzania, and South Africa.

Kate Tellers attended her first Moth event, fortuitously themed Beginnings, in 2007 and has never looked back. Hailed as a "storytelling guru" by the *Wall Street Journal*, she is the director of MothWorks at The Moth, where she has designed programs with nonprofits, including the Bill & Melinda Gates Foundation, the Kellogg Foundation, and the Ashoka Future Forum, as well as Facebook, Ogilvy + Mather, Nike, Google, and the U.S. State Department, and developed stories with her heroes from her Pittsburgh childhood to the present day. She is a regular host and \ storyteller. Her story "But Also Bring Cheese" is featured in the second Moth anthology, *All These Wonders: True Stories About Facing the Unknown*. She lives in Brooklyn with her loud family and dog.

Sarah Haberman has been The Moth's Executive Director since 2013. Prior to The Moth, Sarah held senior management and development positions for Jazz at Lincoln Center, the Columbia Business School, the Whitney Museum of American Art, and the New York Public Library. Before embarking on a career in the nonprofit sector, she spent six years as an acquiring editor in Paris for Robert Laffont-Fixot, a major French publishing house. She is a member of the board of directors for the Herzfeld Foundation in Milwaukee and served on The Moth's Board of Directors until 2013.

ACKNOWLEDGMENTS

The Moth would like to thank:

Our Founder, George Dawes Green.

Our Board of Directors: Deborah Dugan and Ari Handel, The Moth's Co-Chairs, Serena Altschul, Lawrence C. Burstein, Joan D. Firestone, Neil Gaiman, Adam Gopnik, Alice Gottesman, Eric Green, Tony Hendra, Courtney Holt, Anne Maffei, Dr. Alan Manevitz, Joanne Ramos, Melanie Shorin, and Roger Skelton for their extraordinary leadership and commitment to this cause.

Anyone who has ever allowed an audience to get to know them a little better by sharing a significant moment of their life on a Moth stage.

The Moth StorySLAM community, shepherded by beloved local producers in twenty-nine cities. Each week hundreds of five-minute true stories are shared around the world. Eight of the fifty stories in this book are from people we first met at The Moth StorySLAMs.

Our talented musicians, who light up the stage with their sound.

Our incomparable Moth hosts, who bring their nimble wit, emotional intelligence, and fiery energy to audiences night after night – you are our ultimate ambassadors.

Our audience members, listening with open hearts at live events or on headphones, or reading this page right now. You are the essential other half of the storytelling equation.

Our collaborators, friends, and partners in crime: Jay Allison, John Barth, Ann Blanchard, Meryl Cooper, Dan

Green, Joanne Heyman, Kerri Hoffman, Dan Kennedy, Viki Merrick, Sean Nesbitt, Sara Rogge, Paul Ruest, Jake Shapiro, and Kathleen Unwin. And former Moth staff member Katie Sanderson, who left the world too soon.

The hundreds of public radio stations around the country who air *The Moth Radio Hour*, all of our national partners for both the Mainstage and StorySLAM series, and all our regional StorySLAM crews for their tireless dedication.

All our community, corporate, and high-school partners, storytellers, and instructors, who share themselves, listen with empathy, and demonstrate the power of storytelling every day.

Our incredible donors, who make it all possible with their generous support.

Our gifted agent, Daniel Greenberg – thank you for your patience, talent, and wise counsel. You convinced us years ago that The Moth could work in print, and none of these books would have existed without your vision and care.

And our extraordinary editor, Matthew Inman, who has now carried us through three story collections. Thank you for your patience, formidable talent, and grace. Team Fire and Ice 4-EVER!

The Moth staff at the time of publication:
Catherine Burns, Sarah Haberman, Sarah Austin
Jenness, Jenifer Hixson, Meg Bowles, Kate Tellers,
Jennifer Birmingham, Marina Klutse, Suzanne Rust,
Inga Glodowski, Micaela Blei, Sarah Jane Johnson, Aldi
Kaza, Maggie Albert, Larry Rosen, Catherine McCarthy,

Casey Donahue, Michael La Guerra, Liam O'Brien, Michelle Jalowski, Sam Hacker, Lola Okusami, Patricia Ureña, Jessica Cepeda, Timothy Lou Ly, Jen Lue, Lawrence Fiorelli, Chloe Salmon, Jodi Powell, Lauren Gonzalez, Jazlyn Pinckney, Delia Bloom, Emily Couch, and Quinn McNeill.

PERMISSIONS

The Moth are grateful for the following permissions.

"Foreword" adapted from the essay "Novelist Meg Wolitzer on 20 Years of The Moth" originally published in *Newsweek* magazine on June 16, 2017.

"What I Wore to My Divorce" from *Approval Junkie* by Faith Salie, copyright © 2016 by Salient Productions, Inc. Reprinted by permission of Penguin Random House LLC.

"Have You Met Him Yet?" from *Thanks, Obama* by David Litt, copyright © 2017 by David Litt. Reprinted by courtesy of HarperCollins Publishers.

"Seven Shades of Blue," by Beth Nielson Chapman © 1995, 1997 BNC Songs (ASCAP). All rights reserved.

"Thank You for Being a Friend," words and music by Andrew Gold, copyright © 1978 Luckyu Music. All rights administered by BMG Rights Management (US) LLC. International copyright secured. All rights reserved. Reprinted by permission of Hal Leonard LLC.

"I Dreamed a Dream," from Les Misérables, music by Claude-Michel Schönberg; lyrics by Alain Boublil, Jean-Marc Natel and Herbert Kretzmer. Music and French lyrics copyright © 1980 by Editions Musicales Alain Boublil. English lyrics copyright © 1986 by Alain Boublil Music Ltd. (ASCAP). Mechanical and publication rights for the USA administered by Alain Boublil Music Ltd. (ASCAP) c/o Spielman Koenigsberg & Parker LLP; Richard Koenigsberg. International copyright secured. All rights reserved. This music is copyright. Photocopying is illegal. All performance rights restricted. Reprinted by permission of Hal Leonard LLC.

Before television and radio, people would gather on porches, on the steps outside their homes, and tell stories. Their bewitched listeners would sit and listen long into the night as moths flitted around overhead. Storytelling phenomenon The Moth recaptures this lost art each week in cities across America, Britain, Australia and beyond, playing to packed crowds at sold-out live events.

Since its launch in 1977, The Moth has presented tens of thousands of stories, told live and without notes, to standing-room-only crowds worldwide.

Serpent's Tail have published three Moth collections. The two others are:

The Moth – This Is a True Story

The Moth – All These Wonders

www.themoth.org